The College of Law
of England and Wales

LIBRARY & INFORMATION SERVICES

The College of Law, Christleton Hall, Christleton, Chester CH3 7AB
Telephone: 01244 333225

**This book MUST be returned on or before the last date stamped below.
Failure to do so will result in a fine.**

Birmingham • Chester • Guildford • London • York

Renting: The Essential Guide to Tenants' Rights
by Tessa Shepperson

© 2007 Teresa Jeanette Gee

Lawpack Publishing Limited
76–89 Alscot Road
London SE1 3AW

www.lawpack.co.uk

ISBN: 978-1-905261-26-0

Exclusion of Liability and Disclaimer

Contents

About the author

Tessa Shepperson is a solicitor in private practice. She qualified in 1990 and set up her own legal practice, TJ Shepperson, in 1994. Tessa specialises in residential landlord and tenant work, and runs the well-known legal information site Landlord-Law (www.landlordlaw.co.uk), which provides legal information and services for residential landlords and tenants. Tessa lives in Norwich with her husband and son.

Introduction

Despite the optimistic statements issued by government ministers and the Legal Services Commission, it is becoming increasingly difficult for ordinary people to find professional legal advice on housing matters at a reasonable cost. It is essential, therefore, that there are good, alternative sources of information available to help tenants who have no option but to deal with things themselves. There are many excellent online resources (some free of charge) but I think there is still a place for a decent printed handbook which can be carried about and read on the bus.

I was very pleased to be asked to write this guide for tenants. As a result of the increasing shortage of housing advice available, I have gone into quite a lot of detail to help tenants understand and then enforce their rights. Law is a complex and difficult subject and if the information given is to be of any practical use, there is a limit to how far it can be simplified. Most people should have no trouble understanding the information given in this book, although they may have to read parts of it several times.

I have chosen a different way of presenting legal information on housing matters to that traditionally used, which I hope will be more helpful for the ordinary person. To start with, if you are to fully understand tenants' rights in housing law, you need to have some background information, the sort of thing that most solicitors (or at least most housing solicitors) will know as a matter of course. This background information is given in the various sections of Part 1. You will also find in this section a worksheet for you to fill in to work out the type of tenancy you have. This is important, as your rights will often depend on your tenancy type.

However, what most tenants want to know is 'What are my rights?' and this is the focus of Part 2 – the largest section of the book. For this section I have looked at housing law and tried to work out what are the most important legal rights available to tenants. These are then described in some detail, followed in most cases with a 'remedies' section where you can find out how to enforce them (as it is an axiom of our legal system that if you have a right you should also have a remedy to enforce it), and a 'further information' section which will give relevant sources of help and advice.

As you might expect, the most important and largest sections are on matters relating to disrepair, and tenants' rights regarding harassment and eviction, although the 'right to be treated fairly' looking at tenancy agreements and rent matters is also pretty fundamental. These areas of law are very complex, mainly because different types of tenancy are treated in different ways and there are such a lot of different statutes involved. I have done the best I can.

I also thought it would be helpful to have a general description of a tenancy from start to finish, and this is given in Part 3. This is quite a short section; however, hopefully it will mop up some of the points which may not have been covered earlier and will put things into context. Finally, Part 4 gives important information on complaints procedures and how to obtain legal advice.

You will also see quite a few questions and answers (Q&As) scattered through the book. For quite a few years I have run a legal information website on housing law called Landlord-Law at www.landlordlaw.co.uk. One of the most popular parts of this site is the 'Q&A' section where every two weeks I answer ten questions submitted to me by readers. I have taken the questions and answers from here. They are all genuine questions, although I have amended them slightly and removed anything which might disclose the identity of the authors. As they are real questions, they set the legal information in this book in a real-life context, and also serve to illustrate some points not specifically covered elsewhere in the text.

Who are you?

This book is aimed at tenants, although it will also be useful for housing advisers and landlords. Here are some tips for various potential users of the book:

- Social tenants (i.e. tenants of local authorities, housing associations, and other registered social landlords) – most of this book will be relevant to you, save the sections aimed at tenants of private landlords.

- Private tenants – again, most of the book will be relevant to you, save for the sections aimed at tenants of social landlords. However, it is particularly important that you work out what type of tenancy you have, for example before tackling the section on eviction in Part 2.

- Students – the type of tenancy you have will depend on whether you are renting from your college/university or from a private landlord. Have a look at the section on background information on tenancies in Part 1 to find out which is appropriate for you, and use the rest of the book accordingly.

- Landlords – hopefully this book should be useful for you as it is always helpful to know what advice is being given to your tenants! Private landlords, in particular, may find it a useful source of information on their legal obligations to their tenants.

- Advisers – as this book is aimed at a lay audience, I have not included the numerous references which are an important part of the practitioners' textbook, although there are still a lot of statutory references and I have mentioned a few of the most important cases (and others are referred to but not named – see if you can spot them!). Even so the book should still be useful to you as a basic guide, particularly if you are not experienced in this area of law. Hopefully, once you have an understanding of the basics, you will be better able to tackle the less digestible practitioners' tomes.

Whoever you are, I hope that this book will be useful for you. Good luck with your case!

Acknowledgements

I am grateful to my publishers for commissioning this book and to my editors Jamie Ross and in particular Nadine De Souza, for her helpful comments and suggestions during the revision process. Thanks also to all my landlord and tenant clients and the members of my website www.landlordlaw.co.uk who have shared their problems with me, which has helped inform me when writing this book, and to Giles Peaker for his helpful suggestions. Finally, enormous thanks to my husband Graeme for putting up with me while I was writing, and also for his help (as a former councillor) with the 'complaints' section. However, any remaining errors are of course mine alone.

Tessa Shepperson

Important facts

This book contains the information and instructions for landlords letting residential properties. This book is for use in England and Wales. It is not intended for use in Scotland or Northern Ireland.

The information it contains has been carefully compiled from professional sources, but its accuracy is not guaranteed, as laws and regulations may change or be subject to differing interpretations. The law is stated as at 1 July 2007.

Neither this nor any other publication can take the place of a solicitor on important legal matters. As with any legal matter, common sense should determine whether you need the assistance of a solicitor rather than rely solely on the information and forms in this book.

We strongly urge you to consult a solicitor if:

- substantial amounts of money are involved;
- what you want to do is not precisely covered by this book;
- trusts or business interests are involved.

Part 1

Background information

CHAPTER 1

The legal system in England and Wales

In order to understand this book properly, you need to have a basic understanding of where the legal system in England and Wales comes from and how it works. This very short guide is here to help with that understanding.

Common law and statute law

Here is a little bit of history on the development of our current system.

Common law and case law

When William the Conqueror took power in England in 1066 he found a country which had an existing system of justice and government based on local sheriffs. Although he brought in many new ideas and laws, he also kept much of the old system.

Under the feudal system introduced with William, the King was the head of state and source of all justice; however, the King could not personally do everything. Kings would use members of their household to do justice and decide cases on their behalf. Over time these positions became more formalised and they eventually developed into a system of professional judges.

To make their decisions the judges would usually try to find out what the existing custom and practice was in the area and would base their decision on this. Cases started being written down and judges would use these as a reference, basing their decisions on legal points decided in previous cases. Over time the common law developed into the system we have today. If there is no Act of Parliament covering a legal point, judges now look at the case law, sometimes referring to cases decided hundreds of years ago, in order to make their decision.

For many years there were two parallel systems of law. One was the 'common law', developed by the King's judges; the other was known as the Court of Chancery or Equity, and was developed by the King's Chancellor. This is the system described in Charles Dickens' book *Bleak House*. However, the Judicature Acts 1873–5 created one single system of administration, so we do not have separate courts of common law and equity anymore, although lawyers still differentiate between the legal rules developed under these two systems. Both systems were based largely on case law.

Individual case details are found in a series of reports, known as Law Reports, which are printed and which can be found in law libraries. However, as you can imagine, there is rather a lot of case law, so it is expensive to have a complete record, plus it takes up a lot of wall space. So, few libraries, other than those of the professional legal organisations and large legal firms, will have anything like a complete record.

> **Note**
>
> Case law is also used in the interpretation of statute law, particularly where the wording of legislation is ambiguous.

Recently, great efforts have been made to put case law onto the internet. All the House of Lords' decisions made since November 1996 are published online. The British and Irish Legal Information Institute (www. bailii.org) has a huge online database of case law which is freely available. However, the online case reports mostly cover recent cases, and not all of them are included. To look at other cases it is still necessary to refer to the printed Law Reports.

Further information

House of Lords' decisions can be found in the 'judicial work' section of the UK Parliament website at www.parliament.uk. Other case law can be found at www.bailii.org.

Statute law

Even in the earliest days, Kings would sometimes issue proclamations which would affect and alter the common law. However, legislation as we know it today has to be formally approved by the Queen (or King) in Parliament (i.e. the House of Commons, the House of Lords and the Queen/King), and therefore could not exist before the development of the modern Parliament. This began in about the thirteenth and fourteenth centuries and has been developing ever since, eventually resulting in the system we have now, where the House of Commons rather than the monarch has the most power.

These days Acts of Parliament start as a bill which is introduced into either the House of Lords or the House of Commons. Forthcoming government bills are announced by the Queen at the state opening of Parliament every year, although it is also possible for a certain number of bills to be introduced by ordinary MPs, known as 'private members' bills'. To become law, bills have to pass through and be debated in both houses of Parliament. During this time they are also discussed and frequently amended in special committees set up to consider them (known as the 'committee stage'). Bills have to be voted on and passed by a majority in both houses of Parliament. Once this rather lengthy process has been completed, the bill will be formally approved by the Queen, and becomes law. At the time of writing this book, the most recent important housing-related Act of Parliament to have been passed is the Housing Act 2004.

Note on terminology

Statute law means the same as legislation and is made up of Acts of Parliament and their associated statutory instruments (see page 6).

However, bills usually have a long history of development, including much consultation with professional bodies, voluntary organisations and anyone else with an interest in the subject. Frequently, the government will publish a 'white paper' setting out a statement of intent, which is sometimes debated in Parliament. Sometimes this may have been preceded by a 'green paper' setting out proposals which are still being developed, inviting discussion from the public.

Where an area of law is felt to require review, this is often referred to the Law Commission, an independent body set up in the 1960s to keep the law under review and to recommend reform. After carrying out extensive research and consultation the Law Commission will generally publish a draft bill which then may or may not be taken up by the government and made law.

At the time of writing, the Law Commission has recently completed a major project on housing law and has published a draft bill, the Renting Homes Bill, which recommends extensive changes in housing law. The report and draft bill can be found in the public law section of the Law Commission website, as well as in the law reform section of my website at www.landlordlaw.co.uk. The Law Commission is currently working on two other housing-related projects – one on dispute resolution and the other on responsible renting.

Delegated legislation

There has been an increasing tendency in recent years for Acts of Parliament to give a general overview of the new system. The detail of the Act is then set out in delegated legislation or statutory instruments, which are developed usually after consultation, and published often long after the original Act was passed.

For example, the Housing Act 2004 was passed in November 2004 and sets out a new regime for assessing housing conditions and a new licensing system for houses that are in multiple occupation (HMOs). However, these parts of the Act did not come into force until April 2006 when the statutory instruments setting out the details of how these were to work came into force.

More information about the work of Parliament can be found from the UK Parliament section of www.direct.gov.uk.

More information about the Law Commission and its work can be found on its website at www.lawcom.gov.uk.

How to find statute law

All Acts of Parliament and statutory instruments are published by Her Majesty's Stationery Office (HMSO) and printed copies can be purchased from it. However, there are two free sources of statute law online:

1. The Office of Public Sector Information (OPSI) website (www.opsi. gov.uk). Since 1988 all Acts of Parliament have been loaded onto this site and all statutory instruments since 1987. The legislation is as originally published and does not include any subsequent amendments.

2. The UK Statute Law Database (www.statutelaw.gov.uk). Unlike the OPSI site, this site contains all (or most) of the legislation of England and Wales currently in force, going back to the Statute of Marlborough in 1267. Although the site has been in development for some time, it was only made available to the public in December 2006. It is an extremely useful website as it shows amendments which have been made to legislation since it was passed, and also gives other information such as whether parts of the Act are in force. However, note that at the time of writing this book, work is still being done to bring the site up to date and therefore not all of the statutes show all of the amendments. The site has an excellent search engine and it is fairly easy to find your way around.

Law in Wales

As all Welsh readers will no doubt know, Wales was once a separate country with its own government and legal system. In the thirteenth century Wales was gradually conquered by the English, but the administrative and legal system was left unchanged until the reign of Henry VIII. Then, when two Acts were passed in 1536 and 1543, Wales become incorporated with England, its laws were harmonised, and Welsh members were elected to Parliament. At the time these measures were not unpopular with the Welsh as they gave them equality under law with English citizens.

This continued until a new Labour government was elected in 1997 with a manifesto to devolve powers to Wales. Its proposals were endorsed by the

Welsh in the referendum in September 1997, and in 1998 the Government of Wales Act established the National Assembly for Wales. Devolved powers were transferred to the Assembly in 1999. Although Wales is still part of the UK and laws passed by Parliament in Westminster still apply in Wales, the Assembly now has the power to make subordinate legislation which details how laws will apply in Wales. For this reason legislation now often commences at different times in England and Wales. For example, the HMO licensing provisions under the Housing Act 2004, which came into force in England in April 2006, did not come into force in Wales until two months later.

For more information, see the National Assembly for Wales' website at www.wales.gov.uk.

Criminal and civil law

When you talk about 'the law' people often just think of the police and of criminal prosecutions. However, this is only one part of the system. The legal system is actually divided into two halves. One half, the criminal legal system, is about the state prosecuting wrongdoers for breaking the criminal law. The other half, the civil legal system, is about resolving disputes between individuals or organisations.

The relevant legislation will normally make it clear whether the law in question is governed by the criminal law (making the wrongdoer liable for prosecution) or the civil law (where a dispute can be resolved by the courts).

There are quite a few instances in housing law where particular laws (e.g. some offences under the Environmental Protection Act 1990) have a criminal penalty but which do not entitle the tenant to bring a civil claim against a landlord (e.g. for compensation). In other situations a tenant will be able to claim against a landlord for compensation (e.g. for personal injury caused by the property being in disrepair) but the claim will not involve any criminal liability. Finally, there are some situations (e.g. unlawful eviction) where there will be both a criminal and a civil liability, although they cannot be dealt with together in the same court claim.

Criminal law

The purpose of the criminal legal system is to protect society, and prosecutions are generally brought by the state (in the name of the Queen, referred to as 'Regina' in case titles) on behalf of all of us. However, it is also possible for companies and individuals to bring private prosecutions; for example, shops (particularly the larger stores) often bring prosecutions against shoplifters. For some types of offence, other organisations are specifically authorised to bring prosecutions. For example, local authorities will bring prosecutions under the Protection from Eviction Act where landlords have unlawfully evicted a tenant, and the Health and Safety Executive will prosecute landlords who breach the gas regulations.

In criminal court actions, cases will be brought by the prosecution against a defendant. The case can be brought either in the Crown Court (for serious crimes) or in the Magistrates' Court for most other and less serious crimes. Most of the criminal offences associated with housing law are dealt with in the Magistrates' Court. In a criminal claim, the prosecution will have to prove that the defendant is guilty beyond reasonable doubt (this is known as the 'burden of proof').

If the defendant is found guilty, he will be convicted and will receive a sentence (i.e. punishment). The type of sentence allowed for the crime in question will be set out in the relevant Act of Parliament. For housing-related crimes it will generally be a fine, although there are a few housing-related offences (such as flagrant disregard of the gas regulations resulting in the death of the tenant) where the defendant can be sentenced to a term in prison. Once convicted, the defendant will have a criminal record, and this will affect what he is allowed to do in the future. For example, a landlord convicted of a housing-related offence will find it difficult to get a licence to run an HMO.

Civil law

The civil legal system is a complicated system which tries to set out the rights and obligations for all the various situations found in life. Under this system, where there is a dispute which the people concerned are unable to sort out themselves, they can refer it to a judge and he will decide, by referencing to the law, who is in the right.

This is an important part of our civilisation and society. If there is an independent and fair system which people trust to resolve disputes, then they are less likely to take matters into their own hands and use intimidation and violence. The English legal system tries to be fair, and largely succeeds. However, as our lives and society are very much more complex than they were, say 500 years ago, our laws have become more complex to reflect this. It is inevitable that there will sometimes be inconsistencies, and some decisions made by judges may appear 'unfair', perhaps because of the way a statute is drafted. However, often, when this happens, there will be an outcry in the press and Parliament will (eventually) take steps to amend the law and resolve the unfairness, which may not have been apparent at the time that the Act was passed.

The sort of disputes which will be resolved in the civil courts in housing situations include claims by tenants for compensation (e.g. because the landlord has not kept the property in repair) or for the return of their damage deposit, and claims by landlords for possession or for compensation if the tenants have left the property in poor condition. In civil disputes, the person bringing the claim is known as the 'claimant' and the opposing party as the 'defendant'.

Most housing disputes will be dealt with in the County Courts. Very complex and high value claims may be dealt with in the High Court, but this is rare for housing matters. For more information about County Court claims, see Chapter 3.

You will find contact details for all local County Courts, together with a lot of other helpful information and forms, on the Court Service website at www.hmcourts-service.gov.uk.

Some housing matters are dealt with by the Residential Property Tribunal, rather than the County Court. These are mostly challenges to landlords' rent increases, and proceedings under the Housing Act 2004. You will find more information about when the tribunal is used in the relevant sections in Part 2. For more information about the Residential Property Tribunal and its work, see its website at www.rpts.gov.uk.

> **Note**
>
> In many situations it will be important that you obtain legal advice before starting a court action. There are many sources of free advice

for tenants. For more information, see the special section on legal advice in Part 4 of this book.

Further information on civil law

I will now look at two particular areas of civil law which are of great relevance to housing law – the law of contract and the law of 'tort'. This is followed by an overview of the legal remedies for breaches of these types of civil law.

The law of contract

A tenancy is a form of contract, albeit a special form of contract with many of its own rules. However, to help you understand the underlying law, I will outline here some of the basic principles of contract law.

Who can make a contract?

Most adults and limited companies are capable of entering into a contract. However, there are special rules for minors, i.e. people under 18. Some contracts with minors for things known as 'necessaries' (i.e. things which are necessary, such as food, medicine and shelter) are enforceable, and others are not.

Different rules, however, apply to the ownership of land, which includes ownership of a tenancy. Minors are legally incapable of owning land, so any tenancy agreement signed by a minor will take effect as a contract by the landlord to hold the property on trust for the minor, which can then be transferred to the minor when he reaches 18. However, on the minor's part the contract is a 'voidable' one, i.e. he can decide not to go ahead with it if he wishes. Note, though, that the obligation to pay rent is binding on the minor. If he decides not to go ahead with the tenancy at the age of 18 (or at any time prior to this), he will still be liable for the rent for any period of time that he was living at the property.

So far as people of 'unsound mind' are concerned (e.g. people who suffer from some sort of mental illness and who are not responsible for their actions), they can normally enter into and be bound by contracts unless they are subject to an order by the Court of Protection (a special court which looks after the interests of people who are incapable of managing their affairs), or unless they did not know what they were doing when they were making the contract and the other party was aware of this.

Making the contract

A contract is an agreement which gives rise to obligations which are enforceable by law. There must be an 'offer' by one party and an 'acceptance' of the contract by the other party. Once agreement is reached, the contract will be 'binding' and enforceable through the courts.

For the contract to be legally enforceable the parties must exchange something which shows that they wish to be bound by the agreement. The legal phrase is that each party must provide 'consideration'. This is nothing to do with being considerate; consideration is something of value, although it does not have to be a market value. If a landlord signs a tenancy for the rent of a property at £1 per month, he will be bound by this, even if the market rent is £1,000. Consideration has been defined as 'a benefit to one party or a detriment to the other'.

> **Note**
>
> Several hundred years ago, people sometimes used to rent properties out at a rent of one peppercorn (spices were more valuable then) giving rise to the phrase 'peppercorn rent' for a property rented out for a nominal figure.

In tenancy agreements the consideration from the landlord is giving up to the tenant the right to live in the property, and the consideration from the tenant is the agreement to pay rent.

> **Note**
>
> Contracts can be made with limited companies, as well as living people. If your landlord is a limited company, the company is the other party to the contract, not the person who may have actually signed the document on the company's behalf.

Consideration need not be money; for example, it can also be an agreement to do or refrain from doing something. So a landlord could reach agreement with a tenant not to sue him for outstanding rent in exchange for the tenant providing some sort of service (e.g. building work on one of his other properties).

If a person lives in a property as a requirement of his job (e.g. a caretaker who is required to live on the premises), he will not have a tenancy but a licence.

Something that has already been given will not count as consideration for a new contract. So if you have given a present to Mr A of £500, and then want to buy something from him for £500, you cannot force him to give it to you on the basis of the £500 already paid. This will be 'past consideration', i.e. something already done. Unless he agrees otherwise, you will have to pay him another £500.

> **Note**
>
> It is possible to enforce a contract where there is no consideration or past consideration, if it is signed as a deed. This means that the parties have to sign a document setting out all the terms of the contract, the signatures must be witnessed and the document must state that it is signed as a deed.

Contract terms

A contract will have terms. These are things agreed between the parties relating to the contract. If the terms are untrue or are not carried out, this will be breach of contract.

• **Representations:** Sometimes statements are made before the start of the contract which induce or persuade someone to enter into it. These are not terms of the contract, but representations. If these turn out to be untrue, they are known as misrepresentations and sometimes they will entitle the wronged party to end the contract and/or claim damages. For more information, see Chapter 8 on the tenant's right to be treated fairly.

- **Express terms:** These are the terms which are specifically agreed between the parties. In many contracts they will be set out in a document (e.g. a tenancy agreement).

- **Implied terms:** Certain types of contract will also have other terms implied into them by law. For example, contracts for the sale of goods will have implied into them the various implied terms that are set out in the Sale of Goods Act. Tenancy agreements carry a whole raft of implied terms, some of the most important being the landlords repairing covenants, which are discussed in Part 2.

- **Unfair terms:** In a contract made between a business and a consumer, there are now restrictions on contract terms, which must be 'fair' or risk being unenforceable. This is discussed in some detail in Part 2 (the right to be treated fairly).

- **Amending terms:** A party to a contract cannot bring new terms into the contract once it has been made, without the other party's agreement. So a landlord cannot force a tenant to sign a new tenancy agreement if he finds that he has left something out of the contract which the tenant has already signed, or if he wants to change the terms of the contract.

> **Note**
>
> Landlords can amend the terms of an assured or an assured shorthold tenancy (but not other types of tenancy) by serving a special form of notice on the tenant. The notice must give the tenant the right to refer the proposed amendment to the Rent Assessment Committee for review if he does not agree with it. This procedure is not often used, however. You will find definitions of the different types of tenancy in the section on tenancies in Chapter 2.

Ending the contract

There are a number of different ways a contract can be ended (or discharged). These are as follows:

- **Performance:** This is where the subject matter of the contract has been completed or its purpose fulfilled (e.g. if a tenant moves out at the end of a fixed-term tenancy).

- **Agreement:** Parties can agree to end a contract before it has finished (e.g. a landlord may agree to let a tenant leave early). However, you cannot force a party to agree to end the contract if he does not want to.

> **Note**
>
> Although a landlord cannot physically prevent a tenant from moving out, the tenant will normally remain liable for the rent (even though he may not be living at the property) until the tenancy has legally ended.

- **Breach:** A breach of contract does not automatically end it. However, some types of very serious breach may allow the other party to treat the contract as discharged (i.e. ended). So, for example, if the property is in very serious disrepair, a tenant may occasionally be able to treat the contract as discharged and move out.

- **Frustration:** This is where due to a change in circumstances the contract becomes impossible to perform. However, the courts will only allow this in limited circumstances; for example, you cannot use this doctrine to get out of a tenancy of a property in London if your job moves you to Newcastle. Frustration in a landlord and tenant context can only really be used if something happens in relation to the property (e.g. if it burns down).

The law of tort (i.e. civil wrongs)

Tort is a huge area of law, but, unlike contract, most ordinary people have probably never heard of it, or at least will not be familiar with the word 'tort'. I give a brief overview here as many tenants' rights in housing law fall within the law of tort. Basically, a tort is a civil wrong which is not a breach of contract. Therefore, this area of law allows you to sue someone in the civil courts where there is no contractual relationship between you.

For example, if you buy a bottle of ginger beer which contains a decomposing snail and you suffer injury as a result of this, you can sue the shopkeeper who sold it to you for damages for breach of contract. However, if the person who actually drank the ginger beer was not the person who bought it, he will not be able to sue the shopkeeper as there is no contractual relationship between the both of them. However, he will be able to sue the real culprit, the manufacturer of the ginger beer, under the tort of negligence, because the manufacturer has a responsibility to produce products which do not injure people. This is basically what happened in the famous legal case of *Donoghue v Stevenson* in 1932, which founded the tort of negligence.

Most legal claims in landlord and tenant law will be contractual claims as a tenancy is a form of contract. However, there will be situations where it may be appropriate for a tenant to claim under the law of tort. Also, if a claim is made against a landlord by someone who is not the tenant, such as a member of his family or a visitor to the property (e.g. if the individual is injured as a result of the property's disrepair), he will have no alternative but to bring a tortious claim as he will have no contractual relationship with the landlord.

The law of tort (or torts) covers a collection of various legal rights. Below is a brief description of some of the main ones. Others can be found in the rights section in Part 2.

Negligence

This is the largest and the most important area of tort.

For someone to have a claim in negligence the following must be proved:

- **Duty of care:** This will be either where the claimant and the defendant are in a 'special relationship' or where the case falls within the principles developed by case law. Situations where one party owes a duty to another include:

  - One road user to another

  - Employer to employee

  - Manufacturer to consumer (such as in the case of *Donoghue v Stevenson* above)

  - Doctor to patient

  - Solicitor to client

  Traditionally, landlords have not had a duty of care towards their tenants. However, this immunity has been reduced somewhat by statute and case law, so that in some circumstances a claim in negligence may now be possible; for example, where the landlord is also the builder of the property.

- **Breach of the duty of care:** This is something that will have to be proved by the claimant (on the balance of probabilities). Sometimes the court will hold that it is obvious (e.g. there was a case where a sack of sugar fell on someone from a crane operated by the defendant and the court held that this must have been his fault). Also, where the defendant has been convicted of an offence in the criminal courts the claimant will not have to prove the offence again in the civil courts, he can just rely on the conviction (Section 11 of the Civil Evidence Act 1968).

- **Causation:** There must be a causal link between the defendant's act or omission and the loss or damage suffered (known as the 'chain of causation'). If the loss or damage would have occurred anyway, the defendant will not be liable.

- **Remoteness:** In some circumstances the actual loss suffered by the claimant may be considered to be 'too remote' from the negligent act for the defendant to be found liable. The loss must be reasonably foreseeable by the parties at the time.

Negligence is generally used for cases involving physical loss, such as personal injury or damage to property. Pure economic or financial loss cannot normally be recovered in tort, except in exceptional cases.

Occupiers' liability

Under this tort, occupiers have an obligation to ensure that their property is not hazardous to others. The main statute is the Occupiers' Liability Act 1957, supplemented by the Occupiers' Liability Act 1984, which covers injury to trespassers.

The duty is owed by 'the occupier', who is the person who has control over the property. This will normally be you, the tenant, but if some parts of the premises are controlled by the landlord (such as the common areas), then the landlord will be the occupier, perhaps together with you.

The duty is owed to 'visitors', who are people who have express or implied permission to enter the property; for example, the postman, who has implied permission to cross your front garden to post letters through your door. Some people who have a right to enter against your wishes (e.g. police officers entering under a warrant) are also included within the definition of visitors.

The duty is described in the 1957 Act, and is to take such care as in all the circumstances is reasonable to make sure that the visitor will be reasonably safe in using the premises for the purposes for which he is invited or permitted by the occupier (you) to be there.

Therefore, to take the example above, although the postman may have an implied right to go up the path to post letters, this does not entitle him to explore the bottom of the garden. Or as a judge once said in a case, 'when you invite a person into your house to use the staircase, you do not invite him to slide down the banisters'. Note, however, that a greater duty of care is owed to child visitors than to adults.

Under the 1984 Act limited protection was extended to trespassers and people lawfully exercising rights of way.

Nuisance

The tort of nuisance is divided into public nuisance and private nuisance:

- **Public nuisance:** This is where an activity affects a class of people (as opposed to just one person). For example, where quarrying affects the local community by creating dust and vibration and scattering splinters of rock and stone around the neighbourhood.

- **Private nuisance:** This is where the unreasonable use of land interferes with a neighbouring property. This is dealt with in more detail in Part 2, under rights relating to the condition of the property, repair and safety.

Trespass to land

Many people believe that trespass is a criminal offence, due to the number of notices which say 'trespassers will be prosecuted'. However, this is not the case. Trespass is where someone interferes with someone else's land or property, generally by entering it. You can commit trespass even if you do not realise that you do not have the right to enter the land, and even if you do not do any harm or damage. A person who has permission to enter is not a trespasser unless he does something which he does not have permission to do. Certain people have the right to enter land without the owner's consent in some circumstances, such as court bailiffs and the police. Also, trespass can sometimes be justified in emergencies (e.g. if you are escaping from a fire).

A land owner can use reasonable force to remove trespassers, provided they have not obtained full possession of the land (e.g. if they are squatters), in which case force should not be used. In squatter cases, where the squatters make it clear that they will not leave peacefully, a possession order will normally be needed to remove them. Self-help can be used to remove objects, such as overhanging branches, so long as they are returned to their owner.

Trespass to the person

This covers a number of legal torts, such as assault and battery, false imprisonment, and harassment. I do not have space to consider these in any detail here. If you are ever physically assaulted by your landlord, these can be used to base a claim for compensation, but the best course of action (at least initially) is to complain to the police as assault is also a criminal offence.

Defamation

This will not be considered here other than to say that it is a tort and a highly specialised area of law (which very few lawyers will be able to deal with). It is very expensive to litigate, and such claims are best left to celebrities and the media.

Remedies for civil claims (contract and tort)

If a party is in breach of contract or has committed a tort (civil wrong), this will normally entitle the other party to sue, generally for damages/financial compensation. This section gives a very brief overview of the remedies that can be claimed in court proceedings.

- **Unliquidated damages:** This is where the damages are assessed by the judge at the court hearing. They are to compensate a claimant for losses suffered as a result of the breach of contract or civil wrong (i.e. they are not normally given to punish a defendant). If the claimant has not actually suffered any loss as a result of the breach of contract or tort, then nominal damages only will be awarded.

Generally, in contract cases, damages are awarded on the basis that they should try to put the claimant in the position he would have been in had the contract been carried out properly (e.g. that the property should have been in proper repair in the first place). For claims in tort, damages will normally be awarded to try to put the claimant in the position he would have been in had the wrongful act never taken place. Sometimes, this basis is also used to assess damages in contract cases.

In some types of case, the defendant can ask for a reduction in the damages awarded on the basis that the claimant contributed to his own losses; for example, if the disrepair in the property was aggravated by the tenant's failure to allow the landlord access to repair it.

Damages cannot be recovered for losses which are 'too remote'. The loss must be something that was 'in the contemplation of the parties' at the time the contract is made (or the tortious act took place). So if a landlord refuses to go ahead with letting a property to you after you signed the tenancy agreement, he may be liable for your costs of finding another property but will not be liable for additional damages; for example, if you lost your job as a result of this (unless perhaps you can prove that he was fully aware that this might happen).

Damages cannot be awarded if they were not caused by the defendant's breach of contract (or by the defendant's action in tort cases). So if a total stranger breaks a window or if it is broken by something blown by the wind, you cannot normally be held responsible for this (although it may be a good idea to obtain some evidence to prove this).

Someone claiming damages also has a duty to 'mitigate the loss', i.e. if it is possible for him to reduce his loss, he should do so. For example, if you want to leave a property before the end of the tenancy and you find a suitable replacement tenant, a landlord will be expected to mitigate his losses and re-let to the suggested replacement tenant rather than hold you responsible for the rent for the rest of the tenancy.

The main types of loss recognised by the courts are:

- Pecuniary/financial loss
- Pain and suffering as a result of personal injury
- Physical inconvenience (e.g. caused by living in a property while repairs are carried out)
- Distress and injured feelings

Note that not all of these types of loss can be claimed in all cases. Compensation for injured feelings is not normally awarded except in special cases, such as contracts for holidays where the holiday brochure does not match the actual holiday provided.

- **Liquidated damages:** This is compensation for specific sums actually paid by the claimant which can be proved, e.g. by providing a receipt. This could be the value of your items damaged by the ceiling falling in, or your hotel bill if you are unable to live in the property due to disrepair.

- **Possession orders:** These will be awarded by the court in cases where the claimant is able to prove that the defendant is not entitled to remain on land belonging to the claimant.

- **Equitable remedies:** These are specific types of redress which were developed by the old Court of Chancery or Equity (discussed on page 4). All equitable remedies are 'discretionary', i.e. the judge cannot be forced to order them if he does not think it appropriate or practicable in the circumstances. They will not normally be used if the judge considers that financial compensation will be an adequate remedy. The two main equitable remedies you may come across are:

  - **Specific performance:** Where the court orders the defendant to do something. (e.g. to force a landlord to carry out repairs to a property where the landlord is in breach of his repairing obligations).

  - **An injunction:** Where the court orders the defendant not to do something. There are three types:

1   An interlocutory injunction, which is designed to regulate the position of the parties pending a trial.

2   A prohibitory injunction, where a party is ordered not to do something, such as harass a tenant.

3   A mandatory injunction, where a defendant is ordered to undo something he should not have done, such as evict a tenant unlawfully.

...and finally

This has been a very brief overview indeed of the laws of contract and tort and their remedies. Remember that a book could probably be written (and in some cases has been written) about each of the individual points mentioned above, and each has been the subject of many complex cases, some of which have gone all the way up to the House of Lords. For more information it is best to seek advice from a qualified lawyer.

CHAPTER 2

Tenancies and landlords

What is a tenancy?

Essentially a tenancy is the ownership of land or property for a period of time. By granting a tenancy, a landlord effectively 'sells' all of his rights over the property for the duration of the tenancy, other than the right to receive the rent and the right to recover the property at the end of the tenancy.

In the old days before regulation, it was fairly easy for the landlord to recover the property; for example, if any of the terms of the agreement were broken, he could 'forfeit' the lease and repossess. However, because of its political importance, housing law is now heavily regulated and a series of Acts of Parliament have been passed protecting tenants by giving them extra rights, restricting the rights of landlords, and setting procedures which must be followed, for example, before a tenant can be evicted.

The number of Acts of Parliament involved also means that this area of law is very complex, as different Acts apply to different tenancies, and some types of tenancy are exempt from some of the legislation.

However, most of this legislation applies only to 'tenancies'. There are two legal types of occupation of property – a licence and a tenancy.

The difference between a tenancy and a licence

A licence is where an occupier just has permission to occupy the property, which means that he is not a trespasser. However, he does not have most of the legal rights of tenants, and his right to occupy can be ended much more easily. Once his right to occupy has ended, if he stays on he becomes a trespasser and a landlord is entitled as of right to ask the court for an order that the trespasser leaves the property, known as an 'order for possession'. However, if an occupier has a tenancy, this gives him a whole set of legal rights which he can enforce against his landlord including, in many cases, the right to prevent the landlord from recovering possession.

In the past many landlords tried to avoid the housing legislation by granting licences rather than tenancies, so they would be able to evict their tenants if they wanted (e.g. if they wanted to sell the property with vacant possession). Under the Rent Act 1977, which applied to all tenancies before 1989, it was very difficult to evict a tenant.

However, in a famous legal case (*Street v Mountford*) in 1985, the House of Lords decided that when working out whether the occupation is a tenancy or a licence, it is what actually happens during the relationship which is important and which should determine the status of the tenancy, not necessarily what is written on the letting agreement. So if someone has signed a document headed 'licence agreement' but the facts of the occupation show that it is actually a tenancy, then it will be a tenancy and not a licence.

A letting will generally be a tenancy if:

- the occupant pays rent; and
- he has 'exclusive occupation' of the property (or part of the property, e.g. his bedroom), which means that he can lock the door(s) and keep everyone out – including the landlord; and
- it is for a term (i.e. an agreed period of time).

A letting will generally be a licence if one or more of the following apply:

- The occupier shares all of the living space (including the bedroom) with other occupiers.

- The landlord lives on the premises and shares some living space (e.g. kitchen and bathroom) with the occupier – here the occupier is generally known as a 'lodger'.
- The landlord has the right to move the occupier to another room or property.
- The landlord keeps control of the property and has the right to enter it when he likes.
- There are services, such as cleaning and/or meals included with the rent (as in a hotel or in many student halls of accommodation).
- The occupier is required to live in the property by his employer as part of his job (i.e. the accommodation is not just provided as a 'perk').

However, if these points are set out in a 'licence agreement' signed by the occupier but do not reflect what actually happens, then a court may hold that the letting is in reality a tenancy; for example, if the agreement refers to cleaning and meals, but these are not actually provided.

Note that lettings of accommodation on boats and some mobile homes will also be licences, as tenancies can only be granted for lettings of buildings which are permanently fixed to the land (like a house). Whether a letting of a mobile home is a tenancy or a licence will depend largely on how permanent the structure is.

Most student accommodation provided in student halls are licences rather than tenancies as there will be services (such as meals and cleaning) provided and the college or university will retain rights over the accommodation (e.g. to move students from one room to another).

Some lettings made by registered charities and almshouses will also be licences because the occupiers are living in the property due to the fact that they are beneficiaries of a charity; for example, if they are given temporary accommodation by an organisation helping them recover from drug and drink addiction.

This book is mainly about the rights of tenants, rather than the rights of licensees.

Q If a group of sharers sign an assured shorthold tenancy (AST) agreement which forbids subletting, but then subsequently one tenant decides to move out and he replaces himself without notifying the landlord, what legal rights does the new person have? Can he be evicted without going through the courts, and does there need to be an AST for him to be legally considered a tenant?

A Until such time as a new tenancy agreement is signed with the landlord including the new occupant, the occupant will not be a tenant and he will have no direct legal relationship with the landlord. He will be technically a lodger of the remaining tenants. His rights will be against the tenants and not against their landlord. As a lodger he will have no security of tenure against the tenants, who will be entitled to evict him without a court order. If the landlord obtains an order for possession against the tenants, this will be effective against the lodger and if the tenants are evicted by the court bailiff, he will also evict the lodger.

Q I moved into a two-person house on separate tenancy agreements in August 2005. My housemate moved out in October and my landlady started to redecorate the other room straight away, under the understanding that she would later find another tenant, firstly for December, then late January. Between then and two weeks ago she made very slow progress with this. Last week, she informed me that she had split up with her partner and was moving into the other room in the house and has since done so. Is this legal and does it change my rights as a tenant? She has begun to refer to me as a lodger and I hope that this is not my legal status.

A It is not illegal for your landlord to move into the other room of the house in place of getting a new tenant. Unless it specifically states this in your agreement, you will not normally have any say in who the other occupier in your shared house is. However, by doing this, she cannot change the nature of your tenancy or convert your tenancy into a licence. You continue to have the same legal rights that you had when you moved in. You are a tenant and not a lodger. Note that if you and the outgoing tenant had been joint tenants on the same tenancy agreement, the situation would have been different and you would have been entitled to prevent her moving in.

For more information on assured shorthold tenancies referred to in these Q&As and tenancies in general, see further below.

The different types of landlord

Often the rights of a tenant will depend on the type of landlord he has. These are the main types of landlord:

Social landlords

These can be either local authorities and housing action trusts or housing associations, housing co-operatives and similar organisations which are non-profit making.

Social landlords will have an allocations procedure for providing housing. Some of the not-for-profit organisations will specialise in helping particular types of people, such as those with disabilities or special needs.

Most housing associations and other not-for-profit landlords are registered with the Housing Corporation in England or the Welsh Assembly government in Wales, which regulates them. Social housing providers who are registered with these two organisations are known as 'registered social landlords' (often described as RSLs).

Note on terminology

In this book I will generally be using the term registered social landlords for this type of landlord, to include housing associations, housing co-operatives and all not-for-profit housing organisations.

All English registered social landlords are subject to the Charter for Housing Association Applicants and Residents. This sets out what tenants and residents are entitled to expect from registered social landlords. It can be downloaded from the website of the Housing Corporation at www. housingcorp.gov.uk.

Welsh registered social landlords are subject to the Regulatory Code for Housing Associations Registered in Wales. This can be downloaded from the Housing section of the Welsh Assembly government website at www. wales.gov.uk.

Private landlords

These are private individuals and companies who own and rent out property primarily for profit.

Private landlords vary widely from the very good to the very bad. However, many landlords are now members of accreditation schemes. These are usually run by local authorities, universities or colleges, or landlords' associations, generally two or more of these in partnership. Landlords who are members of these schemes have to sign up to a code of practice and are normally required to undergo training. Sometimes properties may be inspected as part of the scheme. Your landlord will probably tell you if he is a member of one of these schemes.

Private landlords will deal with the letting and management of their properties either themselves or via an agent.

Educational institutions

These are universities and colleges which are registered with the Secretary of State (which most are). Although most lettings made by them will be treated as lettings made by private landlords, in two important respects they are treated differently. Tenancies granted to their own students are excluded from the statutory codes (see page 30), and Houses in Multiple Occupation (HMOs) (which will include most student halls of residence) will be exempt from licensing as long as they have signed up to one of the authorised codes of practice. Note, however, that accommodation in student halls of residence will normally be under a licence rather than a tenancy, and are therefore not specifically covered by this book, although some parts (e.g. the sections on HMOs) may be relevant.

> **Note**
>
> Under proposals put forward by the Law Commission and set out in its draft Renting Homes Bill, there would be just two types of tenancy

– one for social landlords and one for the private sector. However, in the meantime. I am afraid it is very much more complex than that.

Further information

The Housing Corporation has a website at www.housingcorp.gov.uk.

For more information about accreditation, see the Accreditation Network UK website at www.anuk.org.uk.

Students can find helpful information (e.g. regarding the codes of practice) via the National Union of Students' website at www.nusonline.co.uk.

Q My girlfriend and I recently moved into a flat with the same landlord as our previous flat. We signed a new six-month contract with the landlord, and that was that. Then when we returned from holiday in August, merely six weeks after moving in, we discovered that the property had been sold and that we had new landlords. This was the first time we had heard of the sale and we were not happy about it, as the previous landlord was very nice and his staff were efficient. Now the current landlord is refusing to take care of repairs and a failed direct debit payment which was the fault of the landlord has meant that we are treated in a very nasty way when we speak to him. Is it legal that he can sell the flat without consulting his tenants and is our contract still legally binding?

A I am afraid that the landlord can sell the property and he does not have to consult with his tenants before doing so. So far as the tenant is concerned, legally the situation is exactly the same. All the tenants' legal rights and obligations remain but are against a different landlord. So you have a legally binding contract, and your new landlord is bound by the repairing covenants in the same way as the old landlord was.

Statutory codes

A short history

Up to 1979

Housing law is very important politically, and over time there has been a series of Acts of Parliament which have amended the original 'common law' governing tenancies. This started at the time of World War I (1914–18), when rent control was introduced and the rights of landlords to evict were restricted. This was mainly to protect the poorer workers, who needed to have secure accommodation so they could do essential work for the war effort. However, because of housing shortages after the war it became politically inexpedient to repeal this legislation, although it was frequently amended.

Attempts to de-control housing in the 1950s caused problems and further measures to protect tenants and to prevent landlords from evicting tenants other than through the courts, were passed in the 1960s. This culminated in 1977 with the Labour government passing two major pieces of legislation: the Rent Act and the Protection from Eviction Act. Both of these are still in force today, although the Rent Act (which sets out a code governing how tenancies operate) only applies to tenancies created before January 1989. However, this series of legislation, although popular politically, made it difficult for landlords to make much profit from renting property. In the nineteenth and early twentieth centuries private renting had been the most common form of housing. This dropped substantially during the twentieth century to 11 per cent at the start of the 1980s (see Table 1 on page 32). Although this was partly due to social changes and the increased ability of people to buy their own homes, the difficulties facing private landlords were undoubtedly a contributing factor.

During the same period (i.e. 1920–80) local authorities were encouraged to provide housing and, as they were considered to be 'model landlords', they were left largely to manage their housing services as they wished. Legislation was more aimed at enabling local authorities to finance and build accommodation than at regulating the landlord and tenant relationship. Rent control did not really exist in the same way as in the private sector, and although it was subject to provisions relating to conditions and public health, local authority accommodation was not subject to the standards local authorities were entitled to enforce against non-local authority landlords. By 1979, 31.5 per cent of all housing in Britain was owned by local authorities.

The third main housing sector today – housing associations and other registered social landlords – has its roots in almshouses and charitable institutions set up from the Middle Ages onwards, plus housing provided by philanthropic commercial organisations and housing co-operatives of various kinds. Up to 1980 most of these organisations provided social housing, often for specific groups such as lone parents or recently released prisoners. Legally they were sometimes treated on the same basis as local authorities and sometimes as private landlords.

After 1979

In 1979 Mrs Thatcher's Conservative government came into power. During the next 20 years new legislation was introduced which has had a profound effect on housing provision.

In the private sector, the government wanted to increase the supply of rented property and believed that the only way this could be done was by relaxing the regulatory framework. A new type of tenancy, a 'shorthold' tenancy, was introduced initially in the Housing Act 1980. However, the system we have today was created by The Housing Act 1988. This introduced assured and assured shorthold tenancies, with landlords being able to recover possession of the shorthold tenancies as of right, so long as they follow the proper procedure. The 1988 Act also removed the 'fair rent' system set up under the 1977 Rent Act, which limits the rent landlords can charge. Landlords are now able to set a market rent, with the tenants having only limited rights to challenge this. The new system was amended slightly by the Housing Act 1996, which made the shorthold tenancy the 'default' type of tenancy.

Although change was delayed by the property crash of the late 1980s/early 1990s, this legislation (along with the introduction of the 'buy-to-let' mortgage) was eventually successful in reversing the decline in private renting, and is the basis of the vigorous private rented sector we have today.

In the public sector, the first changes were brought about by the Housing Act 1980, later consolidated into the Housing Act 1985, which gave local authority tenants similar rights as private tenants not to be evicted from their property. The government also tried to bring rents closer to the market rents charged in the private sector by changing the housing subsidy provisions. However, local authority rents still remain lower than market rents.

The other important change for local authority tenants brought about in 1980 was the right to buy. Under this scheme secure tenants, who meet the qualifying requirements, are able to buy the freehold or leasehold of their home at a discounted price. This right was amended in 1985 and again in 2004, but still remains. The right to buy is a major cause of the increase in the percentage of owner occupiers after 1981, shown in Table 1 below.

So far as housing association/registered social landlord tenancies are concerned, the picture is a complex one, as sometimes they are treated in the same way as secure tenants and sometimes as private sector tenants. Often their precise rights will depend on when their tenancy started, and whether it has been transferred from a local authority.

The other major change insofar as housing associations are concerned is the great increase in their number and the amount of housing they own and control. Since the 1980s, government has encouraged the transfer of local authority housing stock to housing associations, and new laws have made it easier for housing associations to obtain funding than local authorities. Many housing associations have been formed specifically to receive and manage housing stock transferred from local authorities. Tenants on the whole have not objected to this, so long as their rents are guaranteed, their right to buy is protected, and their security of tenure is not affected. Also the new landlord will often be in a better financial position to carry out improvement and repair work, which is attractive to tenants.

The effect of all these changes can be seen in Table 1 below, which gives a summary of the percentage of the different types of housing since 1918.

Table 1

Year	Owner occupied	Local authority	Housing association	Private renting
1918	23%	1%		76%
1981	57%	30%	2%	11%
1991	68%	20%	3%	9%
2005	71%	11%	7%	12%

Comments on the statutory codes

The main statutory codes in operation today are as follows:

- **The Rent Act 1977** regulates most tenancies (other than local authority tenancies) created before 15 January 1989.

- **The Housing Act 1985** regulates secure tenancies from local authorities and housing action trusts, plus some registered social landlord tenancies created before 15 January 1989.

- **The Housing Act 1988** regulates private sector tenancies and most tenancies with registered social landlords created after 15 January 1989. Amended by the Housing Act 1996.

The statutory codes are designed to protect tenants and therefore will not apply to tenancies granted to limited companies, as these are deemed to be businesses which do not need the special protection granted to individuals.

The statutory codes will also only apply to 'dwelling places' (places where people live). The protection given under the codes will be lost if the tenants stop living at the property as their only or principal home (e.g. if a tenant sublets the whole of the property or moves out and lives somewhere else, he will lose the protection of the codes). However, it is sometimes possible for people to live in two places at the same time (e.g. if a family lives in one place and the father has to live elsewhere during the week for his work). Going away on a long holiday or visit will not affect your tenancy so long as you intend to return. However, you may find this difficult to prove if you are away for a very long time. If the protection of the statutory code is lost, then the tenancy will be governed by the underlying 'common law'.

The other main Acts of Parliament protecting tenants are the Protection from Eviction Act 1977, the repairing covenants in the Landlord and Tenant Act 1985 and various provisions in the Housing Act 2004. All of these are discussed in more detail in the appropriate sections below.

The different types of tenancy

It is important to know what type of tenancy you have as your legal rights will often depend upon this.

> **Note on terminology**
>
> **Security of tenure:** This is a legal term describing the tenant's long term right to stay in the property. If you have security of tenure, this means that you cannot normally be evicted unless you have behaved badly (normally by failing to pay the rent) or the landlord is able to re-house you and the judge considers it reasonable to make an order for possession.

How to work out your tenancy type

A tenancy type almost always depends on what the situation was at the time when you first moved into a property (not necessarily the one you live in now) which is owned by your current landlord. The tenancy type is 'fixed' at that time and can rarely be changed. So, for example, if you moved into a property on 19 January 1990 and it was an assured tenancy, and you then moved into another property owned by the same landlord on 20 February 2000, you will still have an assured tenancy. Even if the tenancy agreement you signed had 'assured shorthold tenancy' written at the top.

Likewise, if you rented a room in a shared house which was a protected tenancy under the Rent Act 1977, because you moved in before 15 January 1989, this will not turn into an assured shorthold tenancy because you move to another room in the same house (or to a room in another house owned by the same landlord) in 2003. The fact that you may have signed a number of different tenancy agreements in respect of your property will not change your tenancy to a different type, no matter what it says on the document you signed.

If your landlord has changed, this will not normally affect your tenancy type. For example, if you have a protected tenancy under the Rent Act and your landlord sells the property on to someone else, the purchaser will be your new landlord. He will have exactly the same legal rights and responsibilities towards you as your old landlord did, and will effectively 'step into the shoes' of your old landlord. This will normally also be the same if your property is in the social sector – that fact that the name of your landlord has changed will not affect your legal rights.

There are several types of tenancy covered by this book.

Secure tenancies

This is where the landlord is a local authority or a housing action trust. Tenancies are regulated by the Housing Act 1985. Some tenancies granted by housing associations and housing co-operatives before 15 January 1989 will also be secure. Rents for secure tenancies are generally lower than in the private sector and tenants normally have long-term security of tenure. They also have some rights which are not available to tenants of private landlords, such as the right to buy their property.

Introductory tenancies

These are tenancies granted by local authorities or housing action trusts, which have adopted an introductory tenancy scheme. They were introduced by the Housing Act 1996 (Part 5). Where there is an introductory scheme, all tenancies granted will be introductory tenancies. During the first 12 months of the tenancy the tenant will not have security of tenure (e.g. if he fails to pay rent and the landlord applies to court for a possession order, the judge will have no option but to make the order). Some of the additional rights available to secure tenants, such as the right to buy, are not available during the introductory period. Once the 12-month period has ended, the tenancy will become secure, although there is the power for the landlord to extend the introductory tenancy for a further six months. To do this, he must serve the proper form of notice on the tenant at least eight weeks before the end of the 12-month period.

Demoted tenancies

This is where a tenant's rights are reduced for a period of time (during which time they are similar to introductory tenancies). They were introduced by the Antisocial Behaviour Act 2003 to help social landlords deal with the problem of antisocial tenants. For a tenancy to be demoted the landlord has to serve a notice first, and then make an application to the local County Court for a demotion order. The only landlords who can do this are local authorities and housing action trusts (in respect of secure tenancies) and RSLs (in respect of assured tenancies). Demotion orders will last for 12–18 months.

Assured tenancies

These are tenancies created under the statutory code set up in the Housing Act 1988. They have long-term security of tenure. Since 15 January 1989 all new tenancies granted to individuals (as opposed to limited companies) have, except for a few exceptions discussed on page 38 (e.g. under common law tenancies), been either assured tenancies or assured shorthold tenancies.

If your tenancy started after 15 January 1989 and before 28 February 1997, it will automatically be an assured tenancy unless the special conditions for creating an assured shorthold tenancy (see below) were met. This is because at that time assured tenancies were the 'default' tenancy type.

Assured shorthold tenancies are much more attractive to private landlords (who like to know that they can recover possession of their property without giving a reason if they need to), so most assured tenancies created by private landlords before February 1997 were created by mistake when the landlord did not follow the proper procedures. Very few assured tenancies have been or are deliberately created by private landlords. However, most tenancies granted by housing associations/RSLs are assured tenancies.

Assured shorthold tenancies

This is the standard type of tenancy for lettings by private landlords today, and is regulated by the statutory code set up in the Housing Act 1988. The tenancy must have been created after 15 January 1989.

If your tenancy started after 15 January 1989 and before 27 February 1997, it will only be an assured shorthold tenancy if the landlord served a special notice on you under Section 20 of the Housing Act 1988 before the tenancy was signed **and** if the term of your tenancy was for a period of at least six months without the right for the landlord to end the tenancy earlier (other than via court claims for possession based on rent arrears and the like). If these conditions are not met, your tenancy will not be an assured shorthold but will be an assured tenancy, even though it may have 'assured shorthold tenancy' written on the tenancy agreement. Therefore your tenancy will not be an assured shorthold tenancy:

- if the period of the tenancy was six months less one day; or

- if the tenancy agreement contained a break clause allowing your landlord to cancel during the first six months; or

- (in most cases) if the Section 20 notice is dated the same day as the tenancy agreement, as it will be difficult for your landlord to prove that it was served before the agreement was signed rather than afterwards, or at the same time as you signed it.

If your tenancy started on or after 28 February 1997, it will automatically be an assured shorthold tenancy, either unless a notice was served on you saying that the tenancy was to be an assured tenancy (this is very rare), or unless your tenancy is a common law tenancy (see below).

The main difference between assured and assured shorthold tenancies is that assured shorthold tenants do not have long-term security of tenure. This means that your landlord can evict you from your property without having to give you a reason, so long as he follows the correct procedure, which includes giving you at least two months' written notice. Assured shorthold tenants can also challenge the rent during the first six months after they first move in (see page 120).

Protected tenants/Rent Act tenants

If your tenancy started before 15 January 1989, it will be governed by the statutory code set up in the Rent Act 1977. This means that you will have long-term security of tenure and you cannot normally be evicted. Your rent will also be protected, so long as it is registered under the 'fair rent' scheme. Protected tenancies will pass on to spouses in certain circumstances, or as assured tenancies to some family members. Most protected tenants are elderly and the number of protected tenancies in existence reduces every year. However, there are still quite a few around.

Common law tenancies

There are a number of situations where the statutory codes do not apply and the tenancy is governed by the underlying 'common law'. These are as follows:

Company lets

These have always been excluded from the protection of the statutory codes as the codes were designed to protect individuals.

Tenancies at a high rent or low rent

The high rent exceptions are those where the rent is over £25,000 per annum (i.e. over £2,083.34 per month).

The low rent exceptions are where no rent is payable, or where the rent is under £250 per annum, or £2,500 per annum in Greater London.

> **Note**
>
> If the tenancy was created before 1 April 1990 (i.e. before Council Tax was introduced and when properties paid local tax depending on their rateable value), then if the rateable value on 31 March 1990 exceeded £750 (or £1,500 in Greater London), the property will be a common law tenancy. It will also be a common law tenancy if the rent is less than two thirds of the rateable value as at 31 March 1990.

Resident landlords

This is where the landlord lives in self-contained accommodation in the same building as property rented by the tenant. The accommodation must be self-contained – if the landlord shares living accommodation, then the letting will not normally be a tenancy at all and the occupier will be a licensee or lodger. An example of a resident landlord let is where an elderly lady owns a house which has become too big for her and she has it divided into flats, one of which she lives in herself. If a resident landlord ceases to live permanently in the property, then the tenancy will become subject to the statutory code current at that time (i.e. since 28 February 1989 it will have become an assured shorthold tenancy). The resident landlord exception does not apply to purpose-built blocks of flats; so, if a landlord buys two flats in an apartment block, rents out one and lives in the other one himself, the exception will not apply.

Lettings to students

These are only lettings made to students by the college or university where they are studying (assuming that the college or university comes within the organisations specified by the Secretary of State, which most do). Other lettings to students, for example, by private landlords, will be no different to lettings made to any other type of tenant.

> **Note**
>
> If you live in student halls (which because they are licences are not covered in this book) or other student accommodation, you may find *The Student Housing Rights Guide* by Martin David and Graham Robson, published by Shelter, very helpful.

Lettings where the tenant has lost the protection of a statutory code

This is normally where a tenant, who would normally have a protected tenancy under the Rent Act 1977, or an assured tenancy under the Housing Act 1988, or a secure tenancy under the Housing Act 1985, either makes his main home elsewhere or sublets the whole of the property to someone else. Another situation is where the tenant (or one or more of joint tenants) has given the landlord written notice saying that he wishes to vacate, but then decides to stay on.

....and finally

These are the main types of tenancy covered in this book. The vast majority of residential tenants in England and Wales will fall within one or other of these categories. However, there are some other types of occupation which come within the legal definition of a tenancy. For various reasons, which I explain below, this book will not be specifically looking at these tenancies.

Tenancies not covered in this book

Protected shorthold tenancies

These were created under the Housing Act 1980 and were a forerunner of the current assured shorthold tenancy. However, most tenancies which started off as protected shortholds will by now have been converted to assured shorthold tenancies regulated by the 1988 Act. This will have happened automatically when a new tenancy agreement was granted to them. As there cannot be many protected shortholds now in existence, they are not specifically covered in this book. However, if you have a protected shorthold tenancy, note that the majority of the protective legislation, such as the landlords repairing covenants and the Protection from Eviction Act discussed in Part 2, will apply to you in the same way as they apply to all tenancies. However, the procedure which your landlord will need to follow to evict you is different and is not covered here.

Agricultural tenancies

This is where a person who has worked in agriculture for 91 weeks out of the 104 immediately preceding weeks lives in accommodation which is either directly owned by his employer or where the employer has arranged for the accommodation to be provided. The tenancy agreement, which would otherwise have been regulated by either the Rent Act 1977 or the Housing Act 1989, will be regulated instead by the Rent (Agriculture) Act 1976. As there are so few agricultural workers nowadays (even fewer who are employees), I have decided not to include agricultural tenancies within this book.

Restricted contracts

These were created under the Rent Act 1977 and are where occupiers do not have the full rights of tenants, although they do have some protection. Mainly they arose where services, such as meals, were provided with the accommodation. As no restricted contracts have been created after 15 January 1989 there can be very few left, and so they are not covered by this book.

Tolerated trespassers

A tolerated trespasser is an assured or secure tenant who has had a possession order made against him by the court under which the tenancy has come to an end, but who has stayed on in the property. The law regarding tolerated trespassers is very complex and there are confusing rules about whether a tenancy has or has not come to an end after the making of the possession order. If you have had an order for possession made against you in the past, particularly if this was a suspended possession order made between 2001 and May/June 2006, and have not subsequently signed a new tenancy agreement with your landlord, you may be a tolerated trespasser.

If you are a tolerated trespasser, you will have lost many of the normal tenants' rights, such as the right to have your property kept in repair and (for social tenancies) the right to buy. This area of law has changed recently as a result of some Court of Appeal cases and may change further in the future. If you think that you may be a tolerated trespasser, you should seek professional legal advice, preferably from a specialist housing solicitor. Note that paying off all your rent arrears may sometimes adversely affect your position so make sure you seek legal advice before this is done.

Holiday lettings

Lettings for a holiday are excluded from protection by both the Rent Act 1977 and the Housing Act 1988, so these lettings will be common law tenancies. However, this book is about tenants' rights in connection with their homes. Lettings for a holiday will not be looked at.

Residential accommodation let with commercial property

This is where a person rents living accommodation along with his business premises (e.g. a shop with a residential flat above). The letting as a whole (including the residential part) will be governed by the legislation covering commercial lettings, which is not dealt with in this book.

Note, however, that if the commercial tenant does not live in the residential accommodation and he sublets it out to someone else, that tenancy will be a normal residential tenancy as discussed in this book (it will probably be an assured shorthold tenancy).

Long leases

A lease can be of any length, but generally they are either over 21 years or less than seven years. This book is about short leases – those with a term of less than seven years. However, the vast majority of short lettings will be for terms of a year or less, although the tenants may actually live in the property for very much longer than that. When a lease is 21 years or longer, it is treated differently. It needs to be registered with the Land Registry and it is governed by different legislation. As the legal regime for long leases is different from those of short leases, they are not covered by this book.

Houses in Multiple Occupation (HMOs)

For many years there have been special regulations applying where people who are not family members live in close proximity. Buildings where this happens are known as Houses in Multiple Occupation, generally referred to as HMOs.

The occupiers of HMOs can be either tenants or licensees, and the tenancies can be any of the types discussed above. The important thing is not the type of letting but whether the letting comes within the definition of an HMO. The definition was amended by the Housing Act 2004 and is now very long and complex. Basically a property will be an HMO if two or more 'households' share living accommodation, such as a kitchen, bathroom or toilet. Note also:

- A household is a family unit such as a couple (who can be married or unmarried, including same-sex couples) or relatives (including half-relatives and foster children), plus any domestic staff if they are living rent free in accommodation provided by the person for whom they are working.

- It does not matter whether the occupiers of the property have all signed the same tenancy agreement or whether they have signed separate tenancy agreements for their own rooms. A landlord cannot prevent a property from being an HMO by getting the tenants to all sign one agreement.

- The accommodation must be used as the occupiers' only or main residence. However, the legislation specifically states that the definition will include full-time students, migrant or seasonal workers where the employer provides the accommodation, some refuges and hostels, and some accommodation given to asylum seekers.

The following are exempt under the Housing Act 2004 from the HMO definition:

- Social tenancies (including local authority tenancies and RSLs).

- Halls of residence and other university accommodation if the university is specified as an exempt body (so most university and college accommodation will be exempt). However, most of these will have signed up to a code of standards.

- Dwellings occupied by no more than two people.

- Other exemptions include some religious communities, prisons, care homes, etc.

If a property comes within the HMO definition, the landlord (or manager) will have to comply with the management regulations, and some properties will have to be licensed with the local authority.

Management regulations

These apply to all HMOs. The person managing the HMO (who can be the owner/landlord or someone specifically appointed as a manager) is responsible for the following:

- Providing contact details and displaying these prominently in the HMO.

- Making sure that all means of escape from fire are maintained and kept free from obstruction, that all fire precautions are maintained, and that steps are taken to protect the occupants from injury.

- Maintaining the water supply and drainage.

- Ensuring that annual gas safety checks are carried out and electrical installations are checked every five years, plus the manager must not unreasonably cause any interruption to the gas or electricity supply.

- Maintaining, repairing and keeping clean all common parts and installations, and making sure that common parts have adequate lighting.

- Making sure that each unit of accommodation and any furniture are clean at the start of each occupation and maintaining the internal structure and installations in each letting.

- Providing adequate waste storage facilities and making arrangements for the collection of rubbish.

Non-compliance with the regulations is a criminal offence. This means that tenants cannot sue for compensation (as they could if it were a liability under the civil law). If the regulations are not being complied with, you should complain to the Housing Officer at your local authority, who can enforce them by bringing a prosecution against the HMO manager. Also if the property is one which needs a licence, the landlord may find it difficult to obtain one in future if he does not comply with the management regulations.

Note, however, that tenants also have duties under the regulations not to hinder or oppose the manager in the carrying out of these duties. So you must allow the manager to enter your part of the property if this is necessary and provide any information which he may need. You must not damage the property and you must comply with any rules made (e.g. regarding fire safety and rubbish collection). If not, then you also can be prosecuted and if you are convicted, you will be fined up to £5,000 under the regulations.

Licensing

The Housing Act 2004 for the first time imposed mandatory licensing requirements. However, these do not apply to all HMO properties. At present mandatory licensing applies to all properties where the building or any part of it comprises three storeys or more with five or more occupants living in two or more households. Local authorities also have the power to require licensing for other HMOs, and it is up to the individual authority whether it decides to do this.

If a property needs to be licensed, the landlord must apply to the local authority and pay the relevant fee. Provided that the application is made properly, the proposed manager is someone who is a 'fit and proper person' (e.g. does not have any convictions for housing-related offences) and the property is suitable for the proposed number of occupants, the licence will normally be granted, generally for a period of five years. However, during that time the property will be inspected by the local authority to make sure that it is in a proper condition and that the amenity standards have been complied with.

Again, non-compliance with the licensing regulations is a criminal offence, not a civil wrong or breach of contract, so you cannot sue your landlord for compensation if he is not licensed when he ought to be. However, two of the penalties for non-compliance will benefit tenants. The penalties are:

- The landlord can be prosecuted and on conviction fined up to £20,000.

- If the landlord is convicted, the tenant can then apply to the Residential Property Tribunal for a rent repayment order (assuming that the tenant has actually paid the rent).

- A landlord who should have applied for a licence but has not, will not be entitled to apply to the court for an order for possession under the 'no fault' notice only ground, under Section 21 of the Housing Act 1988.

If you think that your landlord is not complying with the management regulations properly, or he ought to be licensed but is not, speak to the Housing Officer at your local authority, who will investigate the matter for you.

> **Further information**
>
> See also the section on HMOs in Chapter 10 on tenants' rights on disrepair and the condition of the property in Part 2.
>
> The website of the Residential Property Tribunal – www.rpts.gov.uk.
>
> Contact details for local authorities – www.localauthoritydirectory. co.uk.

Other relevant matters

This section looks at a number of legal points and definitions which you need to know about.

Shared houses and 'joint and several liability'

If you are sharing a house or flat with other tenants, there are two ways this can be done. Either all the tenants can sign the same agreement, or they each sign their own tenancy agreement for their own room and shared use of the rest of the property.

Joint agreements

Landlords generally prefer tenants all to sign the same agreement. The reason for this is a legal rule known as 'joint and several liability'. What this means is that the tenants who have signed are all responsible together and individually for the whole of the rent, and for any other money which may become due to the landlord (e.g. for breakages).

So, for example, let us say that four students, Matthew, Mark, Luke and John, all sign a tenancy agreement for the rent of a house at £400 per month. They may agree among themselves that they will each pay £100. However, if John refuses to pay, then the landlord can claim the overdue rent from the other three tenants, as they are all jointly liable for it. It does not even matter if the tenant is actually living in the property. So, as an extreme example, if John moves out, and the other three tenants fail to pay any rent at all, the landlord will be entitled to claim from John the whole of the £400 per month. It will be entirely up to the landlord if he decides to sue for the money, whether he sues just one of the tenants or all of them jointly. Normally he will sue all of them jointly, but it is possible that if one of the tenants is wealthy, say Luke, he will decide to sue just Luke. If, as a result of this, Luke ends up paying to the landlord his co-tenant's share of the rent, he is entitled to claim this back from the other tenants. However, this will not affect his liability to the landlord.

Generally tenants also prefer joint agreements, as they can choose the people they are sharing with. However, if you do this, you must be very careful to choose people you can trust. If you sign a joint tenancy agreement with them, you are potentially making yourself liable to the landlord for their share of the rent.

If one of the joint tenants decides to leave, you will probably want to find someone else to replace him (unless the remaining tenants are able to pay the extra rent). It is best to do this in agreement with the landlord, and get a new tenancy agreement signed with the remaining tenants and the new replacement tenant. Then the outgoing tenant will no longer be liable to the landlord for the rent, as he will have been replaced by the incoming tenant. Remember that the new person will not legally be a tenant until he signs the tenancy agreement.

Contrary to what some people may tell you, there is no legal reason why the new replacement tenancy agreement should not be for the remainder of the original term. So, in this example, if Matthew decides to leave his college course five months into a 12-month tenancy agreement, there is no reason why a new agreement should not be signed with Mark, Luke, John and a new tenant, Paul, for the remaining seven months. However, the landlord may require you to pay for the new tenancy to be drawn up, and for credit reference checks to be made against Paul.

So far as the damage deposit is concerned, Paul will have to pay his share over before Matthew can be refunded. It may be easier for Paul just to pay this to Matthew direct.

Q My brother is renting a student house with two other friends. One of the 'friends' has disappeared leaving arrears, and the agent has turned up saying that they have two days before the bailiffs come in to take their stuff. They are also being told that they have to pay the rest of the rent for the entire duration of the tenancy and leave immediately as they are in breach. Is this completely ludicrous and what should they do?

A If your brother and his friends all signed the same tenancy agreement, then they will all be liable for all of the rent and not just for their own individual share. If they signed individual tenancy agreements for their own room and shared the use of the rest of the house, they will only be liable for their own rent. I suspect that they all signed the same agreement as this is common practice in student lets. So, yes, they will all be liable for the rent of the tenant who has left (although if they have to pay it for him, they are legally entitled to recover it back from him). However, the landlord cannot just come in and take their possessions to pay for this; neither can he evict them without getting a court order. If he tries to do this, it is harassment, which is a criminal offence. Your brother and the remaining tenants can speak to the Tenancy Relations or Housing Officer about this at their local authority. If the landlord persists in the harassment, the Tenancy Relations or Housing Officer can write a letter asking him to stop and if he does not, bring a prosecution. If your brother is a student, he may also be able to get help from the accommodation office at his college or university.

Individual agreements

If tenants are likely to be coming and going at different times, it will normally be more convenient for them to be signed up as tenants individually. Here, their tenancy agreement will be for their own room (or rooms) and for the shared use of the rest of the property. Under this arrangement, they will not be at risk if one of the other tenants fails to pay. There is also much less of a problem if one of them decides to leave before the others, as regularising the paperwork will not affect the other tenants. However, although the landlord will probably consult them when choosing a replacement, the tenants will not ultimately have any control over who the other tenants will be.

Landlords will normally prefer to let properties on joint agreements if they can, as it is administratively easier for them. As tenants are all jointly responsible for the whole of the rent, the onus on finding a replacement if someone decides to leave will be on them rather than on him, plus it will be easier to have the utility accounts put into the names of one or more of the tenants.

> **Note**
>
> If a property is let as a whole, there can be no other lettings in respect of that property until the original agreement has ended. So, in the example, when Matthew leaves, the landlord cannot give an individual tenancy of the back bedroom to Paul, as that is already let out under the original agreement. The only way that Paul can become a tenant is if that original agreement is ended, which is normally done in this situation by replacing it with a new one.

Fixed-term and periodic tenancies

When you are given a tenancy agreement, particularly if it is one given by a private landlord, it will normally be for a specific period of time (e.g. six months or a year). This is known as a fixed term.

However, some tenancies are not for any specific period of time, but are tenancies which run from week-to-week or from month-to-month. These are known as periodic tenancies.

Some periodic tenancies have always been periodic (e.g. most social tenancies); others become periodic if they run on after the fixed term has come to an end, which most tenancies will do if they are not replaced by another fixed-term agreement.

Just because your tenancy runs from week-to-week or month-to-month does not mean that you have less security of tenure. Your landlord will still have to give you notice if he wants you to leave, and you will be entitled to stay in the property until an order for possession has been obtained by your landlord in the County Court. Virtually all of the older pre-1989 tenancies will be periodic tenancies, as their fixed terms will have run out long ago.

Ending tenancies

Most tenancies do not terminate at the end of the fixed term in the tenancy agreement. Before the introduction of the statutory codes they did, and strictly speaking they still do with common law tenancies (i.e. those tenancies where the statutory codes do not apply) – the legal phrase that lawyers use is that the tenancy ends by 'effluxion of time' (i.e. because time has run out). However, even in common law tenancies, if the tenant stays on and the landlord continues to accept the rent, it will be taken that he has agreed to allow the tenancy to continue. However, the tenant of a common law tenancy who has stayed on after the end of the fixed term will not be able to prevent the landlord from obtaining a court order for possession after he has served a special form called a 'notice to quit'.

However, under the statutory codes, a tenancy will continue after the end of any fixed term granted by the landlord. This is known as a 'statutory tenancy' (because it is a tenancy which has been created by statute) as opposed to the preceding fixed-term contractual tenancy granted by the landlord. The statutory codes provide that a new periodic tenancy will take the place of the original fixed-term tenancy, on the same terms and conditions, and with the period of the tenancy being the same as the period for which rent is payable. Therefore, the tenancy will run from month-to-month (if rent is paid monthly) and from week-to-week (if the tenancy is paid weekly). This statutory tenancy can only be brought to an end by agreement or by a court order.

To summarise, the various ways a tenancy can end are as follows:

- Effluxion of time (for common law tenancies only).

- By the tenant moving out at the end of the fixed term, or if he stays on after the end of the fixed term, after having given notice of at least one month ending at the end of a rental period. If the tenant moves out without giving notice, the landlord is entitled to rent in lieu of notice.

- By the tenancy being replaced by a new tenancy agreement (e.g. if the tenancy is renewed or if a new agreement is signed after one or more of the tenants have changed).

- By a court order for possession.

Q Can you please tell me if the act of returning the keys to a rented property constitutes the end of the agreement. I have had an additional week's money taken from my deposit because I did not return the keys on the day my notice ended, even though I had moved out two weeks before. There are no details of this in my tenancy agreement.

A If a tenant fails to return the keys, this is normally taken to mean that he has not given up the tenancy, even if he has actually moved out. After all, as you held the keys you could still enter the property whenever you wanted, and for all the landlord knew you might have deliberately withheld the keys because you still needed to use it. A landlord cannot re-let a property until he has the keys back, unless he arranges to have the locks changed. However, he needs to be careful about changing locks, as the tenant may then claim unlawful eviction, which is a criminal offence. Therefore, it is not unreasonable for your landlord to claim the week's rent from your damage deposit.

Q I have an assured shorthold tenancy agreement, which I have just signed for another six months after a very harmonious first six-month period. A friend has now asked me to house-sit for her starting in a month's time. Is there any way I can break out of my tenancy agreement early without incurring hideous costs?

A I am afraid that if you have signed for a further fixed term, you are contractually bound to the landlord to pay rent for that period. If you just move out, he can sue you for the outstanding rent. However, have a word with your landlord. If the property is in a popular area, he may be willing to re-let to another tenant provided that you pay the costs of re-letting. Alternatively, if you are able to find a suitable tenant to take your place, the landlord should agree to this, subject to your paying any charges (e.g. for getting references for the new tenant).

Sitting tenants

A sitting tenant is a phrase used to describe a tenant who cannot be evicted. In a sense all residential tenants are sitting tenants, because it is a criminal offence to evict a residential tenant other than by obtaining a court order, and in virtually all cases it will take several months to complete the eviction process.

However, the phrase is generally used to indicate a tenant who either cannot be evicted at all, or can only be evicted with great difficulty.

The main types of sitting tenant (i.e. tenants who have security of tenure and who cannot be evicted easily) are those who have protected tenancies under the Rent Act 1977 and assured tenancies under the Housing Act 1988. Plus most social tenants (other than introductory and demoted tenancies) have security of tenure.

Working out your type of occupation

Before you can use the section on tenants' rights, you need to work out what sort of tenancy you have, as this will affect the rights that you are entitled to. This is what a solicitor or other legal adviser would do before giving legal advice. Use these two pages to record the details of your tenancy so you can refer to this while going through the rights section. It will also be very useful for your adviser if you need to take professional legal advice.

- Do you think you have a tenancy or a licence **(see page 24)**?

  ☐ Tenancy ☐ Licence

If you have a licence, there is no need to complete the rest of this list. Much of the information in this book will not be relevant to you.

- What sort of landlord do you have?

  ☐ Local authority
  ☐ Housing association/RSL (including not-for-profit organisations, housing co-operatives, etc.)
  ☐ Private landlord
  ☐ College or university

- What is the date when you first moved into your current property?

  _____

- Tenants of private landlords: If you previously lived in another property owned by the same or one of the same landlords as you have now, when did you first move into the original property?

  _____

  (Note: This is the date that will govern the type of tenancy you have now.)

- Tenants of housing association/RSL landlords: Was your landlord originally a local authority?

  ☐ Yes ☐ No

  If yes, give the date the tenancy transferred.

  _____

- Do you have a written tenancy agreement?

  ☐ Yes ☐ No

  If so, go and get it and keep it (or a copy of it) with this book. You will need to refer to it sometimes when checking your rights. If you have more than one agreement, make sure that you have the first agreement and the current one.

- Does your tenancy agreement give a fixed term?

  ☐ Yes ☐ No

If so, write down the fixed-term dates given in the most recent agreement _____

If this has ended, you will have a monthly or weekly 'periodic' tenancy, depending on how your rent is paid.

- From the information given in Part 1, what sort of tenancy do you think you have?

  ☐ Secure

  ☐ Introductory or demoted

  ☐ Assured tenancy

  ☐ Assured shorthold tenancy

  ☐ Protected (or statutory) Rent Act tenancy

  ☐ Common law tenancy

  Plus

- Is it an HMO?

  ☐ Yes

  ☐ No

Other background information

Letting agents

Many private landlords will employ letting agents to deal with the letting and management of their properties for them; maybe you found your property through a letting agent. Letting agents vary widely in competence and sadly there is as yet no legal regulation. So if you are thinking of finding a property via an agent, it is best to use one who is a member of a recognised organisation, such as the National Approved Letting Scheme (NALS) – www.nalscheme.co.uk; the Association of Residential Letting Agents (ARLA) – www.arla.co.uk; the Royal Institute of Chartered Surveyors (RICS) – www.rics.org; or the National Association of Estate Agents (NAEA) – www.naea.co.uk.

Agency law

There is special area of law called the law of agency, which regulates situations where an agent is used. This is not unique to the letting business – there are many legal cases about shipping agents. This section gives a brief overview of agency law.

The terms generally used in agency law are the **principal** (the landlord), the **agent** (the letting agent), and the **third party** (you, the tenant).

Here are a few important points of agency law:

- If an agent is acting on behalf of a disclosed principal (i.e. if it is clear that he is acting on behalf of a landlord rather than letting his own property), then if the third party wishes to bring a claim then it will be the principal who is liable, not the agent. So, if an agent acts in the letting of a property which subsequently turns out to be in poor condition, and the tenant wishes to make a claim for compensation, then it is the landlord who should be sued, not the agent. Even if it is the agent's fault that the property is in poor condition.

- If an agent makes an agreement with a third party in respect of something which would appear to be within his authority as agent, then the principal is bound by this, even if the agent acted against the principal's instructions. So, if an agent tells you that you can keep a pet in a property, then you will normally be entitled to rely on this even if it later turns out that the landlord had told the agent 'no pets'. A third party is entitled to rely on an agent's assurances, as it is not his fault if the landlord and agent have not sorted out properly what the agent can and cannot do.

- However, this only extends to things which you would normally expect an agent to be able to agree to. So, if a tenant asks to be allowed to build an extension on to a property, this is not normally something an agent would be allowed to agree to. If the agent says he thinks it will be all right, do not rely on this and do not take out a bank loan and start building!

- If an agent does not disclose the fact that he is acting as an agent, then he is personally liable to the third party. Therefore, if an agent lets a property but it is not apparent (and you are not told) that it is not his own property and that he is acting on behalf of a landlord (e.g. if his name goes into the tenancy agreement and he signs it), then if anything goes wrong, it is the agent who is liable and who should be sued, rather than the real property owner.

- Specifically on the subject of damage and other deposits, it will usually be the landlord who is liable for its return and who should be sued, rather than the agent, even though the money may actually be held in the agent's bank account and it is the agent who is the one being obstructive although this changes if the tenancy agreement states that the deposit is held by the agent as 'stakeholder'. However, note that most damage deposits after 6 April 2007 will be held under one of the statutory deposit schemes. For more information about this and deposits generally, see Chapter 7 on the tenant's right to have his deposit returned.

Problems with agents

As the agent is acting on behalf of the landlord, it is the landlord who is generally legally liable for any disputes with his agent. However, if you consider that the agent is acting improperly, you may be able to make a complaint to his professional organisation (if he has one) or to the Trading Standards Office. For more information on this, see Chapter 21 on making complaints.

Q Our letting agent no longer exists, but we are still living in the property and paying rent to the landlord directly. Is the agreement made by the letting agent now void due to the company no longer existing and are we legally still allowed to reside in the house?

A It is difficult to answer precisely without seeing the documents but, yes, you are legally allowed to reside in the house. If your original agreement gave the name of the real landlord, then there is no problem. If, as sometimes happens, the agreement gave the name of the agents as your landlord, then it would be best for a new agreement to be signed with your real landlord as soon as possible, just to regularise the situation. But the fact that he knows you are there and is accepting rent from you would mean that you have a tenancy, even if there were no written agreement at all.

Disability and disability discrimination

Life is considerably harder for the disabled, in ways which people who are not disabled may not realise. Problems include physical or environmental problems (such as difficulties in moving from place to place, entering and moving within buildings, or in obtaining access to services) as well as problems arising from assumptions that people falsely make about disabled people, which affect the way they interact with them.

In order to create a more 'level playing field' for the disabled, various rights have now been set out in the disability legislation, in particular the Disability Discrimination Act 1995.

Under the 1995 Act, disability is defined as 'a physical or mental impairment, which has a substantial and long-term adverse effect on a person's ability to carry out normal day-to-day activities'. More recently the definition has been extended under the Disability Discrimination Act 2005 to include those with cancer, HIV/AIDS and multiple sclerosis. In addition, it is no longer necessary for the mental illness to be clinically well-recognised for someone to be recognised as having a mental impairment and therefore be disabled.

Many disabled people will be registered as disabled with their local social services department and if you are disabled, it is a good idea to register as you will then be entitled to special services, such as reduced fees for facilities and blue badges for parking. However, you do not need to be registered disabled to take advantage of the disability legislation.

The 1995 Act makes it an offence to discriminate against a disabled person:

- by offering a property on worse terms than for a non-disabled person;
- by refusing to sell or let a property;
- by social landlords treating a disabled person less favourably in the maintenance of housing lists;
- by treating the disabled person differently in the way in which he is allowed to make use of the property's facilities;
- by preventing the disabled person from using benefits or facilities;
- by evicting the disabled person or subjecting him to any other form of disadvantage because of this disability.

The Disability Discrimination Act 2005 imposes a duty on landlords and others who manage rented premises to make reasonable adjustments for disabled occupiers. These provisions do not apply to landlords who let six or fewer rooms in their own home. Discriminatory treatment is justifiable under the Act if the landlord can prove that his actions were necessary to protect the health and safety of any person, and in certain other situations.

Claims under the disability discrimination legislation are more commonly raised against social landlords, but they are equally valid against private landlords.

If you are disabled, you may be able to seek help from the Disability Rights Commission. This has statutory duties to:

- work towards eliminating discrimination against disabled people;
- promote equal opportunities for disabled people;
- encourage good practice in the treatment of disabled people;
- advise the government on the working of disability legislation.

It can provide specific assistance to disabled people, including helping them to enforce their rights and arranging for legal advice and mediation where appropriate. It also provides advice and information to disabled people, employers and service providers.

The Disability Rights Commission has a helpful website at www.drc.org.uk.

Special obligations of social landlords

A very large proportion of disabled people live in social housing. Social landlords are being encouraged to do more for the disabled and local authority landlords and most other social landlords are now being required to produce a Disability Equality Scheme and action plan, to be published by December 2007. A statutory code of practice is also being developed.

For more information, see the document '*Housing and the Disability Equality Duty – A Guide to the Disability Equality Duty and Disability Discrimination Act 2005 for the Social Housing Sector*', which you will find on the Disability Rights Commission's website.

CHAPTER 3

Court proceedings

General advice on paperwork

Anything to do with the legal system and legal problems inevitably involves paperwork. It is easy to get in a muddle with paperwork, so follow these simple rules:

- Keep a written record of all meetings and telephone calls. Make sure that these are dated.

- If possible, all paperwork and letters should be printed rather than handwritten as handwriting is often difficult to read. The recipient of your letter is more likely to deal with it if he can read it!

- When writing letters or other documents, write in short paragraphs and use bullet points, as again these will make your document easier to read.

- It is often best to set things out in chronological order.

- When sending out paperwork never send original documents (such as invoices or tenancy agreements). Always send copies. If you send an original document, you may not get it back!

- Keep all paperwork on a matter together, preferably in a folder clearly marked. Correspondence should be kept in chronological order, with the most recent at the top.

- It is probably also wise to keep a printed record of emails and electronic documents. Otherwise, if you have a hard drive failure and have not backed it up, you could lose all your evidence.

- Forget about saving the planet by reducing paperwork. The amount of paperwork for your particular problem is not going to make much difference globally, but not having proper paperwork could make a serious difference to your claim!

- Do not throw paperwork away if you think the problem has been resolved. It may come back and if you have destroyed your paperwork, this will put you at a disadvantage. Ideally, you should keep your paperwork for at least six years.

Court claims

This section gives an overview of how County Court proceedings work. This information is given here (rather than later in the book) because many of the sections on individual tenants' rights in Part 2 discuss court claims, and you will understand these better if you have read this section first. However, when reading, bear in mind that the particular types of claim mentioned are discussed in more detail in Part 2. They are just referred to here to illustrate the different types of procedure.

I will be looking only at civil claims here, as these are the claims tenants are most likely to be personally involved in. Remember that in civil court claims, the person bringing the claim is normally known as the 'claimant' and the person or organisation the claim is brought against is known as the 'defendant'.

Before the claim starts

For almost every type of claim, the court will expect you to have contacted the defendants before the claim starts, warning them that you are considering going to court and giving them an opportunity to resolve the problem first. Also, if there is a complaints procedure available, you should use it (you will find more about making complaints in Part 4). Going to court should always be a last resort, and the courts will frown on 'gung-ho' claimants bringing a legal action without warning on an unsuspecting defendant. Courts are busy and there is a lot of pressure on judges' time, so they are keen to avoid unnecessary and time-wasting cases.

For some types of claim there are special rules laid down setting out what you need to do before issuing proceedings, known as 'pre-action protocols'. There are pre-action protocols if you are bringing a claim against your landlord regarding his failure to keep the property in repair (known as disrepair claims), and when you are bringing a claim for damages for personal injury (e.g. caused by the poor condition of the property). Social landlords will also have to comply with a rent arrears protocol when they are bringing claims for possession based on rent arrears. Protocols set out a list of things which must be done before court action can be issued. For example, the housing disrepair protocol requires you to send the landlord a formal letter giving full details of the repairs which need to be done.

If there is a protocol for your type of claim, the court will expect you to have followed it before proceedings are started. If you do not, you may be ordered to pay the other party's legal costs and the judge may impose other sanctions.

You will find details of all the pre-action protocols on the Department of Constitutional Affairs website in the section for the Civil Procedure Rules at www.dca.gov.uk/civil/procrules_fin/index.htm.

For possession claims, the landlord needs to serve the relevant possession notice on the tenant first, and he must not issue proceedings before the notice period has expired. There are different notices for different types of claim. If the notice is not served or is wrong, often the landlord will not succeed in his claim.

For money claims, it is normal to send a 'letter before action' to the proposed defendant, giving details of the sum claimed and warning that if payment is not made within a specific period of time (traditionally seven or 14 days), you will be bringing court proceedings.

For all other claims, some sort of warning letter should be sent, giving the other party the opportunity to sort out the problem before court proceedings are issued. Very occasionally it will not be appropriate to do this (e.g. if you are seeking an injunction in respect of something which may be removed or disposed of if the defendant gets any warning), but these types of cases are very rare and should not be brought without obtaining legal advice first.

Bringing the claim

To bring a claim you will need to use the appropriate claim form (and provide the court with an extra copy for each defendant) and send this to (or 'file' it at) the appropriate court together with the court issue fee (which varies according to the type of case). All of the court forms are available to download from the court service website at hmcourts-service.gov.uk.

If you are unfamiliar with bringing cases through the courts, it is best to get some guidance before issuing a claim. For simple claims, the guidance leaflets provided by the courts are very helpful, and they are also available online. Alternatively, for a money claim, you can use Lawpack's *Small Claims Kit* (available at www.lawpack.co.uk), or my online kit for damage deposits (available at www.landlordlaw.co.uk). Otherwise, see Chapter 21 on obtaining legal advice.

Note that if you are on benefit or have a low income, you may be eligible for a fee exemption. For more information, see the information leaflet EX160a, available from all court offices or the Court Service's website.

After the issue of proceedings

The court will send you notice of the issue of your claim, and will send a copy of the claim forms and various other paperwork (including in most cases a defence form) to the defendant.

For many types of claim it is possible to apply to the court for a final order without having a court hearing, if the defendant does not file a defence; for example, in claims for money, such as damage deposit claims. However, the court will not do this automatically and you must apply at the proper time (the paperwork sent to you by the court will normally tell you when this is). Possession orders for claims brought by landlords under the accelerated procedure are also normally made without a court hearing. Other types of possession claims are always set down for a hearing.

For most claims where a defence is filed, you will normally have to complete a form, known as an 'allocation questionnaire', and pay a fee (normally the claimant has to pay this). The allocation questionnaire is for you to provide information about the case. This is then referred to the judge for him to make 'directions' on how the case is to be dealt with, such as how long the court hearing will be listed for, whether it needs to be transferred to another court and what documentation needs to be exchanged. For more complex cases there may be a number of short hearings to decide these matters. Court orders on procedural matters made between the issue of proceedings and the trial proper are often referred to as 'interlocutory orders'. It is important that you comply with all interlocutory orders made, as otherwise this may affect your claim.

If you are the defendant in a claim issued against you by your landlord, it is important that you do not ignore it, but that you take legal advice. You may need to file a defence to protect your position.

Settlement

The vast majority of court actions never reach a hearing as they are 'settled' or agreed. In a financial claim (e.g. against your landlord for the return of your damage deposit), you may reach agreement that he repays £400. If the money has been paid and there is nothing more to do, you can simply write to the court and say that the matter has been resolved and that you do not wish to proceed. However, you should not do this if the money has not been paid, otherwise if the defendant fails to pay, you will have to start all over again. In this case you should tell the court what has been agreed and ask the court to put it in a court order. The defendant will have to agree to this. Normally, where a money claim has been agreed, your landlord will not want a judgment registered against him and he will make payment to prevent this happening.

If you are involved in a claim for possession, and the landlord agrees to allow you to stay, then you need to make sure either that this is set out in a court order or that the claim is withdrawn. It is best to get some legal advice here – if possible, you will not want a possession order made against you (although in some types of claim you may not be able to prevent this from happening).

For more complicated claims (e.g. in a claim against a landlord regarding disrepair), the claim may be settled 'on terms'; for example, on the basis that the landlord will do specified repair work and pay the tenants compensation of £3,000. Here, it is normal to prepare a draft court order setting out the terms of the settlement and to ask the court to approve it and make the order. This is best done by a solicitor – even if you are acting in person, it is best to get legal advice on the wording of the final order as you need to make sure that your position is protected. This is difficult if you are not experienced in this type of work, and it is easy to leave something out which will cause problems later.

You should always try to settle a case if you can, as this saves time and money, as well as the worry and stress of a court hearing.

Court hearings

If you are a party in a court case, you can either represent yourself (in which case you will be known as a litigant-in-person) or you can be legally represented, normally by a solicitor. These notes are to help you if you are representing yourself. If you are being represented, your solicitor will advise you what to do.

General matters

If you need to attend a court hearing, make sure that you arrive in time or the hearing may take place without you (although most hearings start later than listed – in my experience, only the cases where you are late start on time!). Try to dress smartly as this gives a better impression. As soon as you arrive at court, look for the lists of hearings (normally found on a noticeboard near the door, or ask someone) and then, before doing anything else, find the usher for your court and tell him that you are there. Once he knows that you are there, he will make sure that you are called when the hearing is about to start, so that you do not miss it.

Most housing-related cases will be heard by District Judges. You call them 'Sir' or 'Ma'am'. Larger trials may be heard by Circuit Judges (who can be recognised by the purple trim on their gowns) and you call them 'Your

Honour'. Many cases will be heard in the judge's room, where you will sit on one side of a table and your opponent will sit at the other, with the judge at the head of the table. If you are in a court room, you will need to sit at the front – the usher will normally show you where (do not be afraid to ask).

When in court be polite and respectful at all times and do not lose your temper (it will not do you any good). The claimant will be expected to present his case first, and call any relevant evidence. The defendant will then present his case and call his evidence, after which the claimant will normally have an opportunity to deal with any points which arose during the presentation of the defence.

You should not interrupt the other party. Allow him to have his say, however strongly you may disagree with it. Make notes on everything, particularly on things you will want to deal with later so you do not forget.

Most cases brought by litigants-in-person will be dealt with fairly informally (compared to trials with professional advocates) and the judge may depart from the standard procedure if he thinks it appropriate. He is in charge and you should follow his guidance. It is his job to see that you are treated fairly and that the correct decision is reached.

Evidence

Evidence is normally given on oath (i.e. a sworn statement). If you lie while giving evidence on oath, this is called 'perjury' and is a criminal offence. If you do not want to swear on the Bible, you can affirm. You will normally be asked if you would like this. If you are not asked, do not be afraid to say (if this is the case) that you would prefer to affirm.

The initial evidence given by someone (i.e. one of the parties to the case or a witness) is called 'evidence-in-chief'. The opposing party (or his representative) is then always allowed to cross-examine (i.e. ask questions based on the evidence given). The person calling the evidence will then be given an opportunity to ask any final questions (called 're-examination'), perhaps picking up on matters dealt with in cross-examination.

In many cases, there will be a 'conflict of evidence', where one party will say one thing and the other party something else. If possible, you should provide 'corroboration' for what you say – this can be documents (letters, bank statements, etc.), the evidence of a witness (who will need to attend the court hearing), photographs or even a video. If you do not have corroboration, this does not necessarily mean that you will lose. Judges are accustomed to weighing up evidence and they generally develop a sixth sense which tells them when someone is not telling the truth. This is an important part of their job. However, they are not infallible, so try to find as much corroboration to back up your case as you can.

Presentation

When presenting a case try to be clear and concise and deal with things in chronological order. If it is appropriate, use chronologies, lists and schedules as they are always helpful, so long as they are concise and easy to read (ideally typewritten bullet points – do not use handwriting unless it is very clear). Explain matters fully and do not expect the judge to be a mind reader.

Be aware that you will need to prove two things for everything you are claiming:

1. That you are legally entitled to it (i.e. that the defendant is liable – known as 'liability'); and

2. That the remedy you are asking for is appropriate. For example, that any sum of money you are claiming in respect of your legal right (known as 'the quantum') is fair and reasonable. In possession claims where there is no mandatory ground (see Chapter 13 for further information), the landlord will have to persuade the judge that it is reasonable for a possession order to be made.

If you are the claimant, you will normally have the burden of proof, which for civil cases is 'on the balance of probability' (as opposed to 'beyond reasonable doubt', which is the burden of proof for criminal cases). This means that you will have to prove to the judge that it is more likely that what you are saying is true than what the defendant is saying. If you are a defendant, then it will normally be your opponent who has the burden of proof.

Note that if the judge stops you when you are speaking and says that you need not say any more, this does not mean that he is denying you your day in court; it normally means that you have won! Conversely, if he has decided not to find in your favour, he will often allow you to say as much as you want so he cannot be accused later of refusing to listen to you.

Judgment

After both sides have presented their case, it is time for the judge to make his decision. Sometimes he will want a bit of time to think about it and will ask you to come back in a few minutes' time. In complex cases he may even ask you to come back on another day. However, usually he will have made up his mind already and will give his decision immediately.

He will generally give a little speech, saying which evidence he preferred and why, and will then say what order he is going to make. It is very important that you write down as much of this as possible. If you think that the judge has made a mistake and you go for legal advice later, one of the first things the adviser will ask is, 'What reasons did the judge give for his decision?' If you have forgotten, then it will be very difficult for the adviser to help you.

Costs

Once the judge has made his decision, he will then deal with legal costs. A winning party is entitled to costs, but this will not necessarily be all that the case has cost him. If you, as a litigant-in-person, are the winner, you will normally (at least for standard cases) only be entitled to any court fees you have paid, plus the costs of attending court (including witness expenses). Therefore, you should make sure that you have all train tickets, parking receipts and the like available at court in case the judge asks for them. You can also make a claim for loss of income caused by attending the hearing, but again you will need some sort of confirmation – a letter from your employer will normally suffice. The judge will normally ask you if you have any costs to claim, but if he does not, you should remind him.

Where the winning party is represented, for most standard cases, the only costs awarded by the court are 'fixed costs', which are sums specified by the court to be awarded for particular types of action. For example, if an order for possession is made against you in favour of your landlord, you will normally be ordered to pay 'fixed costs'. However, the figure awarded will almost always be less than the sum your landlord will actually have paid his solicitor for doing the work.

In complicated cases, the costs figure awarded is generally based on the work actually done by the winning party's solicitor, but unless the costs can be agreed, they will be decided by a judge in a separate (and often complex) court procedure known as 'assessment of costs'. If you are acting as a litigant-in-person in a situation where you have been ordered to pay your opponent's assessed costs, then before agreeing any figures, you should obtain legal advice either from a solicitor or from a legal professional who specialises in this type of work known as a 'law costs draftsman'.

To find a law costs draftsman in your area, see their association website at www.alcd.org.uk.

Court orders

After the hearing (sometimes several weeks later) you will be sent a court order which sets out the decision reached by the judge. Check this very carefully when it is received to make sure that it is correct – mistakes do sometimes happen. If you spot a mistake, write to the court about it and the court will normally amend the order and send out a new one. Make sure that you keep the order safely. If you lose it, the court may be able to send you a replacement, but this will normally take several weeks.

Enforcement

If you win your case, this does not necessarily mean that the losing party will do what he is supposed to do. The courts therefore provide special procedures to force losing parties to comply with the court orders that have been made. This is known as 'enforcement'.

Money judgments

Once a judgment has been obtained, the winner is often known as the 'judgment creditor' and the person who is liable to pay the money as the 'judgment debtor'. Frequently, defendants will fail to pay the money due under a judgment (in the region of 30 per cent of all judgments go unpaid). There are some court enforcement procedures available to force a judgment debtor to pay, but they are not always successful. They are as follows:

- **Bailiffs/sheriffs:** Sending the County Court bailiffs or (for judgments of over £600) the High Court Sheriffs round to 'levy execution', i.e. take the judgment debtor's goods away to sell at auction to pay off the debt.

- **Attachment of earnings orders:** Where the court orders the judgment debtor's employer to pay part of his wages direct to the judgment creditor.

- **Third party payment orders:** Where someone who owes or holds money for the judgment debtor (usually a bank or building society) is ordered to pay this over to the judgment creditor.

- **Charging orders:** Where the judgment debt is registered against a house or flat or other property/land owned by the judgment debtor as a mortgage or legal charge. This can then be enforced by obtaining an order for sale.

- **Statutory demand/bankruptcy:** Serving a statutory demand and then bringing bankruptcy proceedings against an individual or winding up proceedings against a company (although this can be made without obtaining a judgment first).

- **Court summons:** Where a judgment debtor can be summoned to court to answer questions on oath about his assets.

For more information about these enforcement procedures, see the leaflets available from the County Court or via the Court Service's website at www.hmcourts-service.gov.uk.

Possession orders

These are generally enforced by the court bailiff coming around to physically evict you. You will normally be warned of this, either by the bailiff visiting you or by letter. The bailiff has the power to evict whoever he finds at the property (whether or not they are named on the court order) and he can use reasonable force to do this if he is authorised to do so by the property owner.

Other orders

Sometimes, if the losing party to a court order fails to comply with it, the winning party can ask the court to attach a penal notice to the order, which is then re-served on him. This means that if the losing party still fails to comply, he will be in contempt of court, and could be arrested and put in prison. If you wish to obtain or are the subject of a penal notice, you should obtain legal advice.

There are a few other methods of enforcing a court order but they are very rare, are not normally appropriate for housing cases, and in any case they should not be attempted without a solicitor.

Further information

Small Claims Made Easy by Veronica Newman, published by Lawpack.

The Court Service's website – www.hmcourts-service.gov.uk.

Contact details for local authorities – www.localauthoritydirectory. co.uk.

Part 2

Tenants' rights

CHAPTER 4

The right to housing

The Human Rights Act

With the introduction of the Human Rights Act 1998, we now have for the first time an Act which lays down basic rights which people can enforce in the courts. However, these rights can only be enforced against the government and public bodies. In a housing context, this mostly means local authorities and, in some cases, registered social landlords (RSLs). A claim under the Human Rights Act cannot be brought against private landlords.

There have been a number of challenges to eviction proceedings based on the Human Rights Act, but the courts have held that there is no general right to be provided with a home, and that the Act does not guarantee the right to have one's housing problem solved by the authorities. Generally, the courts have found that the Act does not alter the exising laws, for example, regarding the eviction of tenants, so long as those laws are fair and proportionate.

Homelessness

This is dealt with under Part 7 of the Housing Act 1996 (subsequently amended by the Homelessness Act 2002), which sets out how homeless people can receive help and assistance from local authorities. There is also a Code of Guidance which sets out guidelines on the interpretation of the legislation and on good practice. Although this is not enforceable in the same way that an Act of Parliament is, local authorities are expected to follow the code and decisions which do not do so are vulnerable to being set aside by the courts.

The Code of Guidance which applies to England can be found on the website for the Communities and Local Government, and the code which applies to Wales can be found on the Welsh Assembly Government's website.

The law relating to homelessness is complex and could easily take up a book in itself (indeed there are several legal textbooks on this topic). Only a brief outline is given here.

If someone contacts a local authority seeking to be housed under the homelessness legislation, the local authority has a duty to make enquiries to see whether that person is entitled to assistance with housing. If necessary, temporary accommodation will generally be provided while these enquiries are being carried out. The local authority has a duty to provide housing where all the following apply:

- Where the person is either actually homeless or threatened with homelessness (i.e. if it is likely that he will become homeless within 28 days).

- Where the person is eligible for assistance. British nationals are normally eligible for assistance; most persons coming from abroad who do not have a job here are not. However, this is a complex area of law and cannot be summarised easily.

- Where the person is in priority need. People in priority need are basically pregnant women, families with young children, people who are 'vulnerable' due to old age, illness and disability, and people who have been made homeless due to an emergency, such as flood, fire or some other disaster.

- Where the person is not intentionally homeless. A person will be intentionally homeless if he moves out of accommodation voluntarily or if the accommodation is lost due to his own fault (such as failing to pay rent). This is why tenants who are being evicted by their landlord are always advised to stay until they are actually evicted by the bailiffs. If you move out before this (e.g. to stay with relatives), you will lose your right to be re-housed.

- The person has a local connection. This can be because he has lived there in the past, has a job or has worked there in the past (other than with the armed forces), has family there, or there are 'special circumstances'. Note, however, that if you do not have any local connections, then you can generally seek assistance from any local authority.

If these conditions do not apply, the local authority has a duty to provide advice and assistance but it is not under any statutory duty to actually provide housing. If the conditions do apply, the local authority is under a duty to provide accommodation for a period of at least two years.

Other applications for housing

If you are not technically homeless, you can still apply for local authority housing or to be housed by an RSL. However, be warned that in most areas there are long waiting lists. If you cannot wait, then you will have no alternative but to find a property in the private sector.

In neither case do you have a right to demand accommodation. Private landlords can let their properties to whom they please, so long as they do not breach the discrimination legislation. Local authorities must have an allocations scheme, which they will follow when allocating housing. You can find out more about the allocations scheme in your area and also what housing is available from RSLs and from your local authority Housing Officer.

Remedies

If you are homeless or threatened with homelessness, you should contact the Homelessness Officer at your local authority. He will investigate your case and let you know whether you are eligible to be re-housed.

If you are refused housing and you think that this decision is wrong, you can ask the local authority to review it. If you are still unhappy at the decision it comes to, it may be possible to appeal this through the courts. If this happens, you should seek professional legal advice immediately, preferably before the internal review stage.

Local authorities have a statutory duty to give advice and assistance to everyone looking for accommodation, whether or not they are homeless or in priority need. So your local authority's Housing Advice Officer (they may have different names in different authorities) is a good person to speak to if you are looking for somewhere to live.

Further information

For contact details for local authorities, see www.localauthority directory.co.uk.

For urgent telephone assistance, ring Shelterline on 0808 800 4444. This is available seven days a week from 8am to midnight.

For more information on obtaining legal advice, see Part 4.

CHAPTER 5

The right to information about the tenancy

Under the current law you do not need to have a written tenancy agreement to create a tenancy, and there is no general right under which tenants can demand a written tenancy agreement. However, tenants do have the right to information about their tenancy. This right was introduced by the Housing Act 1996, which amended the Housing Act 1988 by introducing a new Section 20A. Under this section you can require your landlord to provide a written statement with the following information:

- The date on which your tenancy began

- The rent payable and the dates on which rent is payable

- Details of any rent review clause

- The length of any fixed term

Provided that your request is in writing, the landlord should provide the information within 28 days; unless it is information he has previously given you, such as in a written tenancy agreement.

One problem about requesting information about an oral tenancy is the fear that your landlord will say in the written statement things which were never agreed with you. The Act specifically says that the statement provided by the landlord 'shall not be regarded as conclusive evidence of what was agreed by the parties to the tenancy in question'. However, if your landlord provides a statement which you think is wrong, you should challenge it immediately, by writing to the landlord saying what you do not agree with and why. If you do not, you may be deemed to have accepted it.

Although tenants have the right to request information about their tenancy, this is not really satisfactory. Therefore, if you are taking on a new tenancy, you should always make sure that a tenancy agreement is signed at the start, and that you are provided with a copy of this at the time you sign it.

However, if you have been living in your property for a long time, and the tenancy agreement has been lost, or there never was one, you are probably better off not signing a new agreement now, especially if you have been living in the property since before January 1989 or have an assured tenancy. Any new agreement presented to you to sign by your landlord will probably contain clauses which were not in your original agreement and which will be in your landlord's favour rather than yours. Your landlord cannot force you to sign a new agreement if you do not want to. If he tries to do this, you should take legal advice.

The future

Under new laws proposed by the Law Commission in its Renting Homes Bill, landlords will have to provide a tenancy agreement for all tenancies and tenants will be entitled to withhold rent for up to two months until this is done. However, it is not known if and when this will become law.

Remedies

If you have requested information about your tenancy in writing and the landlord has refused to provide it, this is a criminal offence. You should speak to the Housing Officer at your local authority, as it is the organisation responsible for enforcing this legislation. Your local authority will write to your landlord on your behalf and if necessary bring a prosecution. Prosecutions are very rare for this type of crime, but they are not entirely unknown.

Further information

For contact details for local authorities, see www.localauthority directory.co.uk.

Q I have recently been made redundant and can no longer pay my rent. I cannot claim Housing Benefit as the council needs a tenancy agreement or letter from my landlord, but I do not hold/have never signed such a document. I have asked my landlord to provide me with one but I have had no luck. I am now running into arrears – what can I do?

A Under Section 20A of the Housing Act 1988, a landlord has a duty to provide information regarding the terms of a tenancy to the tenant, if he receives written notice to do so. Failure to provide this is a criminal offence. I would suggest that you contact the advice service of your local authority. It will help you and will probably write to your landlord for you. He will probably provide an agreement upon threat of prosecution.

CHAPTER 6

The right to information about your landlord

Sometimes you will rent property from an agent and he will refuse to give details about your landlord. If you ask him, he will say that all queries should go through him. This is understandable as often landlords use agents because they do not want to be bothered with the management of their property, and their agents are protecting their privacy. However, you do have a right to know who your landlord is. Sometimes you will know who your landlord is, but you will not have his address. These situations are covered by two pieces of legislation: Section 1 of the Landlord and Tenant Act 1985 and Section 48 of the Landlord and Tenant Act 1985.

Section 1 of the Landlord and Tenant Act 1985

This section says that if a tenant makes a request in writing for the identity of his landlord from the person who asks for his rent or from the last person who received his rent, then that person must provide a written statement of the landlord's name and address within 21 days. It is a criminal offence to refuse to do this.

Section 48 of the Landlord and Tenant Act

This section provides that a landlord must give a tenant written notice (called a Section 48 notice) of an address in England and Wales at which notices, including notices in court proceedings, can be served on him. Until this is done, rent will not technically be due to the landlord.

Although this can provide a defence to possession proceedings, you should not spend the money on other things, because as soon as the landlord serves the notice all the back rent will immediately fall due.

Section 48 notices do not need to be in any particular form. In fact in a Court of Appeal case it was held that the notice does not even have to say that it is in respect of Section 48; just having the landlord's address in the tenancy agreement will be sufficient. However this will not help if the landlord's address is abroad or in Scotland. In that case he will have to either give the address of a friend or relative in England and Wales or use an agent.

Note that the purpose of both sections is to enable tenants to be able to contact their landlord. The address given does not necessarily have to be the landlord's home address; it can be a business address.

Remedies

If the agent refuses to give you your landlord's name and address, this is in breach of Section 1 of the Landlord and Tenant Act 1985, which is a criminal offence, and you can complain to the Housing Officer at your local authority. He should write to the agent for you and, if necessary, bring a prosecution.

If you know who your landlord is but you do not have an address for him in England and Wales, then you can legally withhold the rent until this is provided. However, do make sure that you keep the rent safe so you can pay it over as soon as the address is given to you.

Note that you can also carry out a search at the Land Registry to find out the legal owner of any land which is registered. For more information, see the Land Registry's website at www.landregisteronline.gov.uk.

If your agent is named in the tenancy agreement as the landlord, but you suspect that your real landlord is someone else, you are entitled to treat the agent as if he was your landlord. This is because in agency law, an agent is directly liable to the third party (i.e. you, the tenant) if he acts as an agent for an 'undisclosed principal'. So this means that you can sue the agent personally for any problems with the property if your agent does not tell you that he is acting on behalf of someone else. In this case you will not need to know the name of the actual property owner as the agent will effectively be your landlord.

CHAPTER 7

The right to have your deposit returned to you

There are two types of deposit you may be asked to pay: a holding deposit and a damage deposit.

Holding deposits

This is a sum of money generally paid to the letting agent, before the tenancy agreement is signed. The reason for the payment is to cover the costs of the reference checking and to 'hold' the property for you while these checks are being carried out.

> **Note**
>
> Holding deposits are not subject to the tenancy deposit rules discussed on page 89. This is because they are not held as security in respect of a tenant's liabilities under a tenancy agreement, as the tenancy agreement will not have been signed.

Different landlords and agents vary in how they deal with this payment. However, whatever this payment is called and whatever document is signed by you, the following basic rules should apply:

- If the letting does not go ahead because you change your mind, then the landlord (or agent) is entitled to retain a sum to cover either any expenses and costs incurred by him, or his loss of profit, but not both if this would lead to double recovery.

- This also applies if the letting does not go ahead because your credit reference result is unsatisfactory in a situation where you should have been aware of this (e.g. if you gave false information or have exaggerated your assets).

- If your references are not satisfactory but if you acted in good faith when you gave the information to the landlord (or agent), then you should be entitled to the refund of your whole deposit, less a reasonable sum to cover the actual cost of referencing.

- If your references are satisfactory but the landlord decides to let the property to someone else or decides not to let it out at all, then you should be entitled to a refund of the whole of the deposit held by you.

- If your references prove satisfactory and the property is subsequently let to you, then the landlord (or agent) is entitled to deduct the actual cost of referencing from the holding deposit. Any balance should go towards either the rent for the property or the damage deposit.

However, the landlord (or agent) is not entitled to retain the whole of the deposit, regardless of the expenses incurred by him or any losses caused by any cancellation. Any deductions must be reasonable and relate to actual expenses incurred.

The Office of Fair Trading has confirmed that if the only advance payment taken from the tenant is a sum which just covers the reasonable and necessary expenses incurred by the landlord or his agent, then this can legitimately be retained by the landlord or his agent in full, as it will be a reservation fee rather than an advance deposit. However, it would expect this to be no more than a token amount.

Note that if your references are satisfactory and the landlord (or agent) confirms that the property is going to be let to you, but then refuses to go ahead, you may be entitled to claim compensation for any expenses incurred by you. This is particularly the case if you have signed a tenancy agreement and the agent then tells you that the landlord is no longer willing to let the property. Indeed, if you have signed a tenancy agreement, technically you may be entitled to go to court and apply for an injunction forcing the landlord to go ahead with the letting. However, practically this may not be something you are able or wish to do.

Remedies

If you consider that your landlord or agent is acting improperly, it may be worth complaining to your local Trading Standards Office. If your agent is a member of one of the agents' professional associations, or if you are dealing directly with the landlord and he is a member of an accreditation scheme and/or landlords' association, try complaining to them.

However, the only way to force the landlord (or agent) to refund the money to you if he refuses to pay it voluntarily is to go to the Small Claims Court. Note that where the agent has taken the payment, if you know who the landlord is, you should normally bring your claim against the landlord rather than his agent. However, if the landlord's details were not disclosed to you, then you should sue the agent.

Further information

See the sections in Part 4 on making complaints and in Part 1 on bringing court claims.

Damage deposits

General rules

Most landlords will wish to take a damage deposit from their tenants, to give them a fund of money to use to pay for any breakages or damage to the property at the end of the tenancy. It is normal for this to be equivalent to one, or sometimes two month's rent. Some landlords will require a slightly larger deposit if the tenant has a pet which is likely to cause damage (such as a dog). However, for technical reasons the deposit amount should not be more than two months' rent. The practice has been in the past, and still is for some tenancies, that this money is retained by the landlord (or his agent) and is refunded to the tenant after the property has been checked at the time the tenant moves out, less any sum claimed for damage.

If the landlord wishes to make a deduction from the damage deposit at that time, the tenant is entitled to know what the money is to be used for and to ask for copy estimates and invoices. The landlord is only entitled to charge a reasonable amount for replacements and repair and will be expected to replace like for like if this is possible. For example, he will be expected to replace a broken two-year-old washing machine with a two-year-old washing machine in working order. If he buys a new one, he should make a deduction to reflect this. However, if two-year-old washing machines are not available, he will be entitled to the cost of a new one.

Fair wear and tear

This is an important rule, often misunderstood by landlords. It means that landlords are not entitled to charge a tenant for 'damage' caused by the normal use of the property. So if a flat is let in pristine condition at the start of the tenancy and the tenant lives there for two years, the landlord is not entitled to demand that the tenant redecorate it before he leaves so that it is in the same condition as it was at the start. He is only entitled to have the property back in the condition you would expect after having someone live there for two years. This will vary depending on the type of tenant. So a landlord cannot expect a family with three young children to leave a property in the same condition as an elderly lady living alone would do.

When looking at individual items claimed by landlords, you also need to look at the type of damage. If a carpet gets torn due to people walking on it (e.g. in the hall), then this will normally be fair wear and tear. However, if the carpet has been cut up with a knife or is badly stained (more than one would expect from normal living), then the landlord will be entitled to replace it.

The statutory tenancy deposit scheme

History

For years there have been complaints from tenants and tenants' organisations (such as Shelter) that many landlords unreasonably retain all or part of the tenants' deposits, and that tenants are deterred from claiming these back because they are intimidated by having to bring a County Court claim. In 1998 the Citizens' Advice Bureau published '*Unsafe Deposit*', a report claiming that tens of thousands of private tenants were being cheated out of millions of pounds by unscrupulous landlords. The report called for a statutory tenancy deposit scheme to be set up, modelled on a successful scheme already running in Australia. Partly as a result of this, a pilot tenancy deposit scheme funded by the government was run by the Independent Housing Ombudsman for several years, although it was not well supported by private landlords. Finally, the Housing Act 2004 was amended to include provision for a statutory tenancy deposit scheme.

The relevant sections of the Housing Act 2004 are 212 to 214 in Part 6 of the Act, together with more detailed regulations set out in Schedule 10 (as amended).

Scheme rules

When the scheme applies the rules are as follows:

- The scheme only applies to private landlords and their agents, letting under an assured shorthold tenancy. It does not apply to social lettings, common law and assured tenancies (see Part 1 for more information on tenancy types).
- The scheme only applies to damage deposits paid to the landlord on or after 6 April 2007; or
- Damage deposits taken before 6 April 2007 where the tenancy is renewed after that date, for example by the landlord agreeing to a new fixed-term tenancy.

The types of scheme

There are two types:

1 **Custodial scheme:** The landlord or agent has to pay the money over to the scheme administrators. This scheme is free of charge to

landlords and agents, as the running cost is covered by the interest on the deposit money.

2   **Insurance schemes:** The landlord or agent keeps the deposit money, but informs the scheme administrators of the new tenancy. If he fails unreasonably to return the money to the tenant at the end of the tenancy, money will be paid to the tenant by the scheme administrators. Landlords and agents have to pay to be a member of this type of scheme.

How the schemes will work

·   The landlord or agent will collect the deposit from you.

·   Within 14 days he must give you details of the tenancy deposit scheme being used. There are three schemes available; for more information on these, see above.

·   The landlord must comply with the terms of the scheme he is using, which will either allow him to retain the deposit (for an insurance scheme) or require him to pay it over to the scheme administrators (for the custodial scheme).

·   With some of the schemes, the scheme administrators will also write to you separately to confirm that the deposit has been lodged with them.

·   At the end of the tenancy, the landlord should check the property. If there are any deductions he wishes to make from the deposit, he should try to agree these with you. If an agreement can be reached, he will, if he is using an insurance-based scheme, pay all or part of the deposit (as agreed between you) back to you. If he is using the custodial scheme, the scheme administrators will be informed and will pay the money as agreed between you and the landlord, within ten days of receiving notification.

·   If an agreement is not possible, then the landlord or agent should inform the scheme administrators and the dispute can be referred to arbitration. If he is part of an insurance-based scheme, he will be required to pay the money in dispute to the scheme administrators, and pay any undisputed part of the deposit to you or keep it himself, if that is what has been agreed with you. If the money is held in a custodial scheme, the undisputed part of the deposit will be paid out as agreed between you and the landlord or agent.

- You and the landlord (or agent) will both have to confirm that you agree to the dispute being dealt with by arbitration. It is possible to have any dispute resolved by the County Court instead of by arbitration, but the arbitration procedure is so much quicker and simpler that most people will prefer it, particularly as it is free with no court fees.

- You and the landlord (or agent) will need to provide details to the arbitrator to enable him to reach a decision. This will normally be done on the paperwork alone, without a hearing.

- The scheme administrators will pay out the deposit money as ordered by the court or by the arbitrator within ten days of being notified on the decision.

Your rights if the landlord/agent does not comply

At the start of the tenancy you have the right to contact the relevant scheme administrators to check whether the landlord has registered your tenancy with them. If you discover that the money has not been protected with one of the three authorised schemes, you can apply to the County Court for:

- repayment of the money; or

- an order that your landlord pay the deposit money to the custodial scheme within 14 days; and

- an award of three times the deposit money, to be paid to you within 14 days.

Any Section 21 notice (see page 202 for definition) served on you by your landlord will be invalid if a deposit has been taken and the requirements of the scheme have not been complied with.

The person you pay your deposit to is normally the person who is responsible for ensuring that it is protected by an authorised scheme. However, in some cases you will pay the deposit to an agent, who will then pass it over to the landlord. You should, however, receive notification of the scheme being used within 14 days of the date you made the payment. If this is not done, then it is the person or organisation you paid the deposit money to who are in breach and it is they whom you should claim against.

At the end of the tenancy:

- If your landlord (or agent) refuses to return the deposit to you when you think you are entitled to it, or if he cannot be contacted, get in touch with the scheme administrators and tell them.

- If the money is held in the custodial scheme, the scheme will contact the landlord (or agent) to see what the situation is.

- If the landlord (or agent) fails to respond, the scheme will arrange for the case to be referred to arbitration (or you can go to the County Court if you prefer).

- If the money is held in an insurance-based scheme, the scheme will contact the landlord (or agent) and ask him to pay the money in dispute over to it. If he fails to do this, it will arrange for the case to be referred to arbitration (or, again, you can go to the County Court if you prefer).

- In both cases the regulations provide for the landlord (or agent) to be treated as having given his consent for the matter to be dealt with by arbitration if he fails to respond to the scheme administrators.

- If the arbitrator agrees that the money should be paid to you, the scheme administrators will make payment to you within ten days of receiving notice of this. If the scheme is an insurance-based scheme, it will then try to recover the money from the landlord (or agent) (but this will not affect you).

It will probably very rarely happen, but if your landlord or agent loses his membership of an insurance-based scheme:

- You will be notified by the scheme administrators at least two months before your deposit ceases to be protected and told how this will affect you.

- If you think that your landlord (or agent) is not going to join another scheme, you can consider withholding your rent and bringing a claim in the County Court when your deposit is no longer protected, for the return of the deposit to you and the award of three times the deposit money.

- Note, however, that if you withhold rent, you should keep it in a separate interest bearing bank account until you have obtained the court order entitling you to keep it.

- While the deposit is unprotected, your landlord will not be able to evict you under Section 21.

Dealing with arbitrations

The arbitrator will almost always deal with the case on the paperwork without any meeting or hearing, or visit to the property. It is very important therefore that the paperwork you provide should be as full and helpful as possible. If possible, the arbitrator should have the following:

- A copy of the current tenancy agreement.

- A copy of the inventory.

- Photographs to prove the condition of the property and its contents. Photographs must be very clear, not be out of focus, preferably date stamped, and include a ruler to show the scale.

- Sometimes a video can be used, but again this must be clear and relevant.

- Any evidence you may have to prove that the sums claimed by the landlord are too high, such as estimates for work, and details of prices for contents, such as printouts of details of similar items sold on the internet or the relevant pages of Argos or similar catalogues.

- A written statement giving your own reasons for objecting to the landlord's claim.

- Any statements from others (preferably professional independent people, such as an inventory clerk, builder or surveyor) supporting your claim, and also from any (preferably) independent witness who can confirm the condition of the property. Statements should have the full name and professional qualifications (if any) of the witness, and be signed and dated at the end. Ideally, they should also have at the end, before the signature and date, the words 'I believe that the facts stated in this witness statement are true'.

The current scheme administrators

There are currently three schemes – one custodial and two insurance based. They are The Deposit Protection Service, The Tenancy Deposit Scheme and Tenancy Deposit Solutions.

The Deposit Protection Service

This is the custodial scheme and is run by Computershare Investment Services Plc. It is a large international company and has been running a similar scheme in Australia for over eight years. It has a website at www.depositprotection.com.

The Tenancy Deposit Scheme

This scheme is run by a company called The Dispute Service Ltd, which was previously running a similar voluntary scheme for regulated letting agents. This scheme is aimed mainly at letting agents, although it is open to landlords. It is the only one of the three companies which will be using its own in-house arbitrators. It has a website at www.thedisputeservice.co.uk.

Tenancy Deposit Solutions

This scheme is run in partnership between the National Landlords' Association (the largest landlords' association) and Hamilton Fraser Insurance. The scheme is aimed mainly at private landlords, but it is open to agents. It has a website at www.mydeposits.co.uk.

The Deposit Protection Service and Tenancy Deposit Solutions will be using members of the Chartered Institute of Arbitrators to provide the arbitration service.

Remedies

Before taking any action, check to see if your tenancy is an assured shorthold tenancy or not (for more information on this, see Chapter 2 on the different types of tenancies).

If your tenancy is an assured shorthold tenancy and your tenancy either started or was renewed after 6 April 2007, your deposit should be protected with one of the three tenancy deposit schemes. If you have not received any information from your landlord (or agent) regarding this, you can check with the schemes' administrators. You will find contact details via the schemes' websites given above. If the deposit is not covered by any of the schemes, then your landlord (or agent) is in breach of the scheme regulations and you can go to the County Court to claim the return of your deposit, plus an award of three times the deposit value.

If the person unlawfully holding the deposit is a letting agent or a professional landlord, you can also consider bringing a complaint, either to his professional organisation (if he has one) or to your local Trading Standards Office. For more information, see the section on complaining against letting agents in Part 4.

If your tenancy is not an assured shorthold one (e.g. if your annual rent is over £25,000 per year), then unfortunately the statutory tenancy deposit scheme will not apply, and if your landlord unlawfully withholds your damage deposit, your only remedy is to bring a claim through the Small Claims Court for its return. Write to your landlord first, threatening this and giving him a time limit within which to respond to you. If he does not respond, or if you are unable to resolve the matter, consider bringing court proceedings. It will involve a certain amount of paperwork and possibly a court hearing. However, judges tend to be very sympathetic towards tenants in this situation and if you have a good case, you have a very good chance of success. For more information about court claims, see Chapter 3.

Further information

There is some helpful information about the tenancy deposit scheme on the website for Communities and Local Government at www.communities.gov.uk (follow the link for 'Housing' and then for 'Renting and Letting').

Further information

The websites for the three tenancy deposit schemes are very helpful and contain useful information on the scheme workings. The websites can be found at www.depositprotection.com (The Deposit Protection Service), www.thedisputeservice.co.uk (The Dispute Service Ltd) and www.mydeposits.co.uk (Tenancy Deposit Solutions).

Pre-drafted self-calculating claims forms, for claims against landlords or agents to claim the return of the deposit and compensation when they are in breach of the tenancy deposit legislation, together with instructions, are available for annual members of my online service, www.landlordlaw.co.uk, to download and use.

Tenants whose deposits are unprotected by the tenancy deposit scheme may be interested in my DIY Kit for tenants claiming the return of their damage deposit (Kit 2), also available via www.landlordlaw.co.uk, although for an additional charge.

CHAPTER 8

The right to be treated fairly

It is generally agreed that most landlords are in a stronger bargaining position than tenants. To counter this, various laws and regulations have been passed to prevent landlords and their agents taking advantage of this, to protect the interests of the tenant and to ensure 'fairness'. This chapter looks at some of these laws and regulations.

Advertisements and misleading statements made before the tenancy

The criminal law

It is not always realised that the Property Misdescriptions Act 1991 applies to advertisements for rented property as much as advertisements for properties for sale. Under this Act it is a criminal offence to make 'a false or misleading statement' in respect of any property offered for sale or to rent 'in the course of an estate agency business or a property development business'.

The Act specifically states that this will be a criminal offence only, and the fact that an offence is committed under the Act will not by itself mean that any contract for the property concerned will be void. A breach of this Act will not entitle anyone to bring a civil claim for compensation against the person who placed the advertisement. So, if you want to bring a tenancy agreement to an end and move out because the landlord's advertisement was wildly misleading,this Act will not allow you to do this.

Remedies

Local Trading Standards Offices are the organisations who enforce this Act, so if you think that any advertisement placed was untrue or misleading, you should contact your local office and make a complaint. The Trading Standards Officers will contact the landlord or agent concerned, and if they think that the matter is sufficiently serious, it may consider a prosecution.

Note

Under the Accommodation Agencies Act 1953 it is illegal for agencies to charge prospective tenants for registering with them, or for giving information about available accommodation. If you are charged for these, complain to your local Trading Standards Office.

The civil law

Under the civil law of contract, statements made before a contract is made and which help to induce someone to enter into the contract are described by lawyers as 'representations'. If these statements are untrue, they are known as 'misrepresentations'. If they are sufficiently serious, they may entitle the wronged person to end the contract and/or sue for damages. The main Act which provides for this is the Misrepresentation Act 1967.

The Misrepresentation Act, and indeed this whole area of law, is not easy (even for lawyers) so only a very brief summary can be given here. The Misrepresentation Act applies to all types of contract, and not just tenancy agreements.

For a statement to be a 'misrepresentation' under the Act it must be:

- **A statement of fact:** If a property is described as having double glazing and loft insulation, this will be a statement of fact. However, if the agent describes the property as 'a snug little house' or something similar, this will be what is known as a mere advertising puff – a vague statement of no real effect. A promise to do something may not be held to be a statement of fact, unless you can show that the person making it never intended ever to honour it.

Note

Frequently tenants find that landlords will agree to do certain work before the tenancy is agreed and then fail to do it. This would not normally fall within the misrepresentation rules. Misrepresentation is about people telling you something about the property which is untrue. However, this does not mean that you have no rights regarding the promise. Often you will be able to say that the promise was part of your contract with the landlord, so failure to fulfil the promise will be breach of contract.

- **Some sort of active statement:** An omission to give certain information will not normally count as misrepresentation. The prospective tenant must try to ask all the right questions. Note, however, that if something changes after information is given (e.g. if the boiler breaks down after the agent said that it was working perfectly), it will be a misrepresentation if this is not told to the prospective tenant.

- **A 'material inducement':** The 'representation' must be something which would influence a reasonable person to enter into the contract, such as if you were told that the property was very quiet when it actually turned out to be next to a noisy school. However, something fairly minor will not entitle you to use the misrepresentation rules (e.g. if the light shade in the living room is the wrong colour).

Remedies

If your landlord or agent has made untrue or misleading statements which fall within the misrepresentation rules, this means that the tenancy contract is not 'void' (which means 'not binding') but voidable. This means that the contract is one which can be ended in certain circumstances by the wronged party, but which if it is not so specifically ended, will continue as a binding contract.

There are three ways that misrepresentation can be dealt with (I will give you the legal terms for the types of action involved).

1. **Affirmation:** The misled person may still decide to go ahead with the contract even after learning about the misrepresentation. So if you stay on in a property, you may be deemed to have affirmed the

contract and you will not be able to use the misrepresentation as a reason to move out later. However, you may still be able to claim compensation; for example, if the property is in a much poorer condition than you were led to expect.

2. **Avoidance:** If you discover the misrepresentation before moving in, then you can refuse to go ahead with the tenancy.

3. **Rescission:** This is where, in a landlord and tenant context, you decide to move into the property, you discover the misrepresentation and then you move out. You need to tell the landlord or agent what you are doing and why, and you should not just leave. Note that if you have done anything to 'affirm' the contract (such as make a further payment of rent) or stay in the property for some time, you will normally have lost your right to rescission. However, again, you may still be able to claim compensation in the same way as for affirmation above.

However, misrepresentation is generally a tricky area of law, so unless the misrepresentation is obviously substantial and about something crucial to the property and your use of it, you should obtain some legal advice, preferably from a solicitor or someone with some other legal qualification, such as a legal executive, before taking any action (e.g. before moving out of a property).

Damages/compensation

If you have suffered loss as a result of a misrepresentation, then you will probably be entitled to claim compensation. If you have either never moved into the property in the first place (avoidance) or have moved out (rescission), the damages you would be able to claim will normally be limited to expenses incurred, such as the additional cost of finding somewhere else to live, and your removal costs in the case of rescission. You will also normally be entitled to the return of any deposit or other money paid in advance.

However, do note that strictly speaking you are only legally entitled to any damages if these have been awarded by a court. You cannot just decide that you are entitled to damages and deduct them from the rent under your right of set-off (see Chapter 11 for more information on the right of set-off).

Further information

As this is a difficult area of law, if you think that you may have a claim under misrepresentation, you should really take advice from a solicitor or someone with some other form of legal qualification. An unpaid volunteer adviser is unlikely to know much about it.

If there is no Law Centre or Shelter advice office (manned by a solicitor) near you, I would suggest that you find a firm of solicitors who offer an initial free or fixed-fee interview, just to get their opinion on this point. Be careful, however, about agreeing to let them do any further work for you and make sure that you know precisely what legal costs you are committing to.

Tenancy agreements and documents

Introduction to the Unfair Terms in Consumer Contracts Regulations

When a contract is made between a business and a consumer there is often an imbalance. The business can usually afford lawyers to draft detailed contracts to promote the interests of the business. Most consumers, on the other hand, are unfamiliar with legal documentation, and some may find it hard to read at all. They are also often in a hurry to complete the contract and consider (at that stage) the paperwork to be just a nuisance to be dealt with as quickly as possible.

In the past businesses often took advantage of this situation and produced long detailed contracts, often printed in small type, perhaps in a hard to read colour, which most consumers just signed without even looking at.

However, the purpose of a legal system is to prevent injustice, and we now have legislation in place to assist consumers. This legislation originated from the European Union, who from time to time produce 'directives' which then need to be incorporated into member countries' laws. The directive on unfair terms originally came into force in regulations in 1995 but these were then amended and are currently found in the Unfair Terms in Consumer Contracts Regulations 1999.

It is generally agreed that these regulations apply to virtually all landlord and tenant situations, including tenancies with not-for-profit organisations and charities.

What the regulations do

The regulations exist to ensure that consumers are not put at a disadvantage by the greater bargaining power and legal expertise which many large businesses have. If an individual term in a contract between a business and a consumer is considered 'unfair' under the regulations, then that term is void and of no effect.

For example, if a clause forbidding pets is phrased in a way which, under the regulations, is considered unfair, then the effect of this is the same as if there were no clause forbidding pets at all, and there will therefore be nothing (in the contract) to prevent the tenant from, say, keeping a dog.

Here are the main rules contained in the regulations:

- **Legal rights:** The contract must not try to take away legal rights which the consumer would normally have; for example, tenants have a legal right of 'set-off' (which is dealt with in Chapter 11). A contract term, therefore, which states that rent must be paid without any deductions or set-off will not be effective.

- **Penalties:** If the contract tries to impose any charge or penalty, the contract should make it clear that all charges must be reasonably incurred and be for a reasonable amount. Many contracts have clauses saying that the tenant should pay the landlord's legal or other costs. However, a clause which simply says that the tenant must pay all the landlord's costs will not be effective. The costs may have been incurred for something which the tenant is not in law responsible for, or the landlord may have used a particularly expensive contractor or lawyer. In both these situations the tenant should not be responsible for the actual sums paid by the landlord. In the first case (i.e. where the costs are for something he is not responsible for), he should not be liable at all, and in the second case (where the landlord has used an expensive contractor), he should only be liable for a reasonable amount, which may not be the sum actually paid by the landlord. A contract term needs to make both of these points clear.

Q My landlord charges us interest on late rent payment after seven days from the due date, and also charges us £25 for an administration fee on top of the interest. He said it is on the contract and the £25 fee is due to the bank charging him when he is overdrawn. Is it reasonable? Should I pay?

A Your landlord is not entitled to charge any fees which are not set out in the tenancy agreement. If fees are specified in the tenancy agreement, then they must be fair and reasonable or the relevant clause will be void under the Unfair Terms in Consumer Contracts Regulations 1999. If the clause is void, you do not need to pay the fee. An administration fee in addition to an interest payment will normally be considered unreasonable and the landlord is charging you twice for the same thing. The fact that your landlord may be charged interest on his overdraft will not justify an additional charge. Fees paid by tenants should not depend on the state of their landlords' bank balances! For more information and advice on whether the clauses in your tenancy agreement are unfair, have a word with your local Trading Standards Office, as it enforces these regulations, and it will be able to write to your landlord on your behalf.

- **Prohibitions:** If the landlord has clauses in the agreement saying that the tenant must not do something, then unless it is something the tenant is not supposed to do anyway under the general law (such as causing a nuisance to neighbours), the prohibition should be qualified. This means that the contract term should be worded to say that the tenant should not do whatever it is, unless he has the landlord's written permission, which shall not be refused unreasonably (I generally refer to this as 'the qualifying wording'). To take an example, under the general law there is nothing to prevent a tenant from redecorating a property. However, many landlords will not want this (as tenants may choose an inappropriate colour which would be expensive for the landlords to decorate over after the tenant leaves), and they will wish to prohibit redecoration in the tenancy agreement. However, if the clause includes the qualifying wording, this makes it fair for both sides – the tenant can be given permission to redecorate so long as he uses colours approved by the landlord.

Q My elderly sister is living in rented accommodation and her landlady has recently told her that she is not allowed to use an electric oil-filled radiator she purchased one year ago. The landlady has stipulated that only the night storage heaters provided in the property are to be used. As my sister suffers from arthritis, she cannot be expected to live in cold conditions as the night storage heaters are inadequate. Is the landlady allowed to make this stipulation?

A The landlord is not entitled to interfere in your sister's use of the property, assuming that your sister is a tenant renting a house or flat and is not a lodger renting a room in the landlord's house. If there is a clause in the tenancy agreement regarding the use of heating appliances in the property, this will have to comply with the Unfair Terms in Consumer Contracts Regulations 1999 and must be reasonable. For a prohibition in an agreement to be considered reasonable, it should include the words 'save with the consent of the landlord which shall not be refused unreasonably', or similar. If this is missing, the clause is probably void and unenforceable. In the context of heating appliances, this would allow the landlord to refuse consent to a tenant to use appliances which are a fire hazard (which is reasonable). However, I cannot see that the landlord can reasonably refuse your sister permission to use a safe appliance when she is suffering from arthritis. If the landlord continues to refuse his consent unreasonably, this could be considered harassment (which is a criminal offence) and I would suggest that she seeks the assistance of the Tenancy Relations Officer or Housing Adviser at her local authority. She could also consider asking the local authority to inspect the property and have it assessed under the Housing Health and Safety Rating System, as excessive cold is a Category 1 hazard which the local authority can require a landlord to rectify by the provision of proper heating.

- **Plain English:** Finally, the contract must be written in plain English. If a term contains jargon or is written in a confusing way which will be difficult for the ordinary person to understand, it is likely to be found void.

Q A week after we moved into our flat the landlord pointed out that we are liable to pay the property maintenance charge and all outgoings, even of a novel nature, as stated in the contract, which is actually £75 per month in addition to the rent. This, as you can imagine, was cleverly disguised in our lengthy tenancy agreement, which is not the typical one. Should he have highlighted these extra costs?

A If these extra charges were not apparent from the tenancy agreement, then it is entirely possible that the clause may be invalid under the Unfair Terms in Consumer Contracts Regulations. These regulations state that in contracts between a business and a consumer the clauses must be fair and in plain English. Unusual clauses should be given prominence. If a clause is difficult for an ordinary person to understand, then it will normally be void. I would suggest that you take this tenancy agreement to your local Trading Standards Office, who is the first port of call under these regulations. It will be able to advise you on whether the tenancy agreement is valid or not. If it considers the agreement to be in breach of the regulations, it may pass it on to the Unfair Contracts Terms department at the Office of Fair Trading, which deals with non-compliant agreements.

- **Core terms:** The regulations provide that some terms in a contract will be 'core terms'. These are terms relating to the subject matter of the contract. In a tenancy agreement this will be the names of the parties, the rent and the address of the property. The bulk of the regulations will not apply to core terms. So, for example, the regulations will not protect a tenant who agrees to a very high rent as this will be a core term. However, the plain English rule applies to all contract terms, including core terms; if a term which would normally be a core term is drafted in such an obscure way that it is difficult to understand, this will normally be void.

- **Individually negotiated terms:** The regulations are designed to protect consumers against unfair terms in standard contracts which are imposed on them. They do not apply to terms in a contract which are genuinely negotiated and agreed between the parties. So, for example, if you reach an agreement with your landlord that you can keep your west highland terrier in the property but no other animals, and the contract term specifies this and does not include the qualifying wording, this term will still be valid because it is not a standard term – it was one which was specifically agreed with you.

Do the regulations apply?

There are a number of problems with these regulations. One is that they are not well known. Most tenants (and indeed most landlords) will believe that they are bound by a term in a tenancy agreement if they have signed it, however unfair it is.

Another problem is that it is sometimes difficult to tell whether the regulations will apply to a particular term. The regulations are enforced by the Office of Fair Trading, who have issued guidance. However, some of the terms which it considers unfair are ones which, at first reading, would appear perfectly fair to most non-lawyers (and even to many lawyers who do not specialise in this area of law). You sometimes need to have a specialised knowledge of what tenants' rights actually are before you can see that a clause breaches one of those rights. Also although the Office of Fair Trading can offer guidance, at the end of the day it is up to a court to decide whether a particular term is actually unfair under the regulations or not. This is not a happy situation, as most people would prefer to avoid going to court to argue over a term in a tenancy agreement. Indeed most people do, as there is very little case law in this area.

The best thing to do if you are worried about a particular contract term is to read this book carefully. If, after this, you think that the clause may be void, then seek advice, but make sure that you go to a housing specialist. For further information, see the remedies section at page 117.

> **Note**
>
> The regulations are not retrospective and will not apply to tenancy agreements which were signed before the original regulations came into force on 1 July 1995.

Some particular terms in tenancy agreements

The best source of information is the guidance on unfair terms in tenancy agreements issued by the Office of Fair Trading, and which you can download from its website at www.oft.gov.uk. However, here are some comments on the types of clauses in tenancy agreements which cause the most problems:

Break clauses

This is a clause in the tenancy agreement which will allow it to be ended before the end of the fixed term. Normally, break clauses will provide for two months' notice to be given in writing. A break clause which is just in favour of the landlord will be void – it must apply equally to both landlord and tenant.

Penalty clauses

It is very important that these are fair. Here are some comments:

- A straightforward interest clause on unpaid rent will normally be enforceable so long as the rate of interest is not too high (there have been cases where a rate of ten per cent was considered to be too high and unfair, but this was at a time when interest rates were low). However, the clause may be considered unfair (and unenforceable) if it does not say that interest is only payable on money 'lawfully due', as otherwise it could be interpreted that the landlord is claiming interest on money withheld by tenants under their right of set-off, which would be unfair.

- The clause needs to be specific about how much is to be paid, and any figure quoted must include VAT.

- Sums charged for expenses and fees (e.g. for visits and letters) must reflect the actual cost to the landlord, and be reasonable. There should only be a charge made for letters if they are sent as a result of the tenant's non-payment of rent or some other breach of the tenancy.

- Charges for missed appointments should apply to the landlord as well as to the tenant.

- Any penalty for something which does not protect a legitimate interest of the landlord will be considered unfair.

- Any clauses which give the landlord or his agent a sole discretion to decide on the amount to be paid by the tenant, or to be deducted from the deposit (for deposits not subject to the tenancy deposit scheme), will normally be considered to be unfair.

Charges

Payment for any other charges must be very clear and must only relate to the tenant's use of the property for the period of time that the tenant is renting the property. A clause which allows the landlord to decide how much should be paid will be considered unfair. Here are some examples given by the Office of Fair Trading in its guidance of the sort of charges which will be unfair:

- Clauses requiring the tenant to 'meet all existing and future charges and outgoings in respect of the property'. This is too vague, as it could cover outgoings which would not normally be the responsibility of the tenant.

- General charges for cleaning at the end of the tenancy. Cleaning charges can only be made if the property is left in a dirtier state than when the tenant took it on, taking into account fair wear and tear. A clause which allows the landlord to charge for cleaning, whatever the condition of the property after the tenant has left, will be unfair.

- Compulsory insurance. Sometimes landlords require tenants to take out insurance for their own possessions from a specific insurer (no doubt the landlord is obtaining commission). However, these clauses will be void. It is up to the tenant whether he insures his own possessions; the landlord cannot insist on this.

Landlords' costs and expenses

Any clause relating to refunding the landlord for payments made by him, or for compensation for the tenant's breach of the tenancy agreement, must provide for the charge to be reasonably incurred and be for a reasonable amount.

In particular, any clauses which say that the landlord must be repaid on an indemnity basis, or which use the word indemnity, will be considered unfair. This is partly because the Office of Fair Trading considers that the word indemnity is a legal term which some ordinary people may not understand properly, and partly because it is unfair to force the tenant to pay whatever the landlord may have paid. The sum paid by the landlord for the replacement table, for example, may be unreasonably high. The tenant should only be required to pay what is reasonable.

So far as legal costs are concerned, again any attempt to force the tenant to pay the exact legal fees that the landlord pays will be considered unfair and void. In particular, in connection with court proceedings, a losing party can only be ordered to pay any costs awarded by the court, which is not the same as the legal fees actually paid by the winning party to his lawyers. If there is a court claim where the tenant wins, he should not have to pay the landlord's costs at all. Indeed, the landlord may be ordered to pay his legal fees!

Rent review clauses

Most standard tenancy agreements (e.g. for six months) will not have a rent review clause as the rent will normally be increased by agreement with the tenant, who will sign a new tenancy agreement for a new fixed term at the new rent. However, sometimes landlords will wish to include a rent review clause in the tenancy agreement, particularly those with a long term.

If the rent review clause states that the rent will increase by a specific amount (e.g. if the original rent is £450 and the agreement provides for it to go up to £500 after a period of time (such as 12 months)), it will be difficult to challenge this as it will normally be deemed to be a 'core term' as the tenant will have known the exact amount of the increase at the time that he signed the tenancy agreement. However, if the new rent is not set out in the agreement, then the rent review clause must be fair. Generally, this means that the new rent must be referable to something independent, such as the Retail Price Index or an independent surveyor. Clauses which allow the landlord (or his agent) to increase the rent to any amount he wishes will not be valid.

Notices

The minimum notice periods which landlords and tenants have to give when they wish to end a tenancy are prescribed by law. Any attempt to change this by way of a contract clause will be void. So for an assured shorthold tenancy, any clause saying that a landlord can terminate the tenancy on giving the tenant one month's notice will be of no effect. This is because the period in Section 21 of the Housing Act 1988 is two months. However, if the tenancy is not an assured shorthold tenancy but a common law tenancy (for an explanation of common law tenancies see the different types of tenancy in Chapter 2), the statutory notice period will be different, and a clause providing for one month's notice may be valid. (For more specific information about possession notices, see the eviction section in Chapter 13.

With a fixed-term tenancy, a tenant is entitled to leave at the end of the fixed term without having to give any notice to the landlord, and any term requiring the tenant to do this will be void.

Incorporating other contracts

Some tenancy agreements contain clauses attempting to bind a tenant to the terms of other contracts. For example, the lease of a flat may contain a term saying that the tenant must comply with the terms of the landlord's 'head lease' (i.e. the lease the landlord has with the freeholders who own the building), or a clause saying that the tenant must not do anything which invalidates the landlord's insurance.

Here, the tenant will only be bound by the clause if he is given sufficient information about the other contract, i.e. the head lease or the insurance policy. This can be done either by providing a copy of the relevant contract or policy or by providing an extract setting out the clauses which will affect the tenant. The tenant cannot be expected to comply with the terms of a document that he has not seen. The tenant's right to see the relevant contract or an extract of the relevant terms should be specified in the tenancy agreement.

Terms which interfere with the tenant's use of the property

Although some clauses specifying how the tenant should use the property may be valid, others may not. Some tenancy agreements are far too specific, giving terms, for example, requiring the tenants to wash down working surfaces on a daily basis or clean the windows inside and out every week. These types of clause will normally be void. Under the general law a tenant is expected to maintain the property in a reasonable condition but the landlord is not entitled to seek to control the tenant's conduct during the tenancy, unless there is a valid reason for this.

The following would normally be valid:

- Clauses which go no further than the tenant's obligations under the general law, such as clauses requiring him to keep the property clean and tidy and to give it up at the end of the property in the same condition (fair wear and tear excepted) as it was at the start.

- A clause requiring the tenant to use a piece of equipment, such as a boiler, as provided in the manufacturer's instructions, so long as the tenant is given a copy of these instructions.

- Clauses which are genuine attempts to prevent damage to the property, such as those aimed at preventing condensation (e.g. a requirement that the heating in winter be maintained at a minimum temperature), so long as this is reasonable and it is clear from the agreement that its purpose is to prevent damage to the property.

Smoking

Because of the health and other hazards involved in smoking and also the damage that smoke can do to the decor of a property, a clause forbidding smoking will not normally be considered to be unfair. Indeed the reverse is the case and in order to protect other residents from the damaging effects of smoke and the risks of fire associated with people being allowed to smoke in bed, landlords will be expected either to prohibit smoking altogether or to provide smoke alarms where smoking is allowed.

Pets

As already mentioned, an outright ban on pets will be considered unfair and the clause will be invalid. Any prohibition must provide for the tenant to be able to request leave to keep a pet and for the landlord not to refuse permission unreasonably. As the Unfair Contract Terms Regulations come from an European directive, we are bound by a Spanish case which said that it was unfair to have a blanket prohibition against pets as this would prevent a tenant from keeping a goldfish in a bowl, which would be unreasonable.

Business use

Tenancy agreements generally prohibit the tenant from using the property as anything other than a private residence for him and his family, and this is reasonable. This is because business/commercial tenancies are governed by different legislation and residential agreements are not drafted in the same way as commercial leases.

Allowing other people to stay in the property

A landlord will not want anyone other than his tenants and his family or children living at the property without his consent. He will wish to check and take references for all permanent residents, plus the property may be a house in multiple occupation (HMO), which is licensed for only a specific number of occupants. So it is not unreasonable for a landlord to prohibit anyone other than the tenant and his family from living in the property. However, any contract term which forbids the tenant from having visitors staying overnight will be considered unfair as this would be an unreasonable interference in the tenant's use of the property.

Assignment

Assignment is where the benefit of the unexpired fixed term of a tenancy is legally transferred to another person by deed (for a definition of a deed please see page 13). It is often done for long leases which are purchased at a premium, but very rarely for short lets. In the past it was quite standard in tenancy agreements to prohibit any form of assignment, because a landlord will want to approve any tenants and take references before they take over a tenancy of his property, plus it is generally simpler if the person responsible under a tenancy is the person named in the tenancy itself rather than an assignee. However, the Office of Fair Trading has stated in its guidance that an outright prohibition on assignment (other than during the first three months of the tenancy) will be considered unfair, as a tenant should be able to extract himself from the obligations of a tenancy so long as there is someone else suitable and willing to take it over.

The Lawpack tenancy agreements get over this problem by allowing tenants to end their tenancy, so long as they find a suitable replacement tenant for the landlord. The landlord will then be able to sign a new tenancy agreement with the replacement tenant found by the outgoing tenant. However, unless your tenancy agreement has this sort of clause or some similar way for the tenant to end the tenancy after the first three months, any prohibition against assignment will be potentially unfair and void (i.e. unenforceable). If the prohibition against assignment is void, then, technically, you can assign your tenancy agreement to someone else. In reality, however, this is very rarely, if ever, done.

Note that this problem only arises if you want to leave the property but have several months of your fixed term still to run. If the fixed term has ended and you have stayed on, you can just give a month's notice as discussed at page 251.

Forfeiture clause

This is the clause which says that if you are in arrears for a specific period of time (usually 14 or 21 days), the landlord can 're-enter' the property and end the tenancy. As it is traditionally worded, the clause is unfair as it appears to be saying that the landlord can recover possession without getting a court order. In fact, the word 're-enter' in this context means 're-enter via court proceedings', but ordinary tenants cannot be expected to realise this, so for the clause to be fair, it must specify that the landlord can only recover possession by obtaining a court order.

For example, the forfeiture clause in the Lawpack tenancy agreements say at the end of the forfeiture clause:

> 'If anyone lives at the Property or if the tenancy is an assured tenancy under the Housing Act 1988, the Landlord cannot recover possession of the Property without a court order. This clause does not affect the Tenant's rights under the Protection from Eviction Act 1977.'

If your landlord has not used a Lawpack agreement, the wording may be different, but so long as it is clear that the landlord must obtain a court order for possession, the clause will be valid.

Legally this is an important clause as without it the landlord is not entitled to end the tenancy, such as, for example on the basis of rent arrears, during the fixed term of the tenancy. For more information on forfeiture, see page 224 in Chapter 13.

Clauses allowing the landlord to enter the property

There are two traditional types of clause allowing the landlord access. One is allowing him to inspect the property and carry out any necessary repairs; the other is allowing him to show prospective tenants around during the last few months of the tenancy.

Both of these are situations where it is reasonable for the landlord to be allowed access, provided that the landlord gives at least 24 hours' notice in writing. Indeed, the landlord has a statutory right to access the property to inspect its condition (Section 11 of the Landlord and Tenant Act 1985). Clauses giving the landlord the right to enter the property for any other purpose will only be valid if the reason for the landlord's access is a reasonable one (e.g. to access some of his own possessions which may be stored on the property) and if the landlord is required to give at least 24 hours' written notice. Any clause which appears to allow the landlord to enter the property without giving notice (other than in an emergency) will be void.

Tenants' property left behind

Sometimes tenants leave property behind when they leave. This is a bit of a problem for the landlord as he will need to get rid of it before he can re-let the property. However, any clause which says that the property will become the property of the landlord, or allowing him to deal with it as he wishes, will normally be void. The landlord can deal with the property but he must follow the procedure set out in the Torts (Interference with Goods) Act 1977. This requires the landlord to send the tenant a letter giving information about the goods held and when and how they can be collected. If this letter is ignored, then the landlord can sell or dispose of the goods. If the tenant does not leave a forwarding address and cannot be traced, the landlord is relieved of this obligation. Any clause in the contract which does not follow this procedure will be void. For more information on this topic, see Chapter 14 on the right to your own possessions.

Repairs and redecoration

Under Section 11 of the Landlord and Tenant Act 1985, various repairing covenants (looked at in detail in Chapter 10 on rights regarding the condition of the property, repairs and safety) are imposed on landlords. These repairing obligations cannot be contracted out of other than by the landlord obtaining a court order. So any contract term which provides for the tenant to carry out any of these repairs will be void. Indeed the Office of Fair Trading has indicated in its guidance that even if a clause could be interpreted as extending to requiring a tenant to do work which could come under the landlord's repairing obligations, it will be void.

So far as repairing work which does not come within Section 11, the tenancy agreement can provide for the tenant to do this, so long as the clause is not too onerous. So a clause can provide for the tenant to be responsible for the interior decoration, but a clause requiring the tenant to repaint the inside of the property every six weeks would be void.

In point of fact, normally landlords will not want a tenant to redecorate a property on a short let, as the tenant may decorate it in a way which will make the property more difficult to let out again after he has gone. However, a prohibition against redecoration will only be valid if it contains the qualifying wording.

Statements and presumptions

Sometimes tenancy agreements contain statements to the effect that the tenant confirms or agrees to something, such as that he has been served with a particular document or that he agrees that the property is in a good condition at the start of the tenancy. However, if these statements are buried in the text of the terms and conditions, they will not normally be binding upon the tenant; for example, if the tenant has not actually received the document or if the property is not in good condition.

For such a term to be valid, it really needs to have been specifically pointed out to the tenant and for the tenant to have initialled it to confirm his agreement. Even then, for example, if the tenant really has not been given the document, he may not be bound by the clause, although he may have an uphill task, for example, in court proceedings, to show that he did not appreciate the meaning of the clause.

Guarantees

Although this book is on tenants' rights rather than the rights of guarantors, note that the Unfair Terms in Consumer Contracts Regulations will apply to guarantees in the same way as they apply to tenancy agreements.

The most common clause which is likely to be found void is one purporting to make the guarantor liable after the terms of the tenancy has been changed (e.g. by the rent going up). If the tenant signs a new tenancy agreement, particularly if this increases the rent or changes the tenants' obligations, then this will cancel the guarantee and the landlord must get the guarantor to sign a new guarantee deed.

Tenancy agreements for social landlords

Local authorities, housing associations and other social landlords are bound by the Unfair Terms in Consumer Contracts Regulations in the same way as private landlords. However, their tenancy agreements are more likely to have been professionally drafted by lawyers who know what they are doing, and are less likely to have any obvious unfair clauses.

Social landlords will also often have a consultation procedure which they will follow when it is intended to amend their standard tenancy agreement terms. However, they cannot be prevented from altering their tenancy agreements in a lawful way if the tenants' association does not agree to it.

Adjustments for disabled tenants

Finally, under the disability legislation, landlords are required to respond reasonably to the requests of disabled tenants, and the following requests would normally be considered reasonable:

- To provide tenancy agreements in alternative formats, such as large print, Braille, audio tape or easy read.

- To provide a British Sign Language interpreter during meetings with tenants who use British Sign Language.

- To waive a no pets policy for a disabled person with an assistance dog.

- To spend extra time with tenants who have learning difficulties to make sure that they understand their tenancy agreement and the general rules, etc.

Remedies

If a tenancy agreement contract clause is unfair, then it is void and you can safely ignore it. For example, if your tenancy contains an invalid clause prohibiting pets, legally there is nothing to stop you keeping a dog. You are quite entitled just to ignore the clause and treat the tenancy as if it were not there. However, before doing this, you do need to be sure that the clause you are ignoring really is void under the regulations.

You can also use the fact that a clause is invalid as a defence to any claim the landlord may bring, such as a County Court claim for money allegedly due under a penalty clause that you consider is unfair and void. Again, though, you need to be fairly sure that the clause is an invalid one.

If you are uncertain, it is best to take advice before entering into a possibly acrimonious dispute with your landlord. The best source of advice is a solicitor or lawyer who specialises in this area of law. These are often hard to find, though, and even some housing solicitors are not fully familiar with the Unfair Terms in Consumer Contracts Regulations. A solicitor with the housing charity Shelter may be a good choice, if you are near one of its housing advice offices.

The other course of action is to speak to your Local Trading Standards Office. Although its officers are not themselves experts in this, they can refer the matter to the relevant section of the Office of Fair Trading who police this area of law.

If your landlord is a social landlord, you can also either speak to your tenants' association, if there is one, or follow the in-house complaints procedure.

If you are disabled and you wish your tenancy to be adapted to take account of this, you can obtain advice from the Disability Rights Commission, which has a website at www.drc.org.uk.

Further information

The best source of information is the Office of Fair Trading's guidance, which was last published in September 2005. This can be downloaded from its website at www.oft.gov.uk. It also publishes reports on a quarterly basis giving details of the contracts which have been referred to it and saying how the individual clauses were amended.

Rights regarding rent

A tenant's rights regarding the rent he pays will depend, to a large extent, on the type of tenancy he has and, for some tenancy types, rules have been put in place to ensure that the tenant is treated fairly in relation to rent levels. However, the basic underlying rule is that the rent for a property is a matter of agreement between the parties, which can only be interfered with or set aside if this is specifically provided for in legislation.

Therefore, as a general rule, you should make sure, before signing a tenancy agreement, that you are happy with the rent, that it is an amount that you can afford to pay (or it will be covered by your Housing Benefit payments if you are eligible for Housing Benefit), and that it is a fair rent for the property you are renting. If you find out later that you have made a bad bargain, you may find it difficult to do anything about it.

For all types of tenancy note that the landlord cannot increase the rent during the fixed term of the tenancy, other than by agreement with the tenant, unless there is a valid rent review clause in the tenancy agreement. (For further information see page 109 on unfair terms and rent review clauses.)

Except in the special case of protected/Rent Act tenants (see page 122), a rent can always be increased (or decreased) by agreement between the landlord and tenant. This can be done by:

· The tenant signing a new tenancy agreement at the new rent – this can be done before the expiry of the original agreement if all parties agree (in which case this will have the effect of cancelling the original agreement), although it is generally done after the fixed term has ended.

· The tenant countersigning a letter from the landlord proposing the new rent (or some similar document) to confirm his consent.

· The tenant paying the new rent.

Q I moved into a property taking on an assured shorthold tenancy agreement in June 2006. The landlady is now telling me that I am responsible for rent arrears of the previous tenant, who did not make all his payments. I have gone through my contract and nowhere does it state that I am liable for any previous tenant's costs. She is now threatening me with legal costs. Can she make me pay for a previous tenant's missing monies that I have nothing to do with?

A No, your landlord certainly cannot hold you responsible for a previous tenant's rent! A person can only be responsible for rent due from someone else if he signed the same tenancy agreement with him (i.e. if they are joint tenants), or if he signed as a guarantor. You cannot be held liable for the rent of someone completely separate who just happened to live at the property before you. Even if this was set out in your tenancy agreement, that clause would almost certainly be void. If your landlord continues to threaten you in this way, you should tell her that you will be reporting her to the local authority for harassment, which is a criminal offence.

The statutory rules on rent are different for different types of tenancy.

Assured shorthold tenancies

Generally, the landlord has the right to charge a market rent for the property. However, there is a right, which is little known and little used, for a tenant to challenge the rent of a property during the first six months of the tenancy, by referring the rent to the Rent Assessment Committee (RAC) (sometimes also known as the Rent Assessment Panel) for review. There is a prescribed form for this which must be used, which can be downloaded from the website of the Residential Property Tribunal at www.rpts.gov.uk. However, the RAC will only be able to take action and consider the rent where:

1. a sufficient number of dwellings are let on assured shorthold tenancies in the area to be able to do a comparison; and

2. the rent is significantly higher than the level of rents in the locality (i.e. more than about five to ten per cent).

If the answer to both points is 'yes', then the RAC will decide what the proper market rent for your property is and when any new rent set for the tenancy should start (which cannot be earlier than the date of application). This will then be the only rent the landlord will be entitled to, until he is able to increase the rent after the end of the fixed-term.

This right can only be used once, and is only available during the initial six months of the tenancy. If you are given a further fixed term tenancy agreement for the same property, the right will no longer be available.

One reason why this power is little used is probably that such an application will not make for a happy landlord/tenant relationship, and if you do this, your landlord may decide not to continue your tenancy (something he is entitled to do) after the end of the fixed term.

Assured and assured shorthold tenancies

After the fixed term of the tenancy has expired, the landlord has the right to increase the rent by notice, which must be in the proper prescribed form, available on the Residential Property Tribunal website. This notice will give the tenant one month to object. If you, the tenant, think that the rent is too high, you can refer it to the RAC for review, again using the proper prescribed form (which again can be downloaded from the website of the Residential Property Tribunal). However, it is important that the form is received by the RAC during this one-month notice period. If it is received even one day late, the application cannot be dealt with.

You need to be very sure that the proposed rent is unreasonably high before referring it for review. The RAC may find that the rent is too low, in which case it will increase your rent further. It is a good idea to do some research before submitting an application. The best way to do this is to check the RAC's records for 'comparable' properties in the area. The RAC must make available information concerning its decisions and regarding other rents determined in the area. Factors such as the state of repair of the property, the facilities included in the rent, whether or not it is furnished and whether it is an assured or assured shorthold tenancy will be relevant to whether the properties are directly comparable. It may also be useful to look in local newspapers and estate agents to gauge what rents are being charged. This information will also be useful as evidence to produce to the RAC (e.g. advertisements from local newspapers).

However, a referral to the RAC can only be done where the rent has been increased using the statutory notice procedure. If the rent is increased by agreement (e.g. by signing a new tenancy agreement or a letter from your landlord suggesting a new rent), then this cannot be challenged. Neither can a new rent which is increased via a valid rent review clause. However, as discussed in the section on tenancy agreements above, the rent review clause must comply with the Unfair Terms in Consumer Contracts Regulations and, in particular, must not entitle the landlord or his agent to set any rent they wish.

Case note

In a claim for possession in 2000, a landlord had purportedly increased the rent from £4,680 to £25,000 under a rent review clause in the tenancy agreement, and then tried to evict the tenant for rent arrears. However, the court held that the rent increase clause was invalid, as it was merely a device, masquerading as a provision for an increase in rent, to enable the landlord to bring the assured tenancy to an end when it chose and to obtain possession of the property. The clause was therefore unlawful as it was an attempt to circumvent the mandatory provisions of the Act (*Bankway Properties Ltd v - Penfold-Dunsford and Another*).

Q The letting agency I am with has sent me a letter out of the blue saying that the rent was increased several months ago and I now owe £200 in arrears. I was not notified of this and I have not been given a new agreement to sign. Also, the agency told me that I did not need a new tenancy agreement as my lease ran month-to-month. Please help! I am so confused and I feel like something is not right!

A If the fixed term in your tenancy agreement has expired, then your agents are right – a new agreement is not necessary and your tenancy will run on from month-to-month under the same terms and conditions as the original agreement. However, if the agency wants to increase your rent, it needs to do this by serving the proper form of notice on you (assuming that there is no rent review clause in your tenancy agreement). This notice is in a prescribed form and must give you at least one month's notice. If you do not agree with the rent increase and you think that it is too much, you can refer the rent, during the month's notice period, to the RAC for review. If there is no rent review clause in your tenancy agreement and no notice has been served on you, then your rent has not been increased and you can continue paying at the original rate.

Regulated 'protected' tenancies

Most tenancies which pre-date 15 January 1989 will be subject to the 'fair rent' system. Under this system, a tenant (or a landlord) can refer the rent to the Rent Officer for a 'fair rent' to be assessed. After this has been done, the fair rent assessed by the Rent Officer is the only rent the landlord is entitled to charge. The fair rent will be set out in a notice, which will be served on the tenant, and which will also be recorded in the Rent Service rent register, which can now be accessed online at www.therentservice.gov.uk.

The fair rent can be reviewed every two years upon application (normally by the landlord) to the Rent Officer. Other than this, the rent cannot be changed unless there is a major change at the property (e.g. if the property area rented to the tenant changes or if there are substantial improvements done), when the landlord or the tenant (but it is normally the landlord) can make an early application for the rent to be amended to reflect the changed circumstances.

The starting point for Rent Officers when assessing a fair rent will be the market rent for the property. This will then normally be amended to reflect matters such as the condition of the property and any improvements paid for by the tenant. Generally, you cannot be expected to pay more for a property because of improvements you have made or to pay less for a property because of damage caused by you.

Up until the early 1990s there were very few properties where a genuine market rent could be charged as virtually all residential rented properties were covered by the 'fair rent' scheme. Fair rents therefore gradually reduced to very low levels. However, after the introduction of the assured and the assured shorthold tenancies, there were more market rents available for comparison. As a result, many of the fair rents which for years had been very low began to rise to reflect this. This sometimes caused great hardship – many Rent Act tenants are pensioners on fixed incomes who could not afford the higher rents.

To ameliorate the effect of this, the Rent Acts (Maximum Fair Rent) Regulations were introduced in 1999. Under this, the amount a fair rent can increase at any one time is limited and referable to a complex calculation set out in the regulations. The landlords' organisations were very annoyed by these regulations and a legal challenge was brought which went all the way up to the House of Lords, but the regulations were found to be valid.

Q I am friends with an elderly lady who has lived in the same rented accommodation for over 40 years. She has applied to the council to have her rent of £50 per week paid and has since been told by her landlord that if the council are going to pay, then it will put her rent up. Is this permissible? Obviously my friend is very upset.

A If your friend has lived in the property for over 40 years, then she will almost certainly be a protected tenant under the Rent Act 1977 and her rent is probably regulated (i.e. it is a 'fair rent'). If so, any increase will have to be approved by the Rent Officer. If she does not have a 'fair rent', then she should consider applying for one as soon as possible. She should contact her local Rent Officer and seek his advice. The Rent Service has a website at www.therentservice.gov.uk.

Local authority tenancies

Local authorities have the right to set their own rent levels, but the law requires that they charge 'reasonable rents'. However, the only way to make a legal challenge to a local authority's decision on rent levels is by a legal process known as 'judicial review'. This is a complex type of claim and not really something you can do on your own, plus even if a claim is brought, the courts are usually reluctant to interfere with the local authority's decision.

Any challenge to rent levels set by local authorities should normally be done (at least initially) through the tenants' association or the complaints procedure. However, as the rents set by local authorities tend to be lower than anyone else's, it is not normally the level of rent which is the main cause of complaint for council tenants.

Registered social landlords

Assured and assured shorthold tenants of registered social landlords (RSLs) (including housing associations) are subject to the same rules regarding rent and rent increases as assured and assured shorthold tenants of private landlords.

However, those housing associations which receive funding from the Housing Corporation are expected to set their rents at levels 'which are within the reach of those in low paid employment', i.e. below a market rent. RSL rents are therefore likely to be less than those set by private landlords, but more than rent set by local authority landlords.

Common law tenancies

There is no rent regulation with common law tenancies and tenants have to watch out for themselves. If you sign a tenancy as a common law tenant and find that the rent is unreasonably high, there is no legal form of redress available to you. However, neither is there any special procedure for the landlord to use to increase your rent. Any increase can only be by agreement. Do note, however, that common law tenants do not have any long-term rights to stay in the property after the fixed term has ended, so if you do not consent to your landlord's proposed new rent, he always has the option to evict you so that he can find another tenant.

Does the tenant ever have the right to withhold rent?

The answer is not really, except in exceptional circumstances. Here are some situations where you may think you have the right to do this:

- **Section 48 notices:** As discussed in Chapter 6 regarding the right to information about your landlord, if your landlord does not give you notice of his address in England and Wales, rent is not 'due'. However, it is not a good idea to spend your rent money on something else, as the back rent will become immediately payable once the Section 48 notice has been served (which the landlord can do at any time).

- **Unlicensed landlords:** If a landlord should have obtained a licence from the local authority for a property (usually because it is a licensable HMO) but has not, then you may be able to obtain a rent repayment order from the Residential Property Tribunal. However, you will only be able to do this if you have paid the rent, and the application is made either:

    - within 12 months of the landlord's conviction for an offence of operating an unlicensed HMO that should be licensed; or

    - within 12 months of a order being made on the local authority's application.

    If your landlord is illegally operating a property without a licence, the local authority officer who deals with any action brought against your landlord will be able to advise you regarding rent repayment orders.

    To summarise, you do not have the right to withhold rent just because your landlord is unlicensed. The right is only to obtain a rent repayment order in certain circumstances and after the rent has been paid.

- **Set-off:** In some situations you may be able to 'set off' payments against the rent, that are made to do repair work which the landlord should have done. For further information about this, see Chapter 11.

> **Q** I have received a letter stating that a company has become fixed charged receivers over the property I rent and I am not to pay my landlord. My landlord denies that there is any problem and is requesting my rent as usual. What can I do and where can I find out who I should be paying?

> **A** You need to be careful. I would suggest that you pay neither now but that you keep your rent separate (perhaps pay it into a separate bank account) and tell both parties that you are doing this while you find out who the rent is payable to. I would suggest that you then seek independent legal advice – perhaps speak to your local Citizens' Advice Bureau. If it cannot advise you, it will refer you to a local solicitor who will normally give at least initial advice free of charge.

Some other points about rent

- Rent is payable in arrears unless the tenancy agreement specifies that it should be paid in advance (most do).

- Rent is due on the morning of the day specified in the agreement but is not overdue until midnight of that day.

- If you are paying rent by cash, you should insist on being given a receipt to prove payment. If your landlord refuses to give you a receipt, make sure that someone independent witnesses your payment of rent and get him to sign a statement confirming this, so, if necessary, you will be able to prove at a later date that the rent was paid.

- Where rent is paid weekly, a landlord is obliged by law to provide you with a rent book. However, if this is not done, it does not entitle you to withhold rent. You can complain about your landlord's failure to provide a rent book to the Housing Adviser/Tenancy Relations Officer at your local authority.

- If your landlord refuses to accept rent (perhaps because he mistakenly thinks that he can keep alive a rent arrears claim for possession in this way), keep it in a separate bank account and continue to offer payment to him. You need to be able to show that you have complied with your legal obligations, so that you can defeat any claim the landlord may make for possession based on rent arrears. In particular, do not spend it on other things – just keep it safe.

Q My husband and I have not seen our landlord for five years. We pay our rent every month by cheque, but since January no cheques have been cashed. Do we keep sending them or do we go to the address we are sending them to (this is 25 miles away)? We have written expressing our concern and no reply has been received. Should we be telling anybody?

A To start with, you should make sure that the rent money for the un-cashed cheques is not spent. If you decide not to send any more cheques, make sure that you keep the money so you can pay it over quickly if your landlord contacts you. Then it will not be possible for him to evict you for arrears of rent. It sounds to me as if something has happened to your landlord. If he has died, then someone will be dealing with his estate and at some stage you should be contacted by the executors (who will ask for the back rent). However, I think you should go to the address to see if you can find out what has happened. If the property is locked up and it looks as if no one has been there for a long time, it might be worth speaking to the police. It is not unknown for people to die alone in a house and not be found for a long while. Or he could be in hospital or in prison.

Remedies

If your landlord has tried to increase your rent other than in one of the permitted methods (e.g. if your landlord has just sent you a letter telling you that your rent is going up with effect from next month), this is not an effective rent increase (unless you agree to it) and if you are not prepared to agree to the increase, you should carry on paying your existing rent. Write to your landlord explaining that he cannot increase the rent in this way without your consent, and that you do not agree to his proposed new rent.

If your landlord complains about this and tries to put pressure on you to pay the new rent, this is harassment and you can complain about him to your local authority's Housing Officer. Do not pay the new rent, or you may be deemed to have accepted the increase and consented to it by your action.

Be aware, however, that if you have an assured shorthold tenancy or a common law tenancy, it is fairly easy for your landlord to end your tenancy (without having to give a reason) and if you do not leave after the proper notice period has been given, then he can evict you. He may decide to terminate your tenancy in this way if you do not agree to his proposed rent, so if you want to stay at the property, you may in reality have no option but to agree.

If you have an assured or an assured shorthold tenancy and wish to refer your rent to the Rent Assessment Panel for review, the forms are available to download on the Residential Property Tribunal Services' website at www.rpts.gov.uk. Alternatively, you may be able to find the forms to buy at legal stationers, plus they are also available to members of my website service at www.landlordlaw.co.uk .

Further information

The Rent Service website has useful information about its service, plus the public can now access online its rent register at www.therentservice.gov.uk. There is useful information about the rent review procedure on the Residential Property Tribunal Service's website at www.rpts.gov.uk in the 'Rent Disputes' section.

The right not to be discriminated against

These are the main areas of discrimination which have been legislated against in England and Wales:

- **Age discrimination:** At present the age discrimination legislation only applies to employment, adult education and training; not housing.

- **Race discrimination:** The Race Relations Act 1976 makes it illegal for landlords to discriminate on racial grounds, either directly or indirectly, against people applying to rent accommodation by offering the accommodation on inferior terms, refusing an application for a tenancy on racial grounds, or treating the applicant in any way less favourably than other people.

  Small premises are exempt from these provisions. A dwelling counts as a small premises if the landlord or a near relative lives on the premises and intends to continue living there, and the landlord or near relative shares some of the accommodation with the tenant, and there is, in addition to the accommodation occupied by the landlord or near relative, accommodation for no more than two other separate households if the property is divided into separate lettings, or for no more than six other people in the case of a boarding house. There are other related areas where discrimination is unlawful (e.g. in advertisements for tenants).

  Further advice and assistance can be obtained from the Commission for Racial Equality (CRE), which has a helpful website at www.cre. gov.uk. A Code of Practice on Racial Equality in '*Housing, Commission for Racial Equality*' was published in 2006 and is available from the CRE website.

- **Sex discrimination:** There are similar rules prohibiting discrimination on the grounds of someone's sex in the Sex Discrimination Act 1976. The provisions of the Act are similar to those of the Race Relations Act and cover direct and indirect discrimination and victimisation. It is illegal for landlords to discriminate on the grounds of gender, such as by offering female tenants worse facilities than male tenants. However, the small premises exemption described above applies. It is fairly rare nowadays for this type of discrimination to be a problem in the area of housing law. However, if you feel that you have been discriminated against, you can obtain further information and advice from the Equal Opportunities Commission, which has a website at www.eoc.org.uk.

- **Religious discrimination:** This is prohibited under the Equality Act 2006. This Act set up the Commission for Equality and Human Rights, which is scheduled to come into being in October 2007. In the meantime, there is a website at www.cehr.org.uk where you can obtain further information. In some circumstances you may also be able to seek help and advice from the CRE.

- **Sexual orientation:** As a result of the Human Rights Act 1998 and the Civil Partnership Act 2004, same-sex partnerships are now treated in the same way under the law as heterosexual partnerships. There is no specific legislation prohibiting discrimination against lesbians and gay men. However, the Equality Act provides for regulations to be made regarding discrimination or harassment on the ground of sexual orientation.

  If you feel that you are being discriminated against because you are lesbian or gay, you can seek help from the Equal Opportunities Commission after October 2007. Help can also be sought from other advice agencies, such as the Citizens' Advice Bureau and Shelter. For their contact details, see Part 4.

- **Disability discrimination:** This has already been discussed briefly in Part 1, and will be considered in relation to various aspects of tenants' rights in the various sections below.

  Insofar as tenancy agreements are concerned new regulations came into force in December 2006 which apply to all landlords. We have already considered these at page 117 above.

Remedies and further information

If you feel that you are being discriminated against because of your disability, you can seek help and advice from the Disability Rights Commission, who have a helpful website at www.drc.org.uk.

Discrimination is a huge area of law and it is not possible for a book, which is about tenants' rights in general, to look at it in any detail. If you feel that you are being discriminated against, in any of the areas outlined above, you should seek further advice, perhaps initially from one of the organisations referred to, who will advise you and recommend further sources of help. See also the section on disability discrimination in Part 1.

CHAPTER 9

The right to receive Housing Benefit

Housing Benefit is a complex subject, worthy of a long textbook in itself. This book is mainly concerned with the rights and obligations between landlords and tenants, rather than rights against Housing Benefit Offices (who award the benefit). Therefore, only a brief overview of the system is given here and I will concentrate on how the payment of benefit affects the landlord/tenant relationship.

> **Note**
>
> Housing Benefit is also called 'rent rebate' for council tenants and 'rent allowance' for private tenants and tenants of housing associations/registered social landlords.

Eligibility

If you are unemployed or on a low income, you will usually be entitled to Housing Benefit. This is a national scheme to assist those on low incomes to pay their rent. It is administered by local authorities (although they can contract out). It can normally be claimed by anyone in receipt of any other benefit, or whose income and assets meet the eligibility criteria, although there are some exceptions (e.g. many recent migrants and British nationals who have been living aboard for a long time).

To find out whether you are eligible for benefit and how much you are entitled to, you will need to speak to your local Housing Benefit Office. The sum awarded will depend on your financial and personal circumstances, and an assessment made by the Rent Officer. There are appeal procedures you can use if you consider that your application for benefit has not been dealt with properly. Note that the rent for some secure tenancies will include a small amount for water rates and heating charges. This will not be covered by Housing Benefit and will have to be paid by the tenant.

Payment

Housing Benefit is calculated on a weekly basis, but rent is generally payable monthly. This can make it difficult to work out the exact sum due, unless a record, such as in Table 1 (on page 134), is kept. It is a good idea to do this, so you can make sure that any shortfall is paid promptly, and that you do not fall into serious arrears.

Payment is normally made to the tenant, but you can ask that the payment be made to your landlord direct. This is often a good idea if you do not trust yourself not to spend the money on other debts. Sometimes landlords will agree to limit their rent to the sum paid by Housing Benefit, so long as it is paid to them direct. The Housing Benefit Office can also decide to pay benefit direct to the landlord if 'it is in the interest of the claimant and their family to make payments direct to the landlord'.

Note that if your rent is more than eight weeks in arrears, the Housing Benefit Office will normally pay direct to the landlord if requested by him, and it does not need your consent to do this.

If you receive a Local Housing Allowance (see page 136) rather than Housing Benefit, then this will normally be paid to you, the tenant, unless you are in arrears of eight weeks or more, or you are considered 'vulnerable'. This will be the case if you do not speak, read or write English, have a history of drug or alcohol dependency or gambling, are fleeing domestic violence, leaving care or prison, or have debt problems or a recent County Court judgment.

Clawback

If you, or your landlord, are paid benefit when you are not entitled to receive it, the Housing Benefit Office will want this paid back. The normal way it does this is to deduct it from future rent payments.

It is important, therefore, that you keep the Housing Benefit Office informed of any change in your circumstances so that the benefit you receive is the benefit you are entitled to. As an example, if there is an overpayment and you do not tell the office and you keep the money, and you then lose your job and need to claim again, you may find that although you are entitled to benefit it is withheld to cover the past overpayments. This could mean that you fall into serious arrears and are evicted. Also, keeping benefit when you know you are not entitled to it may be classed as benefit fraud, which is a criminal offence.

Your continuing liability under the tenancy

Private tenancies

Even if you are eligible for Housing Benefit, this does not mean that the benefit you receive will automatically be the full amount of your rent. Sometimes there will be a shortfall which you will be responsible for paying.

Some tenants assume that if the Housing Benefit Office has assessed the benefit they are entitled to receive as being less than the rent in their tenancy agreement, this somehow changes the rent that they have to pay to their landlord. This is not the case. Decisions made by the Housing Benefit Office do not change your legal liability to your landlord under the tenancy agreement you have signed.

For example, if your tenancy agreement states that you are liable for rent of £400 on the 15th day of every month, that is what the landlord is entitled to. If you are paid Housing Benefit of £300 every four weeks, then you will fall into arrears if you do not make up the difference (see Table 1 on page 134). If you do not pay the difference, then the landlord is entitled to sue you and obtain a County Court judgment for the rent arrears. If the rent arrears reach more than £800 (i.e. two months' worth), he will be entitled to serve notice and then evict you under the serious rent arrears ground (for further information, see Chapter 13). Even if you are in arrears because your benefit is less than your rent, or that it has not been paid to you at all, this will not be a reason for the judge to refuse your landlord an order for possession. It is important, therefore, that you do everything in your power to ensure that your benefit is paid to your landlord, and that you make up any shortfall promptly.

Table 1 below shows how a tenant whose rent is £400 per month and who receives £300 Housing Benefit every four weeks can end up with serious arrears over a year. In this case the landlord would have been entitled to bring proceedings to evict the tenant under the serious rent arrears ground (where the rent must be in arrears of two months or more) after August. Note that if your landlord takes you to court for rent arrears, this is the sort of schedule he will be required to produce to the court.

Table 1

Date	Rent due	Rent paid	Arrears
15/01/2007	£400.00		£400.00
12/02/2007		£300.00	£100.00
15/02/2007	£400.00		£500.00
12/03/2007		£300.00	£200.00
15/03/2007	£400.00		£600.00
09/04/2007		£300.00	£300.00
15/04/2007	£400.00		£700.00
07/05/2007		£300.00	£400.00
15/05/2007	£400.00		£800.00
04/06/2007		£300.00	£500.00
15/06/2007	£400.00		£900.00
02/07/2007		£300.00	£600.00
15/07/2007	£400.00		£1,000.00
30/07/2007		£300.00	£700.00
15/08/2007	£400.00		£1,100.00

27/08/2007		£300.00	£800.00
15/09/2007	£400.00		£1,200.00
24/09/2007		£300.00	£900.00
15/10/2007	£400.00		£1,300.00
22/10/2007		£300.00	£1,000.00
15/11/2007	£400.00		£1,400.00
19/11/2007		£300.00	£1,100.00
15/12/2007	£400.00		£1,500.00
17/12/2007		£300.00	£1,200.00

Social tenancies

If you are a council tenant or rent your property from a registered social landlord, then it is less likely that there will be any shortfall. You are also at less risk of being evicted due to delays in Housing Benefit payment, as social landlords are now expected by the courts (under the rent arrears pre-action protocol) to help their tenants sort out any outstanding Housing Benefit problems before bringing proceedings to evict the tenant for rent arrears.

However, if the arrears are due to your failure to pay any shortfall, then you will be vulnerable to being evicted in the same way as you would with a private landlord. Note that you may also have lost any right to be re-housed by the local authority if you fall within the 'priority need' category, if the local authority takes the view that you are 'intentionally homeless' due to your failure to make up the shortfall.

Confidentiality

Your dealings with the Housing Benefit Office are confidential and it will be bound by the Data Protection Act. This means that it is not allowed to provide any information about your application, or any award made to you, to your landlord without your consent.

Most landlords will be anxious for information about your Housing

Benefit payments, particularly if you are in arrears. Therefore, your landlord will often ask you to sign a letter of authority, authorising the local authority to discuss your application and payments with your landlord. You do not have to sign this letter if you do not want to. However, it is usually a good idea to co-operate. The landlord is less likely to evict you for rent arrears if he is able to speak to your Housing Benefit Office and learn when payments are being made. He will also be able to address all his enquiries at the real culprits of any delay, the Housing Benefit Office, rather than bother you about it.

Local Housing Allowance (LHA)

This is a new scheme which only applies to tenancies with private landlords, which is gradually being rolled out across the country. In many ways it is similar to Housing Benefit and it is administered by the Housing Benefit Offices, who can provide you with further information. However, the sum paid is based on a flat allowance which you can find out about in advance. So households who have the same circumstances and live in the same area will receive the same amount, regardless of the size or desirability of the accommodation they actually live in. If you are in an area where this scheme is in operation and your rent is less than the housing allowance you are entitled to, you can keep the difference (and this will not affect the calculation of your other benefits).

At the time of writing, the authorities currently operating the LHA schemes are: Argyll and Bute, Blackpool, Brighton and Hove, Conwy, Coventry, East Riding of Yorkshire, Edinburgh, Guildford, Leeds, Lewisham, North East Lincolnshire, Norwich, Pembrokeshire, South Norfolk, St Helens, Teignbridge, and Wandsworth.

The scheme does not apply to:

- private tenants who live in a caravan, mobile home or houseboat;

- people living in hostels;

- regulated (protected) tenancies, who are excluded from current rent restrictions;

- private tenancies where a significant portion of the rent payable covers meals and services (sometimes known as 'board and attendance').

These, like tenants of local authorities and registered social landlords, will still be referred to the Rent Officer.

Remedies

If you have problems with benefit payments, you should first of all speak to your Housing Benefit Office. Sadly there are major problems with Housing Benefit payments in many parts of the country, and there are often long delays. The best source of advice and help with Housing Benefit problems is usually your local Citizens' Advice Bureau or any money advice service associated with your local Citizens' Advice Bureau office. Its advisers are usually extremely knowledgeable and will be able to advise you and write letters on your behalf.

Local authority tenants and tenants of registered social landlords should speak to their Rent Officer, who will normally be able to help. If you are dissatisfied with the service received, you can follow the complaints procedure discussed in Part 4.

If you think that the sum awarded to you as benefit is incorrect, or that there is some other problem connected with the award and/or payment of your benefit, there is an appeals procedure you can follow. Your local Citizens' Advice Bureau adviser or Rent Officer will help you with this, should it prove necessary.

Further information

You will find helpful information on both Housing Benefit and the LHA scheme on the website for the Department of Work and Pensions (DWP) at www.dwp.gov.uk.

There is a very detailed manual on Housing Benefit on the DWP website at www.dwp.gov.uk/housingbenefit/manuals/hbgm/index.asp.

For other information, it is best to consult your local Citizens' Advice Bureau, Shelter office, Law Centre or local authority housing adviser. Note that these advisers will generally be better than solicitors in solicitors' firms, who, on the whole (with a few honourable exceptions), tend not to be very knowledgeable about the Housing Benefit system.

CHAPTER 10

Rights regarding the condition of the property, repairs and safety

Your right to have your property kept in good repair is a very important right. It may be the reason why many of you have bought this book. However, unfortunately, this is a very complex area of law. If you have not already done so, I would suggest that you read first the background chapter on the legal system in England and Wales in Part 1, in particular the information on civil law, as this will help you understand the law relating to property repairs.

The main reason why this area of law is so complex is that there are so many different types of law and legal rights involved. Some rights come from the common law and others from statute. Some of these are rights (either contractual or non-contractual) that allow the tenant to sue the landlord direct, and others are repairing and other obligations which come under the criminal law system where the landlord can be prosecuted by the local authority (or some other public body). There are different considerations, procedures and often remedies associated with each of these. Finally, there are some circumstances where the landlord will have a claim against the tenant, if the tenant has not complied with his obligations under the tenancy, and the condition of the property has deteriorated as a result, and this is looked at briefly at the end of this chapter.

Probably the clearest way to set things out is to look at the different individual areas of law involved, which is what I have done below. However, usually any one problem will come within several of these areas, and you will have to choose which of a number of possible courses of action to follow. For this reason, particularly for serious problems, it is important to obtain specialist legal help before any formal steps are taken, as your advisor can help you make the right decision on to the course of action you should take.

> **Note on terminology**
>
> **Disrepair:** This is where a property is in a poor state of repair. It is generally used in the context of a tenant claiming against his landlord for breach of the landlord's legal obligations to keep the property in repair.
>
> **Dilapidations:** This is where a landlord claims against the tenant where the condition of the property at the end of the tenancy cannot be justified under the 'fair wear and tear' rule (discussed in Chapter 7) and the tenant is therefore in breach of his obligations under his tenancy.

Rights under contract

If you are a tenant, there will be a tenancy agreement. Either this will be a written document or you will have an 'oral' tenancy, where there is no documentation. In both cases, repairing obligations either will be express terms (i.e. specifically mentioned) in your tenancy agreement, or will be implied into the tenancy by either the common law or statute.

> **Note**
>
> Your landlord's repairing obligations are not conditional upon your paying rent and your landlord will be expected to keep the property in repair even if you are in serious arrears. However, bear in mind that if your landlord has not been receiving rent, it may be difficult for him to pay for the repair work to be done.

Rights at the start of the tenancy

Under common law, for furnished properties, there is an implied term that the property is fit for habitation on the day the letting starts. This will include things that were wrong with the property at the time you moved in but which you did not find out about for a while. The property will be considered unfit if it:

- is infested with bugs;

- has defective drainage or sewerage systems;

- is infected;

- has a lack of safety; or

- has an insufficient water supply.

The property will also be considered unfit if it fails to comply with the statutory definition of fitness. For properties let before 6 April 2006, this was set out in Section 604 of the Housing Act 1985. For properties let after that date, the relevant law is that found in Part 1 of the Housing Act 2004, which set up the Housing Health and Safety Rating System (see page 153).

Note that any contract terms which seek to exclude this right (e.g. a clause purporting to confirm that you have checked the condition of the property and are satisfied that it is in good condition before you have moved in) will normally be void.

Unfortunately, this right only applies to furnished properties and not to unfurnished properties.

> **Remedies**
> If you move into a property and find that it is not fit, you are entitled to move out immediately and you will not be liable for rent. However, it is important that you leave before paying any rent as payment of rent will be considered an acceptance of the condition of the property. So if rent is paid weekly, you should leave during the first seven days. If you have paid rent in advance of moving in, then it is arguable that this should not be deemed to be an acceptance of the unfitness if you had not had an opportunity to discover the problems.

If you have lost the right to move out, you will still be able to claim compensation for breach of contract. For further information on this, see the section on enforcement in Chapter 3.

Obligations of the landlord under the tenancy agreement

The statutory repairing covenants

These come under Section 11 of the Landlord and Tenant Act 1985, which inserts obligations or 'covenants' into all tenancy agreements for tenancies for a term of less than seven years. Section 11 is very important and is the basis of tenants' rights against their landlord as regards repairs. Under this section the landlord is responsible for keeping in repair the structure and exterior of the property; and the installations for the supply of water, gas, electricity, sanitation, space heating and heating water.

Repair work to the structure and exterior of the property

Note that the work must be 'repair'. You will not be able to force the landlord to rectify what might be a design fault in the building, or to improve it. Generally, 'structure and exterior' includes:

- A partition wall between your property and another house or flat.
- The path and steps leading to a house (but not the paving of the backyard).
- The roof of a house, including any skylights and the chimney.
- The walls, together with any cement rendering.
- Any external joinery (and failure to paint this so as to protect it from rot will be covered).
- Windows.
- The outside walls and the outside of inner party walls of flats. Also, the outer side of any horizontal divisions between flats, which can include the roof, if appropriate.

Installations for the supply of gas, electricity, water, sanitation, heating and hot water

This will include water and gas pipes (including guttering), electrical wiring, water tanks, boilers, radiators and other space heating installations (e.g. vents for underfloor heating).

When does Section 11 apply?

Section 11 applies to all tenancies of residential accommodation which started after 24 October 1961 and where the term is for a period of seven years or less. This means the fixed term specified in the tenancy agreement. Many tenancies last for far longer than seven years, but they are still protected by Section 11 as they either have a succession of short fixed terms (such as six months or a year) or they run on from week-to-week or month-to-month after a fixed term has finished.

For all tenancies where the section applies, the provisions of Section 11 will form part of the tenancy agreement, whether or not this is actually mentioned in the written tenancy document. If the provisions of the section are not mentioned in the document, it will be an implied term.

A landlord is not allowed to exclude the provisions of the section unless he has obtained a court order permitting this (which is very rarely done), so any contract term which tries to pass responsibility for the repairing obligations set out in Section 11 over to the tenant, or which tries to reduce the landlord's obligations in any way (e.g. by requiring the tenant to notify the landlord of any repairs needed within a strict time limit) will be void.

> **Note**
>
> One of the confusing things so far as tenants are concerned is that tenancy agreements will frequently contain no details of these important rights, so tenants are often unaware of them. The Law Commission has recommended reforming the law to make it a requirement that all landlords provide a written tenancy agreement which will have to include prescribed terms, including details of the landlord's repairing obligations under Section 11. However, at the time of writing this book, there is no indication when or if this will become law.

Some further comments on Section 11

- It has been said in case law that the landlord should be required to put the premises into repair if it was not in good repair at the start of the tenancy.

- Installations should be in working order at the start of the tenancy.

- The landlord must keep the property and installations in repair throughout the tenancy.

- The requirement under Section 11 is regarding 'repairs' – a tenant cannot require a landlord to make improvements. In some cases it will be difficult to say whether any particular work is repair, improvement, maintenance or renewal. If there is a dispute and no agreement can be reached, then ultimately this will be something for a court to decide. There is a lot of case law on this.

- The Act also specifies that when deciding the standard of repair, the age, character and prospective life of the property and the locality in which it is situated must be taken into account. This means that a tenant cannot expect a property to be put into a perfect condition, unless possibly it is a very expensive letting in an upmarket part of town. For most properties, the landlord will just have to do repairs to a standard that would make the property fit for occupation.

- The landlord is not obliged by the Act to rebuild a property which has been destroyed by fire, flood or inevitable accident.

- The section will not apply to any property of the tenant.

- The landlord cannot be forced to carry out repairs if the damage has been caused by the tenant himself and if he does the repairs, he can claim the reasonable cost of them back from the tenant (e.g. by deducting them from the damage deposit).

- For tenancies which started after 15 January 1989, Section 11 also extends to installations which service the tenant's property, but which are located outside it, so long as the landlord owns or has control of the installation. An example of this is where a landlord owns a building with several flats with central heating and the boiler which services them all is kept separately in the basement (and the basement is not included in any of the lets).

- If a landlord needs to gain access to another property to get repairs done, but is unable to obtain permission to do this, then this will give him a defence to any claim by the tenant. So, if the boiler mentioned above is located in one of the flats and the occupier of that flat will not let the landlord in to repair it, the landlord will have a defence.

- The landlord will not be liable under Section 11 until he has received notice of the disrepair. It is best to give notice in writing by way of a letter, making sure that the letter is dated and that you have kept a copy.

- Where a landlord is bound by Section 11, he will also have a right to enter the property to inspect it at reasonable times, after giving not less than 24 hours' notice.

> **Note**
>
> If the landlord's suggested inspection time is inconvenient for you, there is no reason why you should not object, and ask him to arrange another appointment. However, you should not refuse to allow the landlord in at all. If you do this, you may lose your right to claim compensation (as it will be your fault that repairs were not identified and carried out) plus if the property deteriorates because essential repairs are not done, the landlord may be entitled to claim compensation from you.

The common parts of properties

Many tenancies involve the tenant using or needing to use property which is shared with other tenants or occupiers (e.g. halls, passageways and paths, stairways and lifts, and shared accommodation). If there are no specific 'express' terms regarding these areas, the following terms will be implied into the tenancy agreement:

- They must be maintained by the landlord so as to prevent injury to the tenant or to the property let to him (e.g. preventing dampness getting into a flat).

- If a tenant is given a contractual right to use another part of the building, not included in the property rented to him (e.g. a shared toilet or kitchen area), then the landlord must maintain that area.

- The landlord must maintain facilities which are necessary for the tenant's use of the property, such as lifts and rubbish chutes.

- If there is disrepair, this may breach the tenant's right to 'quiet enjoyment' (for more information, see Chapter 13). An example of this is if a landlord fails to keep a property watertight and the tenant's property becomes damaged.

- The parts of the property retained by the landlord must not interfere with the tenant's property.

- For tenancies which started after 15 January 1989, the provisions in Section 11 discussed above apply also to installations which affect the tenant's property but are located outside of it, if they are under the landlord's control.

As the common parts of the property are within the landlord's control, the landlord is obliged to carry out any repairs, whether or not he has been informed of them by the tenant (unlike repairs to the tenant's property, where the landlord is only liable after the tenant has given him notice). However, you should still give notice to your landlord of any necessary repairs, and keep a copy of your letter in the normal way.

If there are any 'express terms' in your tenancy agreement regarding any of the matters discussed above in connection with Section 11, note that if your landlord tries to take away any of your rights, those terms in your agreement will be void. They will only be valid if they state accurately what the law is, or if they give you greater rights.

Additional obligations under the tenancy agreement

If the work that needs to be done is not covered by the sections discussed earlier, then take a look at your tenancy agreement. Sometimes the tenancy will make the landlord responsible for matters over and above the repairing obligations prescribed by law; for example, it may say that he will be responsible for the maintenance of the kitchen 'white goods' (e.g. fridges and washing machines) or the garden. Note that there are many small items which some landlords may routinely deal with but which they will not be strictly liable for, such as fixing floor coverings and redecoration. Unless your tenancy agreement provides for these you will not be able to force your landlord to deal with them if he chooses not to.

Remedies

The rights discussed here all relate to the tenant's contract with his landlord, so the various remedies appropriate to contractual claims (discussed in Part 1) can be used, such as a claim to the County Court for an order that the repairs be carried out or a claim for compensation. However, it is very important that you notify your landlord of the problem before taking any action, as he will not be legally liable (and you will not be entitled to use any of the enforcement procedures) until you do so. Make sure that you keep a copy of your letter and that you are able to prove that it was sent or delivered to him. Note, also, that the pre-action protocol which is discussed below will apply and must be complied with before any court action is started.

For further information on court action, see the background information on court proceedings in Part 1 and also the general section on enforcement for repairing obligations below. Note also that, provided the proper procedures are followed, you may also have the right to get the repairs done and set off the cost of the repairs against your rent. For more information on set-off, see Chapter 11.

Rights under tort

A tort is a civil wrong which is not a breach of contract. I would suggest that before you read this section you read the section on the law of tort in Part 1 (page 15). Bear in mind that generally these rights are less commonly used than the contractual rights discussed here.

Negligence

This has already been discussed in Part 1. Traditionally, landlords have not had a 'duty of care' towards their tenants. In some cases, for example, if the landlord is also the builder, a claim can be made. However, because of this traditional immunity, it is wise for claims in negligence to be made in conjunction with another claim and not on their own.

Private nuisance

This is where something in one property interferes with the use and enjoyment of a neighbouring property. This legal rule can only be used by property owners. This includes tenants, as they have a legal interest under their tenancy, i.e. they are deemed to 'own' it for the period of their tenancy. However, it does not include family members and visitors, other than the spouse of the tenant.

> **Note**
>
> You can also claim against your neighbours in nuisance, but this book is looking specifically at your rights as a tenant, so we are only considering claims against your landlord.

So, if your landlord has retained control over part of the building where you rent your flat, then he will be liable under the tort of nuisance if defects in the retained part, or your landlord's use of the retained part, causes interference with your use of your flat. This will also apply if the landlord lives next door; for example, if you rent one of two adjoining houses.

The sorts of thing which can be covered by the tort of private nuisance include disrepair which affects the use of your property, noise, bad smells, and possibly pest infestation if these enter or arise from an area controlled by the landlord. The nuisance must go on for a long time. If your landlord does very noisy repair works every night in the basement of the building where you rent a flat, that will be actionable, but not if he just does it once. There must also be some sort of harm to you resulting from the nuisance for there to be an actionable claim. Therefore, if the nightly noise in the basement prevents you sleeping, you will have an actionable claim, or if the landlord has control of the roof and gutters but does not maintain them, resulting in rainwater leaking into your property and causing damage, you will have an actionable claim.

Unlike personal injury claims in negligence, you will not normally be able to claim in nuisance if you are unusually sensitive. So, if you are an exceptionally light sleeper, then you will not be able to claim regarding the noise in the basement if most people would be able to sleep through it.

However, the intentions of the defendant are important in private nuisance claims. If you can show that the landlord's actions are done deliberately to affect you, you may be able to claim in situations where otherwise the landlord's actions would be reasonable. In one case (not a landlord and tenant situation) a defendant hung metal trays and hammered on the wall to disrupt music lessons given by his neighbour.

Note

Remember that you will also be liable under the private nuisance rules. So, for example, if you are very noisy, your landlord would (if he lived next door) be able to claim against you in nuisance, as would your neighbours.

Remedies

A claim would have to be made to the County Court for an injunction for the landlord to stop the behaviour complained of. Damages can also be claimed but generally an injunction will not be granted if damages are awarded. In some circumstances you can act to remove the nuisance yourself (e.g. if a radio is left playing loudly in the basement, you can probably go and switch it off). However, in most situations it is wise to take legal advice before taking any action (e.g. before going onto the landlord's property where you do not have a right of access).

The Defective Premises Act 1972

This Act gives duties to landlords and builders/improvers to do work safely and properly, and gives landlords liabilities where damage or injury results from disrepair. It is often used alongside actions for negligence and for breach of contract.

Advantages in using this Act are:

- that the tenant does not have to serve notice on the landlord first for him to be liable;

- the rights extend to anybody 'who might reasonably be expected to be affected'. This could include members of the family or visitors.

Wherever possible, claims should not rely on this Act alone but should be used in conjunction with another claim; for example, in negligence or (where claims are made under Section 4 of this Act) the landlord's repairing obligations under Section 11 of the Landlord and Tenant Act 1985. I will now have a look at some of the main sections of this Act.

- **Section 1:** Under Section 1 of the Act, people who carry out work to a property on or after 1 January 1974 or who are connected with such work (e.g. landlords, builders, architects, surveyors and specialist subcontractors) are under a duty to ensure that the work is done in a professional manner with proper materials and that the property is fit for habitation when completed.

  The term 'fit for habitation' is not defined in the Act but will include safety for occupation, sufficient water supply, infestation by bugs or pests, adequate drainage and infection. The Act can also be used if there is an omission when carrying out repair work (such as failing to incorporate a damp proof course in a newly built wall) or if that work has been carried out badly.

  The duty under Section 1 is very strong because the person who carries out the work will not be able to argue as a defence that it was 'reasonable' to believe that the work was adequate. This duty is owed to the person for whom the property was provided and to subsequent tenants and owners and anyone else who has a legal or equitable interest in the property.

  Note, however, that the duty is not owed where properties are built or first sold under the terms of a scheme approved by the Secretary of State that provides insurance cover for defects in the state of the building. The only scheme currently approved is that of the National House-Building Council. However, this covers virtually all private residential developments, so effectively in the private sector the Act will only apply to conversions and alterations.

> **Note**
>
> Builders may also be liable where, as a result of their negligence, personal injury is caused to subsequent occupiers of the property. Local authorities can be liable if the injury or damage has arisen from its negligent failure to check work plans for the site or to enforce building regulations.
>
> Further information about the National House-Building Council can be found on its website at www.nhbc.co.uk.

- **Section 3:** Under common law landlords were not liable for defective work carried out prior to the letting of a property. However, this was changed by Section 3 of the Act, which abolishes the immunity that landlords had. This means that a duty of care is owed in negligence by the landlord for any repair, maintenance, construction or other work done in relation to a property. The duty of care is owed to the tenant, members of the tenant's household and visitors. It only relates to tenancies that started on or after 1 January 1974.

- **Section 4:** Under this section landlords who are contractually obliged to repair or maintain a property (such as all landlords to whom Section 11 applies) owe a duty of care to anybody who could reasonably be affected by disrepair arising from the breach of their repairing covenants. The duty is also owed if the landlord has a right to enter the property to carry out repairs (again this will apply to all landlords subject to Section 11) and is triggered if the landlord knows or ought to know of the defect (e.g. because he should have spotted it in his inspection visit), regardless of whether or not he had been told about it by the tenant.

  However, the duty will not be owed if the loss or damage is not reasonably foreseeable, or if it is caused by the tenant's failure to comply with his obligations, or if the defect is hidden and undiscoverable. It does not cover problems which are not caused by the landlord's failure to do repairs (e.g. condensation).

Breach of building regulations

A claim can also be made against the landlord if he has done work to the property which was subject to building regulations which have not been complied with, and this causes harm. A claim can also, in some circumstances, be made against local authorities if they do not enforce the regulations properly.

> **General remedies in tort**
>
> Claims are normally made to the County Court for damages and/or for an injunction. In some circumstances, as indicated above in the relevant sections, self-help is available. However, legal advice should normally be obtained before you use a self-help remedy. For more general information on remedies in tort, see the background information on the legal system in Part 1.
>
> You should also seek professional legal help before attempting to use any of the rights under tort discussed here, and certainly before bringing any legal proceedings.

Rights under public/criminal law

As well as his direct liability to you, his tenant, your landlord is also liable under the criminal legal system for various offences under statute. Although these are dealt with through the criminal system, and cases are brought in the Magistrates' Court, they are not normally brought by the police. Most often cases are brought by local authorities, sometimes by Trading Standards Offices, and other organisations such as the Health and Safety Executive (HSE). Sometimes cases can be brought by you!

However, it is important to remember that in all these types of case, the focus is on the landlord's failure to comply with public standards, rather than his direct duty to you. Sometimes, a compensation order may be made as part of the proceedings, but this is incidental to the main purpose of the case, which is punishment by the state for your landlord's failure to comply with the relevant statute. A conviction under one of these statutes also does not necessarily mean that you will then be able to bring a civil claim against the landlord – this will depend very much on whether the subject matter of the prosecution is something for which the landlord is liable to you under the law of contract or tort.

The Housing Health and Safety Rating System (HHSRS)

It is not generally realised that all residential property owners (not just landlords) have a duty to maintain their property to certain standards. This was previously set out in Section 604 of the Housing Act 1985, but from 1 April 2006 this was replaced by the new HHSRS in Part 1 of the Housing Act 2004.

This new system is a radical change from the old. Section 604 set out a standard of fitness which all properties had to be assessed against. Under the new system there is no single standard; assessors instead will look to identify hazards and their likely impact on the health and safety of the occupier or visitor. If serious hazards are identified, then there are powers available to local authorities to force landlords to remedy them.

A hazard is any risk of harm (including temporary harm) to the health or safety of an actual or potential occupier of accommodation that arises from a deficiency in the property. The underlying principle is that 'any residential premises should provide a safe and healthy environment for any potential occupier or visitor'.

Therefore, all properties should:

- be designed, constructed and maintained with non-hazardous materials;
- be free from both unnecessary and avoidable hazards; and
- provide adequate protection from all potential hazards.

At the time of writing there are 29 identified hazards against which properties will be assessed. These fall within the following areas:

- Physiological requirements, such as damp and mould growth and excess heat and cold.
- Non-microbial pollutants, such as asbestos, carbon monoxide and lead.
- Psychological requirements, such as overcrowding, unauthorised intruders, lighting and noise.

- Protection against infection, i.e. hygiene, sanitation and water supply.
- Protection against accidents, such as falls, electric shocks and burns, collisions, cuts and strains.

As the system is looking at general safety, hazards are assessed on the basis of their effect on the most vulnerable class of occupiers rather than on the actual people living at the property. For example, when looking at the hazard of excess cold (perhaps the hazard which will have the most impact and which many properties are least likely to comply with) the assessor will be looking at its effect on the elderly rather than on (for example) the group of four 18-year-old students living there at the time of the inspection.

If you think that your property is likely to contain any of the hazards indicated above (and your landlord refuses to take any action), you should contact someone in the Environmental Health Department of your local authority (sometimes this is dealt with by a department called Private Sector Housing). The department will arrange for an Environmental Health Officer (EHO) to come out and inspect your property. If you put your complaint in writing, it is legally obliged to do this.

When doing his inspection the EHO will give each hazard a rating which will be expressed through a numerical score. These will be entered into a computer program which will work out the result of the inspection for the property. If the result shows that there are hazards at the property, the action taken by the local authority will depend on whether the hazards assessed are Category 1 or Category 2. If they are Category 1, the department must take action. If they are Category 2, then it only has a discretion to take action if it considers it appropriate. It is not legally obliged to take action.

The normal action taken will be to serve an improvement order on the landlord, ordering him to carry out remedial works. If these works are not done within a specified time, then the landlord can be prosecuted in the Magistrates' Court. Note that in some areas it may take the local authority some time to arrange for an inspection, so if the disrepair needs urgent action you should use the remedies under contract and tort discussed above, or use your right of set-off discussed in Chapter 11.

HHSRS and social landlords

It is not possible for a local authority to enforce the powers under the Act against itself. However, it should carry out inspections of its own property where asked to do so.

Other registered social landlords (RSLs) are subject to inspection and enforcement in the same way as private landlords.

Note, however, that there is an official standard – the Decent Homes Standard (see further below) – which all social landlords (including local authority landlords) are supposed to comply with. Part of this standard provides that properties must be free of Category 1 hazards. Local authorities when receiving a complaint about a dwelling owned by an RSL, should first consider their plans for complying with the Decent Homes Standard, before deciding what action to take.

Further information

There is a vast amount of information on the Communities and Local Government website at www.communities.gov.uk and this is the best place to look for further help and guidance. You should be able to find a long PDF guidance document for landlords and property-related professionals on the HHSRS, plus there is a whole subsection of the 'Housing' section of the site devoted to decent homes. This is particularly recommended for tenants of all social landlords.

The Decent Homes project

The government is looking to generally improve the standard of housing in the public sector and this is being implemented under the Decent Homes Project. This sets out a general standard of what is a decent home, and aims to make all social housing comply with this by the end of 2010.

The standard provides that a decent home will meet the following criteria:

- It meets the current statutory minimum standard for housing (i.e. it would satisfy an inspection under the HHSRS).
- It is in a reasonable state of repair.

- It has reasonably modern facilities and services (in particular, kitchens and bathrooms).

- It provides a reasonable degree of thermal comfort (i.e. it has effective insulation and effective heating).

Private landlords are also expected to conform to the Decent Homes Standard, but as the standard is not specifically enforceable by tenants, for example, through the courts, it is less helpful in the private sector.

For more information, see the Communities and Local Government's website at www.communities.gov.uk. There is a whole subsection of the 'Housing' section on decent homes, including some helpful FAQs.

The Environmental Protection Act 1990

This Act deals largely with various aspects of pollution and statutory nuisances and measures to control them. So far as landlords and tenants are concerned, the most important section of the Act is Part 3, which looks at statutory nuisances. A statutory nuisance is where premises are in a state which makes them prejudicial to health. Specific nuisances include:

- Premises in such a state as to be prejudicial to health or a nuisance.

- Smoke emitted from premises.

- Fumes or gases emitted from premises.

- Accumulation or deposits of noxious waste.

- Animals kept in such a manner or place as to constitute a nuisance.

- Noise emitted from premises.

Local authorities (generally via the Environmental Health Departments) are generally the organisation which will enforce this Act. They have a duty to investigate complaints and if, as a result of their inspection, they find that there is a statutory nuisance, they are legally bound to take action.

Generally, the local authority will serve an informal notice first, and if this is not acted on, proceed to the service of an abatement notice. This can be done even if the nuisance is not in existence at the time of the service of the notice, so long as it is reasonably likely that it will reoccur. There is a right of appeal against an abatement notice. However, if it is not complied with, the landlord can be prosecuted in the Magistrates' Court and if convicted, fined.

Note

The statutory nuisance rules discussed here are different from the private nuisance rules discussed in the tort section (on page 149). Private nuisance is a civil wrong and you can sue in the civil courts. Statutory nuisances under the Environmental Protection Act are a criminal offence and are dealt with through the criminal law system. They could, of course, be about the same thing (e.g. the noisy repair works in the basement discussed before). In law, there are often different ways of dealing with the same problem.

Remedies

If you consider that your property comes within the definition of a statutory nuisance, you should contact the Environmental Health Department of your local authority and ask it to carry out an inspection. Once this has been done, depending on the results, it will have to decide, if the property is problematic, whether it is best to bring proceedings against the landlord under the HHSRS or under the Environmental Protection Act.

Using the Act against local authority landlords

If the landlord is the local authority, then EHOs will not be able to bring a claim, as this would be against their own authority! However, in these circumstances you can, if necessary, take action yourself.

If you decide to do this, you must take legal advice first before taking any action. These proceedings are complex and you will need independent expert evidence (e.g. from an EHO (not one from the local authority concerned)) and medical evidence (e.g. if your health has been affected by the nuisance). Also, after taking advice, you may find that this is not the best course of action for your particular problem. However, basically this is the procedure:

- You serve a notice of intention on the person responsible for the nuisance (for local authorities this is normally the Chief Executive or

Town Clerk). The notice must be in writing, containing details of the matter complained of, and it must make it clear that unless the nuisance is abated or a reasonable proposal for abating the nuisance is given, proceedings will be commenced without further notice. The notice must be for 21 days, and court proceedings cannot be commenced until the notice period has elapsed.

- Note that the nuisance must be continuing at the time the summons is issued. If it has stopped you are unlikely to succeed, even if it is probable that the nuisance will occur again.

- If this is ignored, you should apply for a summons in the Magistrates' Court. This is called the 'laying of information'. You will need to complete a form providing details of the problem and the person or organisation responsible. You will need legal help at this stage as an incorrectly completed application can affect your right to compensation.

- There will then be a hearing, at which independent witnesses (such as neighbours or EHOs) may be called upon to verify the existence of the statutory nuisance. This must be proved to the criminal standard of proof (i.e. beyond reasonable doubt). If it is proved, then the court must make a nuisance order against the landlord requiring works be carried out either to abate the nuisance within a specified time limit, or to prevent a recurrence of the nuisance. The court can also impose a fine on the defendant landlord and order compensation. Note that the nuisance must be continuing at the time the summons is issued. If it has stopped, you are unlikely to succeed, even if it is probable that the nuisance will occur again.

Other specific hazards/problems

Gas safety

Gas safety is very important – tenants have died due to carbon monoxide poisoning from faulty gas appliances. Under the Gas Regulations, landlords are obliged, where there are gas installations in the property, to have these checked by a CORGI-registered gas installer. He will provide a certificate, a copy of which must be given to tenants when they first go into the property. The landlord must also arrange for further inspections annually (again by a CORGI-registered installer) and for copies of the certificates to be provided to you, the tenant.

> **Note**
>
> If you are unhappy about the service provided by the person who carried out the check (e.g. if you think he has missed a problem), CORGI will sometimes arrange for appliances to be re-checked, by way of monitoring the service provided by its installers. For further information, contact CORGI.

It is most important that you co-operate with your landlord in allowing access for these inspections to take place. They are for your safety. Also, if you do not co-operate, the landlord will no longer be liable if you suffer loss and injury (such as personal injury) as the problems will have been largely caused by your failure to allow the inspections to take place.

The landlord is also responsible for the cost of maintaining gas installations and the flues supplying them, the cost of the inspections, and of any necessary repairs. Any attempt to transfer any of these obligations to the tenants, such as by way of a contract term in the tenancy agreement, will be void.

> **Remedies**
>
> If your landlord has not provided you with your certificate or you feel that the regulations are not being complied with, you should contact your local HSE. It administers these regulations and will contact your landlord and, if necessary, bring a prosecution against him.

> **Further information**
>
> You can find contact details of your local HSE in the telephone directory or via its website at www.hse.gov.uk. You can find out more about CORGI via its website at www.trustcorgi.com/consumers.htmx.
>
> There is also a gas safety advice line you can ring on 0800 300 363.

> **If you smell gas or are worried about gas safety, you can ring National Grid Transco on 0800 111 999 at any time.**

Electricity

Strangely, there are no specific regulations regarding safety checks for electrical installations (apart from those in HMO properties, see page 165 below), unlike gas. Therefore, your main recourse will be under the landlords repairing covenants under Section 11 (see page 142).

However, there are regulations regarding the condition of electrical equipment in the Electrical Equipment (Safety) Regulations 1994. Under these regulations, suppliers (e.g. the landlord or letting agent) have a statutory duty to ensure that they only supply electrical equipment that is in a safe condition, so as to prevent risk of injury and/or damage to property. However, there is no mandatory requirement for equipment to be safety tested or for a safety certificate to be issued. There are also regulations regarding the safety of plugs and sockets.

Remedies

If you have any complaints regarding the condition of electrical appliances in your property, which the landlord refuses to deal with, you should speak to your local Trading Standards Office, which administers these regulations. It can contact your landlord and, if necessary, bring a prosecution in the Magistrates' Court.

Note that due to changes in the building regulations, most electrical work must now be done by a competent electrician rather than your landlord, or indeed you (unless of course either of you are an electrician).

See also page 165 on Houses in Multiple Occupation regarding electrical inspections for HMOs.

Further information

NICEIC acts as the electrical contracting industry's independent voluntary regulatory body for electrical installation safety matters throughout the UK and maintains and publishes registers of electrical contractors that have been assessed against the scheme requirements. You can find out more about them and about electrical safety generally on its website at www.niceic.org.uk.

Furniture and furnishings

All furniture provided by landlords in properties let to tenants must comply with the furniture regulations (the Furniture and Furnishings (Fire) (Safety) Regulations 1987 and the amendments made in 1988). Basically, these provide that all furniture must be fire safety compliant and carry the proper labels. Items covered include padded headboards, sofas, mattresses, pillows, cushions, nursery furniture and cloth covers on seats.

Some items are exempt, in particular, furniture made before 1950, curtains, carpets, duvets and sheets.

Remedies and further information

The best people to speak to about these regulations are your local Trading Standards Office, who will generally have some very helpful leaflets explaining the regulations in more detail. It also enforces the regulations, so if your landlords are not complying, it will deal with this for you. You can find details of your local Trading Standards Office in the telephone directory or on its website at www.trading standards.gov.uk.

Radon gas

This is a clear, odourless, naturally occurring radioactive gas that escapes naturally from the rock beneath the earth's surface and can cause lung cancer if it builds up in high concentrations. It is a hazard that can be rated under the HHSRS, whose operating guidance indicates that radon levels in excess of $200Bqm^{-3}$ in a dwelling would be considered a Category 1 hazard.

Further information

See the Radon Council website at www.brad.ac.uk/acad/envsci/radon_hotline/HOME.HTM.

Asbestos

This is a group of fibrous materials which in the past was widely used in building, but which is now banned. Sometimes it can produce very small fibrous dust particles that can cause asbestosis, lung cancer, mesothelioma and eventually death. It is still found in many older buildings. If you think that you may have asbestos in your building, you should contact your local authority and ask it to test for it (asbestos is a hazard under the HHSRS). You should also tell your landlord. Even if the asbestos is not in a dangerous condition, your landlord has a duty to manage the risk. He should label the asbestos, seal it or remove it depending on its condition. Any repair work lasting more than two hours must be done by someone licensed by the HSE.

If your landlord is a social landlord, then joining together with other tenants to complain and demand action is often more effective than one tenant complaining alone.

Further information

See the section on asbestos on the HSE website at www.hse. gov.uk/asbestos/index.htm.

Vermin

If these were in the property from the start, or the infestation is due to disrepair, or the vermin have entered your property from property controlled by your landlord (e.g. the common parts), then they are the responsibility of the landlord. However, local authority Environmental Health Departments also have a duty to control vermin so if your landlord fails to take any action, you should contact them. Some infestations may also come within the definition of a statutory nuisance and you may be able to take action under the Environmental Protection Act 1990. Local authority tenants and tenants of RSLs may also be able to exert pressure on their landlords through their local councillor (for more information on this, see Part 4 on complaints).

Damp

This is often a problem in rented properties. The responsibility for sorting it out depends on the cause of the dampness. If it is caused by a structural defect (such as a lack of damp-proof course, poor ventilation or a hole in the roof), the landlord may be responsible under the HHSRS. If the dampness is caused by damage to the structure of the walls, your landlord will be responsible for repairs under Section 11. However, dampness can also be caused by condensation produced by drying clothes indoors or the heating system not being used effectively. In this case it may be you who is wholly or partly to blame. If you have a problem with damp, it is best to get some professional advice; for example, by consulting the Environmental Health Department's Housing Officer at your local authority.

Q This is my second year living in a student house. The house does not have gas central heating and does tend to get cold in the winter months. However, this year we have noticed that some rooms are much colder than last year already. The bathroom is particularly cold, so cold in fact that you can see your breath in there, even in the middle of the day, and the walls have started to get black mould growing on them. We believe this may be due to the fact that nothing in the bathroom dries out as it is so cold. This is the first year that this has happened, and we fear that it is only going to get worse. What are the legal requirements surrounding the heating of a rented student property? There is a heater in the bathroom, but it is electric, and is very old, and we are frightened that it may set on fire if it is switched on due to the damp environment. Please help!

A I would suggest that you contact the Housing Officer at your local authority and ask that an EHO comes out and assesses your property under the HHSRS. Under this system, properties are assessed against various hazards – one of which is excess cold. If the hazard is found to be in the Category 1 level (i.e. serious), the local authority will serve an improvement notice on your landlord, asking him to carry out works to bring your property up to the required level. If this is done, ask the EHO for a copy of the report as you may be able to claim compensation from your landlord. You should, however, seek independent legal advice before bringing any legal claim against your landlord – your Students' Union may be able to assist.

Additional rules for Houses in Multiple Occupation (HMOs)

Before reading this section, you should read the general section on HMOs in Part 1. Note that this section will only apply to the private sector as social landlords are exempt from the HMO legislation under the Housing Act 2004.

Management regulations

HMOs are subject to all the legal requirements regarding the condition and repair of the property as set out above. They are also subject to additional regulations, such as the management regulations (mentioned also in Part 1) which apply to all HMOs, and not just those which are licensed. The management regulations provide, so far as the condition of the property is concerned, the following:

- **Fire safety:** The landlord/manager must make sure that all means of escape from fire are kept free from obstruction and maintained in good order and repair. Any fire-fighting equipment must be kept in good working order, and (unless there are four or fewer occupiers) notices indicating the location of means of escape from fire must be displayed in prominent positions so that they are clearly visible to occupiers.

- **General safety:** The landlord/manager must take reasonable measures to protect occupiers from injury, with regard to the design of the HMO, its structural condition and the number of occupiers. In particular, he must ensure that roofs and balconies are safe or take measures to prevent access, and windows with low sills have bars or other safeguards.

- **Water supply:** The water supply and drainage system must be kept in good, clean and working condition. In particular, cisterns and tanks must be covered, and fittings must be protected from frost damage. The landlord/manager must not do anything to interfere with the supply of water or drainage.

- **Gas safety:** The gas regulations will apply as they do to all residential lettings, and the landlord/manager must supply a copy of the latest gas certificate to the local authority within seven days of receiving a written request.

- **Electrical safety:** Every electrical installation must be inspected and tested at least every five years by a qualified electrician and a certificate obtained. This must be supplied to the local authority within seven days of receipt of a written request. The landlord/manager must not do anything to interfere with the supply of electricity.

- **The common parts:** The landlord/manager must maintain the common parts of the HMO in good and clean decorative order, in a safe and working condition, and reasonably clear from obstruction. In particular, all handrails and banisters must be kept in good repair and additional ones added, if necessary, for safety. Stair coverings must be kept securely fixed and in good repair. Windows and other ventilation must also be kept in good repair. There should be adequate light fittings and all fixtures, fittings and appliances used in common by occupiers must be kept in good and safe repair and in clean working order. However, this does not apply to items of occupiers (including tenants and licensees), which they are entitled to remove (e.g. their own possessions).

- **Outside areas:** Outbuildings, yards and forecourts used by occupiers must be maintained in good repair, clean condition and good order, and gardens must be kept in a safe and tidy condition. Boundary walls, railings and fences, etc. must be kept in good and safe repair so that they are not a danger to occupiers.

- **Unused areas:** If any part of the property is not in use, the landlord/ manager needs to ensure that areas directly giving access to it are kept clean and free from rubbish.

Note that the 'common parts' for which the landlord/manager has responsibility include entrance doors (including to the occupiers' own rooms), stairs, passages and corridors, lobbies, entrances, balconies, porches and steps – basically, the parts of the property used by occupiers to gain access to their own accommodation and any other part of the property shared by occupiers.

- **Living accommodation:** The landlord/manager must ensure that living accommodation and furniture for the occupiers' own use is in a clean condition at the start of the tenancy, and that the internal structure and any fixtures, fittings or appliances are maintained in good repair and clean working order, including windows. However, this does not apply to damage caused by the occupier failing to comply with the terms of his tenancy agreement or if he fails to conduct himself in a reasonable manner, or to things he is entitled to remove from the property (e.g. his own possessions).

- **Rubbish disposal:** The landlord/manager must ensure that suitable and sufficient litter bins and/or bags are provided, and to make arrangements for the disposal of rubbish with regard to the local authority collection services.

Note that standards of maintenance and repair required by these regulations will depend on the age, character and prospective life of the property and the locality in which it is situated. So, posh central London shared properties will need to be maintained to a higher level than tatty bedsits in rundown inner city areas.

Perhaps the most important new requirement under these regulations is the requirement for the checking of electrical installations every five years. However, there is no requirement that the electrician should have any particular qualification (e.g. by NICEIC). Neither is there any right for the tenant to be provided with a copy of a certificate of inspection. However, local authorities can require a copy to be provided to them. So if you suspect that the electrical checks are not being done. you should speak to the Housing Officer at your local authority.

Although these regulations place requirements on landlords and their managers, they also place obligations on you, the tenant, as follows:

- Not to do anything that will hinder the landlord/manager from meeting his duties.

- To allow the landlord/manager to enter the units of accommodation at reasonable times to carry out his duties.

- To provide any information to the landlord/manager that he may reasonably require in order for him to meet his duties.

- To take reasonable care to avoid damage to anything which the landlord/manager is under a duty to supply, maintain or repair.

- To store and dispose of litter in accordance with the arrangements made by the landlord or manager.

- To comply with reasonable instructions in respect of means of escape from fire and fire precautions.

Licensing

Some HMOs, mostly the larger HMOs, need to be licensed with the local authority. At the time of writing, buildings consisting of three or more storeys and occupied by five or more tenants in two or more households have to be licensed. However, individual local authorities have the power to order that additional classes of property be licensed. To find out whether your property needs to be licensed, contact your local authority.

Before a property can be licensed, a local authority will have to be satisfied that the person managing the HMO (which may not necessarily be the landlord) is a suitable person, that the property is suitable for the proposed number of occupants, and that the property meets the standards set out in the regulations. The local authority can also set additional standards for its area. This is a summary of the basic standards in the regulations (note that these will only apply to those HMOs which require a licence):

Kitchen facilities:

- There must be kitchen facilities in each room or a suitably located shared kitchen.

- Kitchens must have a sufficient number of sinks with hot and cold water and draining boards, installations or equipment for cooking food, electrical sockets, worktops, cupboards and refuse disposal and refrigerators.

- Shared kitchens must have adequate freezer space or a separate freezer, appropriate extractor fans, fire blankets and fire doors.

Washing facilities:

- There must be individual bathing and toilet facilities or shared facilities suitably located in relation to the living accommodation.

- For four or fewer occupiers there must be one bathroom with a bath or shower and one toilet which may be situated in the bathroom.

- For five or more occupiers, there must be one separate toilet with a washbasin and at least one bathroom for every five occupiers.

- For five or more occupiers, each unit of living accommodation must contain a washbasin or sink.

Other amenity standards:

- There must be the appropriate number and type of fire precaution facilities and equipment.

- Each unit of living accommodation must be equipped with adequate heating.

- All of the bathrooms must be suitably and adequately heated and ventilated.

- Baths, showers and washbasins must have hot and cold running water.

- Bathrooms and kitchens must be of adequate size and layout.

> ### Remedies
>
> If your landlord ought to be licensed but is not, you should contact your local authority. Note that in some circumstances where your landlord has been operating an HMO without a licence, you can apply to the Residential Property Tribunal for a rent repayment order. However, this is only where the local authority has taken action first (e.g. to bring a prosecution). You will need to speak to your local authority about this. Landlords of properties which ought to be licensed but are not, cannot use the 'notice only' Section 21 procedure to evict tenants. If this applies, you can defend any claim for possession by your landlord under Section 21 on this basis.

> **Further information**
>
> The basic information on licensing is set out in Part 2 of the Housing Act 2004. The two regulations referred to here are the Management of Houses in Multiple Occupation (England) Regulations 2006 (SI 2006 No.372), which applies to all HMOs, and the Licensing and Management of Houses in Multiple Occupation and other houses (Miscellaneous Provisions) (England) Regulations 2006, (SI 2006 No. 373).
>
> For contact details for local authorities, try www.localauthority directory.co.uk. You will find more information about HMOs and licensing on the Communities and Local Government's website at www.communities.gov.uk.

Conclusions on disrepair claims

As you can see, the whole area of repairs and disrepair is a very complex one. Here are some concluding points.

Keeping records

As always, if you have a disrepair problem, you should start by keeping detailed records of everything (e.g. take photographs or a video of the problem). Keep a special folder where you can store all of the correspondence and telephone attendance notes so that they do not get lost. Keep a diary detailing all the problems you have had; this can include contact with the landlord or his agent about the problem, and any comments they make. Keep a record of every visit, telephone call and meeting, including all visits to the property by surveyors, Housing Officers and contractors.

Keep any belongings which have been affected, such as clothes that have been affected by damp. You should also keep full details and proof of money paid for any extra expenses you have incurred as a result of the disrepair. For example, keep receipts or evidence of comparable prices (e.g. a catalogue) for items damaged or destroyed (e.g. by damp), together with details of when and where any items were purchased; keep records of any extra electricity used for heating (keep your utility bills), cleaning equipment purchased, meals out/takeaways purchased if you have no fridge or cooking facilities, and so on. If you go to court, you will need these to prove your claim for 'special damages' (explained on page 21).

If other people witness the problems, make sure that you have their names and addresses so that you can contact them later, if necessary. It is a good idea for them to write down what happened and if they do, make sure that they date and sign their statements.

Note that it is not unknown for contractors (e.g. those employed by social landlords to carry out repair works) to claim 'no access' without turning up, and failing to meet their appointments. Keeping proper records will help you deal with this, if it happens.

See also the general advice on paperwork in Part 1.

Experts

It may also be appropriate for you to get an expert to do an inspection and report. Initially, it is probably a good idea to ask the local authority's EHO to carry out an inspection. For complex civil claims, you will probably have to commission someone to write a report at some stage. This can be either a surveyor or an environmental health practitioner.

> **Note**
>
> Surveyors will have the initials MRICS or FRICS after their names (FRICS is the superior award). Environmental health practitioners should be members of the Chartered Institute of Environmental Health (MCIEH). On the whole, judges tend to prefer surveyors, so consider using a surveyor for County Court cases which are likely to be defended, especially where the cause of the disrepair is likely to be in dispute.

However, it is best to obtain legal advice before commissioning any report, as your solicitor will usually be able to recommend someone good, and will be able to ensure that the report covers all the relevant points. Bear in mind also that the pre-action protocol (discussed below) provides the parties to jointly get a report from an expert, so it may be best to wait until this stage before instructing an expert.

Legal advice

As this is such a complex area of law it is always advisable to get some professional legal advice before taking any action, particularly legal action. You need to be very sure, before going to court, that the disrepair is something that the landlord is legally responsible for. You will need advice on which of the many avenues of approach is the most suitable for your case, and you need to be sure that any action taken is done properly; for example, for court claims that the pre-action protocol is complied with (discussed below, page 173).

Remedies for disrepair

To a certain extent, these will depend on what the problem is and how serious it is.

- **Moving out:** For serious disrepair problems, you may be entitled to move out of the property altogether, particularly if you have only just started renting and you were not aware of the problems, or the extent of the problems, before you moved in. However, particularly if you have been living in the property for a while, you should seek legal advice before moving out.

- **Complaining to your landlord:** Before you start any of the procedures discussed in this chapter, you should tell your landlord about the problems, in writing, and ask him (or the officer concerned for social landlords) to arrange for the repairs to be done. You should give your landlord a reasonable period of time to do this. What a 'reasonable period' is will depend on what the problem is. Some repairing problems can be dealt with fairly quickly, but others will take your landlord more time to arrange. However, whatever the problem is, it is reasonable to assume that some action should have been taken by your landlord within a month, even if the landlord has only been able to seek estimates for the work. If it looks as if your complaint is being ignored, you should then try to take the matter further.

- **Complaining to the local authority (private landlords):** If you are not going to move out, and your landlord has not taken any action on your complaint, unless the disrepair is serious and needs urgent action, a good course of action is often to contact your local authority and ask it to carry out an inspection. This is free of charge, and you will normally be able to ask for a copy of the report. It will help you find out whether there really is something wrong with your property. If there is a Category 1 hazard and/or an environmental health problem, the local authority must take action against your landlord. If there is a Category 2 hazard, it may take action if it considers it to be appropriate. However, note that it will generally take the local authority some time to arrange for an inspection visit, so this approach will not be appropriate for urgent cases. Bear in mind also that the local authority report will have been prepared for the purposes of the HHSRS rather than (for example) a civil claim for disrepair.

- **Complaining (social landlords):** If your landlord is the local authority, then you can still ask its Environmental Health Department to carry out an inspection. However, the department will not be able to take legal action against its own organisation. You should then follow the complaints procedure described in Part 4. This should also be followed for other registered social landlords. Alternatively, you can just start the complaints procedure without getting the EHO's report done first. Note that for serious disrepair problems you should also obtain legal advice as soon as possible, without waiting for the complaints procedure to be completed.

- **Self-help and set-off:** For information, see Chapter 11 on the tenant's right of set-off.

- **Going to court:** If complaints achieve nothing and the repairs are not something you are able to deal with yourself, then probably your only action is to consider going to court. This will normally mean a claim in the County Court. Here, for most disrepair problems, you should be able to ask the court for:

  - an injunction ordering the landlord to carry out the repairs;

  - compensation for your inconvenience and distress caused by the disrepair; and

  - any expenses you have suffered (e.g. for replacing clothes and other possessions destroyed by damp);

- a claim for compensation for personal injury, if the disrepair has caused you any physical injury (e.g. a broken leg through falling down a damaged staircase, or asthma caused by damp);

- an order in respect of your legal costs if you succeed in your claim. Note, however, that this may not cover all of your costs.

You should read the section on court claims in Part 1 for more general information. Do note the following points:

- If you are bringing a claim for disrepair, you will need to comply with the housing disrepair pre-action protocol. This is part of the Civil Procedure Rules (CPR) and can be downloaded from the website for the Department of Constitutional Affairs at www.dca.gov.uk.

- You do not need to comply with the protocol if you are raising disrepair as a defence to a claim for possession based on rent arrears. It only applies to claims where the tenant is taking the lead.

- If you also have a claim for personal injury, you may also need to comply with the separate personal injury pre-action protocol. This is probably not required if the injury is slight and you will only be using a GP's letter as evidence of injury. However, for more serious injuries and particularly where there are longer-term consequences, the protocol must be followed. This can also be downloaded from the Department of Constitutional Affairs' website.

- For most claims, particularly serious and expensive claims, the court will want to see some sort of evidence from an expert to prove the disrepair.

- Your claim form will need to set out the legal basis of your claim (e.g. that the landlord is in breach of his statutory repairing covenants under Section 11 of the Landlord and Tenant Act 1985), as well as list all of the the things you are claiming (e.g. an injunction, compensation, etc.). The judge can only award you something if you have asked for it.

The disrepair pre-action protocol

This exists to ensure that there is a full exchange of information between the parties before court proceedings are issued. This is done by the tenant sending an 'early notification letter' and later on a 'letter of claim' setting out the full details of the matters complained of. In many cases this will prevent court proceedings being issued altogether. Indeed, this is the aim of the protocol as there is tremendous pressure on court time, which the courts are trying to reduce as much as possible. Therefore, you will receive little sympathy from the judge if you go ahead with a claim for compensation or repairs without following the protocol. Generally if you have not followed the protocol your claim will be postponed (described by lawyers as 'stayed') while the protocol procedure is followed and you may be ordered to pay the landlord's legal costs.

The protocol is clearly written and provides sample letters. However, it is easy to make a mistake if you are not familiar with court work. Also, if you need to go to court, the court claim form must be carefully drafted to make sure that it includes everything that you are entitled to. Unless you really know what you are doing, you should not do this without professional legal help. However, this can be expensive so you should first look to use one of the following:

- **Shelter:** Shelter is a housing charity and it provides a free telephone helpline you can ring on 0808 800 4444. This will give you initial advice and will help you to find a local adviser. Shelter runs local housing aid offices where you can obtain more detailed help from a solicitor or other legal adviser (these are also free of charge). In many cases these advisers will be able to act for you in legal proceedings. To find an office near you, ring the helpline or visit the website at www.shelter.org.uk.

- **Law centre:** Many towns will have a Law Centre, which will almost always be able to give advice and support for housing disrepair claims. This is a free service. To find your local Law Centre, see Part 4. You can see a recent list of addresses at www.landlordlaw.co.uk/page.ihtml?id=217&step=2&page=links.

- **Citizens' Advice Bureau (CAB):** There are many more CABs than there are Shelter Officers and there will almost certainly be one near you. However, only a few CABs will specialise in housing work and you need to make sure that the person you see is experienced in this. Generally, it is best just to use the CAB for initial advice and to assist you to find a suitable solicitor.

- **Legal Aid solicitor:** If you are on a low income, you may be eligible for advice and assistance from a solicitor who does Legal Aid. However, unfortunately few solicitors now offer this service so you may find it difficult to locate one. The best source of information is the Community Legal Services Direct's website at www.clsdirect.org.uk.

- **A solicitor under a no-win, no-fee agreement:** Many solicitors offer these for personal injury claims; some will also offer them for disrepair claims. You will need to sign a complicated agreement which your solicitor will explain to you. You will also need to take out insurance to cover you for your landlord's costs if you lose your case, and for medical reports. It is generally best to go direct to a solicitor rather than via a claims company. The Law Society runs a telephone helpline for personal injury claims called Accident Line on 0870 607 8999.

For more information on legal help, see Part 4.

Financial compensation

Any sum awarded to you at court for compensation will vary depending on the type of disrepair, the type of property involved, and the course of action you have taken to obtain compensation.

Generally, you will receive a higher award by taking your claim to the County Court, rather than via a claim under one of the criminal law jurisdictions (e.g. under the Environmental Protection Act). This is because the purpose of the criminal law jurisdiction is to uphold standards and punish landlords for wrongdoing, rather than compensating individual tenants.

When making an award in the civil courts, frequently the sum awarded by the judge will reflect the level of rent paid and will often be a proportion of the total rent for the period of time you experienced the problem, to reflect the diminution of 'enjoyment' of the property as a result of the disrepair. So the same problem may attract a much higher award for a tenant of an expensive central London apartment than for the tenant of a low value bedsit. You will only be awarded 100% of your rent in very serious cases, normally where you have had to move out of the property altogether.

For example, if your property has no hot water and heating in the winter due to a non-functioning boiler, you will probably receive a basic award in the region of 30% of your rent for the relevant period of time. However, you will also be able to claim your expenses incurred because of the non-functioning boiler, for example additional heating bills and the like.

Note that if you have caused any aspect of the disrepair yourself or made it worse (e.g. by not allowing the landlord in to do inspections), any award made to you will be reduced accordingly.

Further information

Contact details and websites have been given in the various sections above.

There is an excellent practitioners' book published by Legal Action Group called *Repairs: Tenants' Rights* by Jan Luba and Stephen Knafler. Unfortunately, the most recent edition was published some time ago in 1999 but it is still a very helpful book.

To find your local authority, see www.localauthoritydirectory.co.uk.

Q Our landlord has indicated that he would be willing for us to have cavity wall insulation fitted at our expense to the house we are renting to help with the damp and the exorbitant heating fees. However, he has also intimated that should we undertake this work he would then put up our rent. Can the landlord put up the rent when the improvements have been made at no cost to him?

A Frankly, I would not advise any tenant to carry out and pay for expensive improvements to someone else's property. If the works are done, ideally it should be following an agreement (preferably drafted by a solicitor) that the landlord will reduce the rent to allow for the improvements you have done to his property, and that he will allow you to stay in the property for an agreed minimum period of time (to prevent a situation which happened in one case I know of, where the tenant was evicted shortly after carrying out costly works). If, by any chance, you are a protected or statutory tenant under the Rent Act 1977 (i.e. if you have been living in the property since before January 1989), you should ensure that a fair

> rent is registered before the works are done. When the rent is reviewed the Rent Officer will not take any improvements paid for by you into account when assessing the new rent.

The rights of disabled people to request changes to their property

Since the Disability Discrimination Act 1995 came into force, it has been illegal for landlords to treat disabled tenants less favourably than non-disabled tenants because of their disability, without justification. For more general information on disability discrimination, see Chapter 2.

From December 2006 new regulations came into force bringing new duties for landlords to make reasonable adjustments to properties for disabled people; for example, by providing a temporary ramp for a wheelchair user who has a small step up into his flat.

However, note that landlords can only be required to do what is reasonable. It will not normally be considered reasonable to require a landlord to make expensive adaptations to premises which will inconvenience other tenants. Just because you are disabled and the proposed change will benefit you, does not necessarily mean that you are entitled to demand it. Also, what it is reasonable to expect from a large professional or social landlord may not be reasonable for a small private landlord with only a few or just one property.

In particular, landlords and managers of rented premises cannot be forced to take any steps which involve the removal or alteration of physical features of the property. However, the regulations have set out things which are not to count as 'physical features' and which a disabled tenant is entitled to ask to have done. These are:

- The replacement or provision of any signs or notices.

- The replacement of any taps or door handles.

- The replacement, provision or adaptation of any doorbell or door entry system.

- Changes to the colour of any surface (such as a wall or door).

In addition, landlords cannot unreasonably withhold consent from disabled tenants who need to make physical adjustments to their homes for disability-related reasons. However, the tenant must pay for the alterations and must ask permission from the landlord. This right of individual tenants to make adjustments will not apply to the 'common parts' of properties, such as stairs or hallways of communal blocks of flats.

Remedies and further information

Generally these rights can only be enforced by court action. If you are disabled and your landlord is refusing to agree to reasonable adaptions to the property, your best course of action is to seek advice from the Disability Rights Commission, which has a website at www.drc.org.uk.

Dilapidation claims – where landlords can claim against the tenant

Before ending this chapter on the condition of the property, it is probably appropriate to have a short section on your rights when your landlord seeks to claim against you for damage to the property.

This sort of claim is normally dealt with at the end of the tenancy where the tenant leaves the property in a poor condition and the damage deposit (discussed above at Chapter 7) is insufficient to cover the cost of repair and the replacement of broken items.

For this sort of claim it will normally be essential for the landlord to have a good inventory, ideally one which provides details about the condition of the property and its contents, rather than just a list of furniture. As it will be the landlord bringing the claim, he will normally be the one who has to prove to the court that the damage was caused by you, and that the sum he is claiming is reasonable. Here are a few points on dilapidations claims:

- The landlord cannot claim against you for items which were damaged before you moved into the property or after you moved out. If you challenge him, he will have to prove that the damage was done during the period of your tenancy.

- If the landlord did his final check several weeks after you left, it is open to you to argue that the damage was not done by you.

- The landlord cannot claim for damage occasioned by 'fair wear and tear'.

- There is a technical rule (in Section 18(1) of the Landlord and Tenant Act 1927) which says that the landlord cannot claim more than the diminution caused to his reversion (i.e. the value of the property when he regains possession) by the state of the premises at the end of the tenancy. So if the property should have been worth £100,000 when he got it back, but due to the damage to the property done by the tenants it is actually worth £70,000, he will not be entitled to claim more than £30,000 from the tenants. Note that the rule does not include damage to the property contents, but just to the property itself.

- If the landlord has had repair work done, the court will normally accept the invoices as being evidence of the value of the damage to the landlord's reversion, provided it was reasonable for him to do the work and the sums charged were reasonable.

- If the landlord has not had any repair work done, he may have difficulty proving his case. If he has no invoices or estimates for the proposed work, the court may dismiss his claim.

- Sometimes landlords will also seek to claim for rent lost as a result of having to carry out the repair work. However, to claim this he will have to establish how long it would reasonably have taken him to let the property if it had been in a proper condition, and then show that the works that were completed extended this period.

- You may be entitled to ask the court to reduce any sum awarded to reflect 'betterment', i.e. the fact that after the works are done the landlord will be getting back a property in a better condition than he was entitled to expect.

Further information

Hopefully, few readers of this book will have caused such damage to their property that the damage deposit is insufficient to cover it! However, if your former landlord is making a big claim against you, the best thing to do is to obtain legal advice as soon as possible. See the guidance in Part 4 on obtaining legal advice.

CHAPTER 11

The right to make deductions from the rent (set-off)

In some circumstances a tenant is entitled to make deductions from his rent if his landlord has failed to comply with his repairing obligations. However, you need to be very careful when exercising this power, as if it is done incorrectly, it could make you vulnerable to a claim for possession based on rent arrears.

> **Note**
>
> Any attempt by your landlord to take away your right of set-off by any term in your contract (e.g. requiring rent to be paid without any deduction or set-off) will be void.

First of all, the right can only be exercised in respect of repairing work your landlord is legally obliged to do. This means work covered by Section 11 of the Landlord and Tenant Act 1985, and/or repair work the landlord is required to do under the terms of your tenancy agreement discussed in Chapter 10.

If you are certain that the repair work is the responsibility of the landlord, and if the landlord wrongly refuses to get the work done after he has received proper notification, you can then consider getting the work done yourself and claiming the cost back from the rent. You should, as far as possible, follow the procedure below:

- Write to your landlord explaining that you are going to do the work yourself unless the repairs are done within a reasonable time (such as two/four weeks, depending on the type of repair involved).

- Once this time has passed, get three quotes for the work.

- Send the quotes to your landlord with a letter explaining that you are going to go ahead with the cheapest quote unless your landlord arranges for the repairs to be done (or at least started) within a certain time (such as a further two to four weeks, depending on the type of repair work).

- Once this time has passed, arrange for the work to be done by the company that gave the cheapest quote.

- Pay for the work yourself and send a copy of the receipt to your landlord. Ask your landlord to refund the money.

- If your landlord does not give you back the money, write and explain that you are going to deduct the money out of your future rent.

In some circumstances it may be acceptable to withhold rent for a period of time so that you can 'save up' to get the work done. However, if you do this, the withheld rent should be kept in a separate (preferably interest-bearing) bank account so it can be paid to the landlord immediately, if necessary. If you are considering doing this, it is a good idea to take some legal advice first.

The right of set-off is limited to situations where you have given the landlord prior notice of what you intend doing. If you just go ahead and do the work without informing him first, then you will not normally be entitled to recover the cost of the work.

Be aware also that you **cannot** use this procedure to deduct compensation for damage or personal injury suffered as a result of the disrepair. If you are unable to reach agreement with your landlord regarding compensation, your only alternative is to obtain a court order. If you just make a deduction and your landlord sues you for arrears of rent, you can counterclaim for damages, but the sum deducted by you will probably be different from any sum awarded by the court.

> **Note**
>
> **Improvements:** You should check carefully before carrying out any

work in or to the property, be it redecorating or more substantial work. Unless it is specifically agreed with your landlord in advance, you will not be entitled to recover the cost of the work from him. Indeed, many tenancy agreements specifically prohibit any sort of building, decorating or other work in the property without the landlord's prior written authority. If work is done without this, your landlord is quite within his rights to recover from you the cost of putting the property back to its original condition.

Further information

See Part 4 for information on obtaining legal advice.

Q My family and I have lived in a property which has been beset with problems for a few months. We have been inconvenienced by workmen coming into the house every week to fix issues such as flea infestations and roof leaks, and I have had to take time off work to move furniture. As a result, I have withheld my rent for the current month as compensation for the inconvenience, and have written to my landlord explaining my reasons. He is demanding the rent and is not prepared to compensate me. I have three months of my shorthold tenancy to run, and I do not mind if the landlord wants to serve notice. If I stick to my guns, what are the potential legal repercussions?

A Strictly speaking, you are not entitled to make deductions yourself from your rent for inconvenience and stress under your right of 'set-off'. However, the only way your landlord can force you to pay the rent is by bringing proceedings in the County Court. If he does this, you can then counterclaim for damages for compensation for the inconvenience you have suffered, asking the judge to consider your case and award you damages, to be offset against your landlord's rent claim. I would be surprised if the judge did not award you at least some compensation from what you have said. However, it is impossible to say whether this would be more or less than one month's rent. If you write to your landlord saying that you are not going to pay the money and that if he sues, you will counterclaim for damages, he may decide not to take the matter any further, as he will not want the inconvenience of a court hearing. Just to be on the safe side, however, I would suggest that you keep a diary of events to prove the problems you have encountered, should this ever be necessary, and get written confirmation from your employers of the time you have had to take off work because of it.

CHAPTER 12

Rights regarding overcrowding

Your rights will depend on whether the overcrowding is as a result of the landlord's action in putting too many people in the property, or whether you have caused the overcrowding yourself by having more people living with you than your property was designed to accommodate.

There are two technical definitions of overcrowding. They will not be discussed in detail, but they involve either (1) too many people or people of different sexes who are not partners, sharing the same room, or (2) where the size of the room is too small for the number of people sleeping in it.

Sometimes overcrowding is permissible, such as where a family living in a small house have more children, or their children grow up, or if the additional people are only staying at the property temporarily, or if the local authority has given permission.

If none of these apply, then either the occupier or the landlord will be committing an offence.

Landlords' liability

If it is your landlord who is responsible, then you should report the matter to your local authority, as local authorities are under a general duty to enforce the overcrowding legislation. Your local authority will carry out an inspection and, if appropriate, serve either an abatement notice on your landlord or an improvement notice under the Housing Health and Safety Rating System (HHSRS).

If your landlord is the local authority, then as well as initiating the complaints procedure discussed in Part 4, you are also entitled to apply for a transfer. When allocating accommodation, a local authority must give preference to people living in overcrowded conditions.

If it is not reasonable for you to continue living in the overcrowded accommodation, you may also be able to make a homelessness application. If you fall within the category of priority need, your local authority may be obliged to re-house you. For further information, see Chapter 4.

Note that local authorities have special powers regarding overcrowding in Houses in Multiple Occupation (HMOs) under the Housing Act 2004.

Tenants' liability

If it is you who is responsible for the overcrowding, then you may be making yourself liable for eviction. This is particularly the case with protected tenants under the Rent Act 1977, as they will lose their protection if the property is illegally overcrowded.

If you are a local authority tenant, note that under the Housing Act 1985 local authorities have the power to evict tenants where the property is illegally overcrowded and the tenants have not abated the overcrowding within 14 days of being served notice. Eviction must be applied for within three months of the notice expiring, if it has not been complied with. The court must order possession between 14 and 28 days of the hearing.

Remedies

If your landlord is responsible, you should contact your local authority, report the matter and seek its advice. If your landlord is the local authority, then either follow the complaints procedure or ask for a transfer to alternative accommodation (or both). If you are responsible for the overcrowding, then you should either arrange for some of the people living with you to move out, or move to a larger property.

For further information, speak to your local authority's Housing Officer, or one of the advisers suggested in Part 4.

CHAPTER 13

The right to live in the property undisturbed

This is an important right. It covers both harassment and tenants' rights in connection with eviction proceedings, and these two topics are dealt with separately below (although there is a certain amount of crossover). However, first I will have a look at where this basic right comes from in both the civil and the criminal law.

Civil law – the covenant of quiet enjoyment

All tenancy agreements have a clause, generally to be found in a section (usually a rather short section) on the landlord's obligations under the tenancy agreement, which runs something like this:

> 'The Landlords will allow the Tenant peaceably to hold and enjoy the Property during the term without unreasonable interruption from the Landlord or any person rightfully claiming under or in trust for the Landlord, subject to the Landlord's right to take any lawful steps to enforce his rights against the Tenant if the Tenant breaks any of the terms of this Agreement.'

This clause is known as the 'covenant of quiet enjoyment'. This does not mean that the tenant has to be quiet or that he has a right to 'enjoy himself' in the property. It means that the landlord must allow the tenant to live in the property without interference from the landlord, other than by lawful methods. The two main lawful methods are: agreement with the tenant, or by a court order.

The covenant of quiet enjoyment applies to all tenancy agreements. If it is not specifically written into the tenancy agreement, it will be implied. Any clauses in the tenancy agreement which interfere with the effect of it (e.g. a clause allowing the landlord to enter the property using his keys whenever he likes) will be void.

If your landlord breaches the covenant of quiet enjoyment, you can bring a claim in the County Court seeking financial compensation or damages, and an injunction either to stop the harassment or to let you back into the property if you have been evicted.

'Derogation from grant'

There is also a legal rule that if a landlord has granted a tenancy to someone, he should not then do anything to deprive the tenant of this. Lawyers call this a breach of the implied obligation not to 'derogate' from the grant of a tenancy. This is an additional claim that should be included in the claim form if you are bringing legal proceedings against your landlord.

The criminal law – the Protection from Eviction Act 1977

This important Act specifically prohibits the following and makes them a criminal offence:

- Physically evicting a residential tenant other than by court proceedings.
- Doing anything to cause the tenant to give up possession.
- Preventing a tenant from exercising his rights under the tenancy agreement.
- Doing anything which will interfere with the 'peace or comfort' of the tenant or members of his household.

- Withdrawing or withholding services which are reasonably required for the occupation of the property as a residence.

With the last two, the offence is committed if your landlord knows, or had reasonable cause to believe, that his conduct is likely to cause you to leave the property or discourage you from exercising any right or remedy you may have in respect of the property. The fact that the Act specifically states 'or had reasonable cause to believe' means that even if your landlord's actions were not done for the specific purpose of making you leave the property, if it was something which was likely to make you decide to go, then he will still be guilty of an offence.

A criminal offence under the Act is not committed if your landlord (or his agent) reasonably believed that you had already left, or had reasonable grounds for thinking that he was entitled to withhold or withdraw the service.

> **Note**
>
> This Act also applies to residential occupiers who are not tenants. So licensees, such as people renting accommodation on boats, and people who are required to live in certain accommodation because of their job (where occupiers are licensees), will also be protected. Note that lodgers (people who share living accommodation with their landlord) are not protected.

Someone who commits an offence under the Act will be liable to be prosecuted under the criminal law and if convicted, can be fined or (for serious cases) imprisoned for up to six months, or both. Prosecutions will be in the Magistrates' Court.

Q I have a friend staying with me for a few days. After I had left for work my landlord showed up at the property with no warning and proceeded to let himself in with his own key. He then questioned my friend about who she was! He then phoned me and told me that I cannot have anyone stay as it is against his rules. This is not in the contract. What should I do? Do I have a right to have a friend stay if I choose? Can the landlord just let himself into my property?

Your landlord should not let himself into your rented property with his keys while you are out. He also cannot object to your having a friend to stay (although he is entitled to object if she moves in permanently). Any contract term forbidding this will be void under the Unfair Terms in Consumer Contracts Regulations 1999. Your landlord's conduct will almost certainly be deemed harassment under the Protection from Eviction Act 1977, which is a criminal offence. You should tell him that he must never enter the property again without your express permission. You could also complain about him to the Tenancy Relations or Housing Officer at your local authority, who will write to him on your behalf and, if necessary, bring a prosecution in the Magistrates' Court.

Harassment

What behaviour is harassment? Here are the main types of harassment which can occur. These will be harassment under both the civil and criminal law:

> **Note**
>
> Here it is assumed that you are a tenant in the private sector, as social landlords are unlikely to harass their tenants (other than perhaps by failing to do repairs, but for more information on this see Chapter 10).

- **Physical eviction:** This is the worst case scenario where you are locked out of the property and your possessions are either destroyed or put outside in bin bags, etc.

- **Cutting off services:** This is where your landlord arranges for one or more of the essential services, such as electricity, to be cut off. Note that if the service is cut off by the service provider because you have not paid your gas or electricity bill, the landlord will not be at fault. However, if your rent includes an element for gas and electricity and your landlord cuts off the service because you have failed to pay your rent, he will be in the wrong.

- **Damaging the property/failure to maintain:** This is where your landlord does something to damage the property, such as taking out doors and windows. Although this sounds extreme, some criminal landlords have been known to do this sort of thing, to force tenants to move out. However, on a lesser scale, it will also be deemed harassment if your landlord fails to do essential maintenance to the property (e.g. failing to repair the boiler or electrical faults).

- **Entering the property without consent:** This is frequently a problem. Often landlords simply do not understand that once a property has been let to a tenant, they lose most of their rights in respect of it (except for the right to receive rent and the right to get the property back after the tenant has left) and they cannot just go in and out as they please. The only occasions when your landlord is entitled to enter the property without a specific invitation from you is when carrying out the regular inspection visits (where he has to give at least 24 hours' notice in writing) and in a case of emergency.

- **Inspection visits:** Although landlords are authorised by statute to enter your property to carry out inspections, they have to give you at least 24 hours' written notice, and you are entitled to object to the inspection visit if you wish, in which case the landlord should not enter. If you are objecting because you want to be present and the proposed appointment is inconvenient for you, your objection will be perfectly reasonable. However, you should not prevent your landlord from carrying out any inspection visits at all, and you certainly should not prevent him from carrying out any necessary repair work. This would put you in breach of your tenancy agreement and may make you vulnerable to eviction. Also, if you suffer loss or injury as a result of any disrepair, you will not be able to claim against your landlord in damages as it will be your fault that no repair work was carried out.

Note also that inspection visits must genuinely be for the purpose of inspecting the condition of the property, as opposed to (for example) intimating you or spying on you. Generally, landlords will carry out an inspection visit quarterly. If they are more frequent (e.g. monthly), then this could be deemed to be harassment, unless there is a reasonable explanation. For example, if the landlord wishes to monitor some repair works, more frequent visits may be appropriate.

Q We rent our house through a lettings agency. We have always kept it neat and tidy, paid rent on time and, in fact, improved the property; However, our letting agency insist on inspecting the property every quarter, which we find somewhat humiliating. Is there anything we can do?

A I am afraid that you will probably have to put up with this. One of the reasons that landlords use letting agents (and one of the things they are paying for) is to ensure that someone is checking up on their property periodically, which as you will appreciate is a valuable financial investment. For example, the agents may spot some small item of repair, which you may not have noticed, which, if done quickly, could prevent expensive repairs later. Although you are good tenants and look after the property, it is not unknown for good tenants to stop looking after the property, perhaps if they have a major disaster in their life such as a bereavement, or they take in an unsuitable lodger who causes problems. Quarterly inspections are quite usual and are considered a reasonable period (as opposed, for example, to monthly inspection visits). If you have been in the property for several years, though, without problems, the agents may agree to reduce their inspections to every six months, but the landlord would have to consent.

Q Our landlord sent a maid around to clean the property after an inspection where he found the property 'unacceptably dirty and untidy'. He informed us that he was coming around for the inspection. However, he did not tell us that the maid was coming around three days later. It later transpired that he had left a telephone message that we had not picked up on BT Callminder. Does our landlord need to inform us before sending around workmen and if so, does the missed call (about 36 hours in advance) count as proper notice?

A Your landlord should give you at least 24 hours' written notice of any inspection visits or of any visits from workmen to do repairs (and some tenancy agreements provide for a longer notice period). A telephone message will not suffice. However, unless this is provided for in the tenancy agreement, I cannot see that he is entitled to send someone around to clean the property without your specific consent. Cleaning does not come within his responsibilities and he cannot insist on you agreeing to this. I would suggest that you write to your landlord (keeping a copy of the letter) saying that in future can he please provide written notice of any visits either from himself or from workmen. If you do not want the maid coming around, you can then say that this is not something he is entitled to do. If you are happy with the maid, make the point that if he wants to do this it must be at his expense, as the cleanliness and tidiness of the property during the period of the tenancy is a matter for you. If you want inspection visits to be at times when you are at the property, you are entitled to insist on this. Tell him that if he continues to come around, or send round workmen or maids without giving you proper written notice first, this is harassment, which is a criminal offence. If your landlord ignores you, you can complain about him to the Housing Officer at your local authority, who will write to him on your behalf.

- **Intimidating behaviour:** This can be anything. Perhaps the most obvious is your landlord coming around and shouting at you; for example, because you have not paid your rent. However, this can be any behaviour which puts you in fear or affects the way you use the property.

Q My landlord has claimed three times that I have not paid the rent and he has threatened me with legal action – each time he has found that the error lies with him and his administration. I am fed up of making calls to the bank and checking direct debits. Do I have any legal rights regarding these false accusations, which happen every month when the pay goes out?

A If this happens again, I would suggest that you write to your landlord saying that you consider this to be harassment, and can he please not do this again before checking the situation properly. If this has no effect, I would suggest that you speak to the Tenancy Relations or Housing Officer at your local authority. They are empowered to enforce the harassment legislation. They will write to your landlord for you on your behalf and, if necessary, they can bring a prosecution.

Remedies

Both the civil and the criminal systems can be used in connection with harassment problems.

- **Local authority assistance:** For most cases you will be best off going to see the Tenancy Relations Officer or Housing Officer at your local authority. Local authorities are the main organisations empowered to enforce the provisions of the Protection from Eviction Act 1977. The Officer will write to your landlord for you and, if necessary, bring a prosecution at the Magistrates' Court. Often a landlord is not aware that he is breaking the law, and a letter from the local authority will stop the offending behaviour.

- **Self-help:** For situations where your landlord is persistently entering the property without your consent, after being asked (in writing) to stop, the most obvious thing to do is to change the locks. Most tenancy agreements will prohibit this, but it can be justified if the only reason you are changing the locks is the landlord's own breach of the covenant of quiet enjoyment. In particular, female tenants who are frightened by male landlords letting themselves into their property without giving notice should, if the landlord continues to do this after being asked to stop, have no hesitation in changing the locks.

  The same applies if the person entering the property is your landlord's agent or someone who has been given a key by the landlord.

- **County Court claims:** In many (but not all) cases of harassment, you will be entitled to claim compensation from your landlord. In serious cases, you can also ask the court to make an injunction forbidding the landlord to continue the offending behaviour, or to let you back in if you have actually been evicted. Bringing a court claim is not a simple matter, however, and if you are thinking of this, you should get legal advice before taking any action. If you are looking to claim compensation, it is very important that the claim form is drafted properly so this should be done by a solicitor experienced in this type of work.

Further information

See the sections in Part 1 on background information on bringing court claims and in Part 4 on obtaining legal advice.

The following websites may also be of interest:

- **Victim support:** This is a national charity which helps people affected by crime. If you have suffered serious criminal harassment, then this service can help you recover from the experience (www.victimsupport.com).

- **Harassment law:** This is a website run by barrister Neil Addison which contains advice on other types of harassment (www.harassment-law.co.uk).

Q We have given the appropriate notice of our intention to leave our flat at the end of the current tenancy period. Unfortunately, our landlord has entered the property without our knowledge to show around a letting agent and is now giving only an hour's notice of prospective tenants looking around in our absence. Is there any law regarding the amount of notice landlords are supposed to give before entering a flat that is occupied?

A The landlord's right to enter to let to prospective tenants should come from the tenancy agreement and you need to check this. If there is no clause providing for this, then you are entitled to refuse access. Even if there is a clause in the tenancy agreement, it should provide for reasonable notice to be given to you of at least 24 hours or the clause is likely to be void under the Unfair Terms in Consumer Contracts Regulations 1999. Certainly the landlord is not entitled to enter the property without giving you any notice at all. This is harassment, which is a criminal offence. You could threaten to report him to your local authority, which is the prosecuting authority for this type of offence. Also, if your landlord continues to enter without your agreement, I think you would be entitled to change the locks.

Eviction

This is an important complex subject. The information is set out in the following way:

- First, I look at unlawful eviction and advise you about what you should do if your landlord tries to evict you without following the proper procedure.

- I then deal with the various stages that your landlord should follow if he is dealing with the procedure properly.

- The first is the service of a possession notice on you. Different notices are used for different types of tenancy and for different types of claim, and these are all discussed.

- There is then a short section on the procedure for demotion of tenancies – this is used for social tenancies only, and cannot apply to you if you rent from a private landlord.

- I then go through the possession procedure in detail, from the service of documents upon you, through preparing for and attending the hearing (if any), up to physical eviction by the bailiffs (if the case gets that far).

- Note that the pre-action protocol, which all social landlords must comply with for claims for possession based on rent arrears, has different requirements for the three different stages of the proceedings (before the service of notices, after the service of notices, and after the issue of proceedings), and these different requirements are considered separately in the relevant sections below.

To understand the eviction section properly as it applies to you, you need to know what sort of tenancy you have. If you have not already done so, you should read the sections in Chapter 2 on the different types of tenancy, and complete the section on 'working out your type of occupation' at pages 53 and 54. You will probably need to refer to this as you go through the text.

Unlawful eviction

The first point to make is that under no circumstances can your landlord physically evict you from the property without a court order. You have the statutory right to stay in the property until you are evicted through the courts, even if you have not paid the rent or are in breach of your tenancy agreement.

Your right as a tenant to be evicted only through properly conducted court proceedings is a very important right. The eviction procedure is sometimes referred to by lawyers as 'due process'.

If your landlord threatens to evict you without going to court, or if he actually evicts you other than through officers properly appointed by the court, then this is a criminal offence under the Protection from Eviction Act 1977 and you should speak immediately to the Housing Officer at your local authority. Your landlord will have committed a criminal offence for which he can be prosecuted. Local authority Housing Officers will deal with this for you and may also be able to find you temporary accommodation. Be warned, however, that prosecutions are quite rare and the penalties are surprisingly low (generally a fine of less than £1,000) for what many people would consider to be a serious offence.

You should also seek immediate legal advice with an organisation such as Shelter, a Law Centre, the Citizens' Advice Bureau, or a firm of solicitors which specialises in housing work (your local authority's Housing Officer may be able to help you find a suitable firm). If you have been physically evicted, you will be entitled to an injunction under the civil law allowing you back in and probably a court order for financial compensation. These organisations will help you with this. Alternatively, you could just ring Shelterline on 0808 800 4444 and ask for advice.

Unfortunately, the police are generally unwilling to help tenants who have been unlawfully evicted, considering this to be a 'civil matter' (even though unlawful eviction is a criminal offence).

If you are looking to bring a County Court claim against your landlord, note that it is important that this is drafted properly and all the legal points are included. If this is not done, it could affect the level of compensation you are awarded. You should, therefore, take legal advice before issuing proceedings, and you should be represented by a solicitor who understands and is experienced in this area of law.

Eviction through court proceedings

For your landlord to evict you properly, he must (in most cases) first serve the proper form of notice on you, and then (in all cases) issue proceedings for possession. However, if your landlord is a social landlord and is evicting you because you have not paid your rent, he must also follow the pre-action protocol for rent arrears claims.

The pre-action protocol – introduction and initial requirements

In order to reduce the number of cases going through the courts, the court rules include pre-action protocols for certain types of case. These set out procedures which must be followed by the claimant landlord before claims are issued. If the protocol is not followed, claimants are normally penalised in some way, perhaps by having their case stayed or even dismissed, and frequently by being ordered to pay all or part of their opponent's legal costs, i.e. the tenant's.

The pre-action protocol for possession claims only applies to:

- social landlords, such as local authorities and registered social landlords (RSLs); and

- rent arrears claims made by social landlords.

So it will not apply, for example, if your landlord is evicting you because of your antisocial behaviour. However, rent arrears claims form the majority of possession claims by social landlords going through the courts.

Here is a brief outline of what your landlord (assuming he is a social landlord) will need to do to comply with the protocol, prior to possession notices being served:

- Your landlord must contact you (and each of your co-tenants if you have any) shortly after you fall into arrears to discuss the cause of the arrears, and any entitlement you may have to benefits.

- If possible, your landlord should try to agree an affordable repayment programme with you. If this is agreed, it should be confirmed in writing and you should be told of the consequences of not complying with it (basically you will put yourself at risk of being evicted).

- Your landlord must provide you with rent statements in a comprehensible format at least quarterly.

- For tenants who have difficulty in reading (presumably not you as you are reading this book), the landlord must take steps to ensure that the tenants understand any information given to them.

- The landlord also has to consider whether you are 'vulnerable' (e.g. due to disability or mental incapacity) and if you are, take appropriate action. (Note that if the rent arrears have been caused by your disability, it will normally be very difficult for the landlord to evict you.)

- If appropriate, your landlord should try to arrange for your arrears to be paid by Housing Benefit and he should help you with your benefit claim.

- Possession proceedings should not be started against you if you can show that the arrears are only due to non-payment of benefit and that you have done all that you can to progress your claim,

- The landlord should provide you with details of suitable agencies (such as the Citizens' Advice Bureau) that you can contact for general help with debt problems.

One of the main benefits of this protocol will be to prevent the ludicrous situation of local authority landlords aggressively serving notices and bringing possession proceedings based on rent arrears, when the sole cause of those arrears is the failure of their own Housing Benefit Office to deal with your Housing Benefit claim.

If your landlord is a social landlord and serves a possession notice on you without complying with the points set out above, then he will be in breach of the protocol, and this may affect his ability to obtain a possession order against you at court.

Additional general tips

Here are some additional tips for tenants of social landlords (although they may also be helpful to some private tenants) to follow when dealing with notices and claims for possession:

- Make sure that you keep all your appointments with Rent or Housing Officers.

- Do not allow yourself to be pressurised into agreeing to a repayment programme which you cannot afford, particularly if you are on benefit.

- If an unrealistic offer is made to you, counter it with an offer of a payment you are sure that you can afford, and keep records of your correspondence and discussions with the Rent Officer.

- Bear in mind that the usual court-ordered rate where someone is on benefits is in the region of £3.00 per week over the rent payments.

- If you can afford to make any rent payments straight away, do so and keep on making payments. This is important as if the case ever goes to court, it will show that you are taking the problem seriously.

- Before seeing a solicitor try to obtain a rent statement for the past year.

- Also, when you visit a solicitor, make sure that you take your tenancy agreement, any letters from the landlord about arrears and possession, the notice seeking possession and (if proceedings for possession have started) the claim for possession form.

I will now take a look at the various possession notices that can be served.

Possession notices – the right to be told before court action is started

In virtually all cases, your landlord must serve the proper form of possession notice on you, and the notice period must have expired, before he can issue legal proceedings for possession. The only exceptions are as follows:

- Where a Section 8 notice would normally be served; either
  - in cases of serious bad behaviour by the tenant (where a notice may sometimes be served at the same time as proceedings are issued); or
  - in claims for possession under one of the possession 'grounds';
- But in both of these cases, only where the judge considers it 'just and equitable' to dispense with the notice requirement. Note, however, that he cannot do this for possession claims based on the serious rent arrears ground for assured tenancies.
- Common law and Rent Act protected tenancies where the landlord is bringing proceedings to 'forfeit' the tenancy for non-payment of rent.

The reason why there is a requirement for a notice to be served on you is so that you are given warning of what the landlord intends to do and can either rectify the problem (if appropriate) or arrange for alternative accommodation.

Judges take very seriously a tenant's right to stay in his home, and generally will require landlords to follow the proper procedure. They are normally unwilling to grant an order for possession unless notice has been given, and then only where the notice is properly drafted and gives the correct notice period. Many tenants have successfully defended possession claims because of faults in the landlord's notice.

Sometimes even though the landlord may think he has given you the proper notice period, because of the way the notice has been served, he may not have done. If the notice was served by being hand delivered to you, but it was, in fact, put through the letter box rather than being given to you personally, it will normally be deemed to have been served the next working day. If the relevant notice period expired on the day it was delivered, the notice period may therefore be one day short (or longer if it was delivered on a Friday), and the notice will be invalid.

I will now detail the different types of notice that may be served.

> **Note**
>
> For general information about tenancy types, see Chapter 2. You need to know your tenancy type when reading this section.

> **Q** My landlord stopped paying his mortgage and I am told that the bailiffs will arrive on 1 September. I have been paying my rent as normal, although my contract has run out. Do I have any rights at all or should I get out on 31 August before they come in and change the locks?

> **A** Unfortunately, in this situation there is nothing you can do, and you should make arrangements to move out. Technically, you will have a claim against your landlord for breach of contract as he has caused you to be evicted, but practically this is probably not worth bothering about. If you find it difficult to find alternative accommodation, speak to the Homelessness Officer at your local authority, who may be able to assist. You may be eligible to be rehoused by them, particularly if you have children.

Assured and assured shorthold tenants

Section 21 notices

This is the notice which you are most likely to receive if you rent in the private sector. As you will probably be aware, if you are a tenant in an assured shorthold tenancy, your landlord has the right to evict you after the fixed term of your tenancy has ended, provided the correct procedure has been followed. The first part of this procedure is service of this notice, which must be drafted strictly in accordance with Section 21 of the Housing Act 1988. Note that if your tenancy is an assured rather than an assured shorthold tenancy, then this notice will be void and of no effect.

There is no prescribed form for Section 21 notices, i.e. there is no specific format, wording or layout for the notice that is required by law. The notices must just be in writing and contain the information set out in the relevant part of Section 21. This information will vary depending on whether the notice is served before your fixed term has ended, or after it has ended.

If it is served before your fixed term has ended, then:

- the notice will need to comply with the provisions of Section 21(1);

- it must give you at least two months' notice; and

- it must expire on or after the end of your fixed term (i.e. it should not give an expiry date which is before the end of your fixed term).

> **Note**
>
> Sometimes landlords will serve a Section 21 notice as a standard procedure at the start of the tenancy. However, if the notice is served at or before the time your tenancy agreement is signed, it is arguable that it is invalid, as you cannot be given notice to end a tenancy which has not yet started.

If the notice is served after your fixed term has ended (i.e. if you have a periodic tenancy), then:

- the notice will need to comply with the provisions of Section 21(4);

- it must give you at least two months' notice; and

- it must give an expiry date which is not earlier than two months after the notice was given to you; and

- the expiry date must be the last day of a period of your tenancy; and

- the notice must state that possession is required by virtue of Section 21 of the Housing Act 1988; and

- if your tenancy period is longer than one month, then a longer notice period may be needed (this will apply to very few tenancies).

Landlords have had most problems with the requirement that the date be the 'last day of a period of the tenancy'. Many landlords simply do not realise this is needed and give a date which is just two calendar months from the date of service. In most cases, these notices will be invalid.

For example, if your tenancy started on 18 May for a period of six months, the fixed term will end on 17 November. If a Section 21 notice is served after this, then Section 21(4) will apply. The notice must give a date which is the 17th of the month and not less than two full months from the date of service. So the actual notice period will be between two and three months, depending on when in the month the notice is served. If the notice was served on 15 January, the date should be 17 March. If the notice is served on 19 January, the date should be 17 April.

However, many printed Section 21 forms (e.g. the Lawpack Section 21 form) now include special wording which provide a formula for working out the correct date if the date written in the notice is incorrect. If your landlord has used one of these forms, then the notice will normally be valid even if the wrong date has been put by mistake.

Note that Section 21 notices will continue in force indefinitely until they are cancelled by the landlord giving you a new tenancy agreement (or renewal). Your landlord can therefore base a claim for possession on a notice served several years ago; he does not have to use the notice immediately. However, as soon as he gives you a new tenancy agreement, the old Section 21 notice will be cancelled and he will have to serve a new one.

Dealing with Section 21 notices

If you are hoping to be re-housed by the local authority, then you should take the notice to the Homelessness Officer. However, be aware that most local authorities are under tremendous pressure to re-house tenants, and have insufficient properties available to them to do this. Realistically they are unlikely in most cases to re-house you until your landlord has obtained a court order. In any event, you should not move out. If you do, you will almost certainly lose your right to be re-housed. For further information, see Chapter 4 on your right to housing.

If you think that there is a fault in the Section 21 notice served on you, then you should seek professional legal advice. However, if you have an assured shorthold tenancy and a properly drafted Section 21 notice has been served on you, you should start looking for alternative accommodation as you will not normally be able to defeat your landlord's claim for possession.

Q Our landlord has died and the new owner now wants us to leave. Our tenancy agreement is for one year, and six months have passed. What kind of notice to quit should we expect to receive within the law?

A Your landlord cannot normally evict you before the end of the fixed term of your tenancy agreement, unless you fall into arrears with the rent. He will need to serve a notice under Section 21 of the Housing Act 1988 requesting you to leave at the end of the fixed term. The notice will have to be in the proper format. Unless such a notice has been served, you have the right to stay on. Even after the notice has been served on you, the landlord cannot force you to leave until after he has obtained a court order for possession. However, if the landlord does this, you will be responsible for some of the costs. If a notice is served on you, it is always a good idea to seek legal advice just to make sure that the landlord has served notice in the proper form.

Section 8 notices

This is the notice that needs to be served if your tenancy is an assured or an assured shorthold tenancy and your landlord wants to evict you under any of the 'grounds' for possession set out in Schedule 2 of the Housing Act 1988. The most common ground is the serious rent arrears ground, which is Ground 8.

Note

Coincidentally there are two 'eights' – Section 8, which is the section of the Housing Act which requires the notice to be served, and Ground 8, which is the particular ground which covers serious rent arrears.

Here are some points on Section 8 notices:

- The notice must be in the prescribed format. For example, if any of the notes are omitted from the form, it will be invalid.

- The notice also needs to set out in full the wording of the ground being cited in the notice. If any of the grounds are omitted, or if any of the wording in the ground is omitted, the notice will be invalid.

- The notice has to give a date before which possession proceedings cannot start; this date must not be earlier than either two weeks (for the 'bad tenant' type grounds) or two months (for all other grounds) from the date of service of the notice. So if the notice is served on 2 January, the expiry date should be on or after 16 January for the 'bad tenant' grounds and should be on or after 2 March for the other grounds (remembering that if the notice is served other than by handing it to you personally, it will not be 'deemed served' until one or more days later, and the notice period must allow for this).

- Section 8 notices have a 'life' of 12 months. If proceedings are not started during that period, your landlord will have to serve a new notice. He will also have to serve a new notice if he has given you a new tenancy agreement (or renewal) since the last notice was served.

- Note that although the notice should set out all the grounds relied on by the landlord, it is possible for him to add additional grounds to the court proceedings (although he cannot add Ground 8 at that stage). However, generally the grounds referred to in the notice are the things which will form the basis of any court claim.

If a Section 8 notice is served on you, you should take this very seriously. Your landlord is unlikely to serve this notice unless he is seriously contemplating possession proceedings.

I set out below the main grounds that may be given with some comments:

> **Note on terminology**
>
> **Mandatory** grounds are where the judge must make a possession order against you if your landlord proves the case; **discretionary** grounds are where the judge has a discretion whether or not to make an order for possession. The most commonly used mandatory grounds are Ground 8 and the grounds for possession set out in Section 21.

Mandatory grounds

- **Ground 1:** This is the 'owner occupier' ground. The landlord is entitled to possession if he has lived in the property as his only or principal home in the past, or if he is intending to live in the property as his only or principal home after possession has been recovered from you. For it to be a mandatory ground, the landlord needs to have given you an earlier (Ground 1) notice either in the tenancy agreement or beforehand, saying that he may be using this ground. If the Ground 1 notice was not given, the judge has a discretion to waive the requirement for this, if he thinks this would be 'just and equitable'.

- **Ground 3:** This is used for out-of-season holiday lets.

- **Ground 4:** This ground relates to lettings by educational establishments of properties which are normally let to their students.

- **Ground 5:** This ground relates to lettings of properties which are intended for occupation by ministers of religion.

Again, for these three grounds (3, 4 and 5), the landlord needs to have given you written notice at the start of the tenancy saying that the ground may be relied on. Unlike Ground 1, the court has no discretion to waive this requirement, so if the landlord did not give you the notice, he will not be entitled to possession under the ground. However, if these grounds are properly made out, there is no defence, so you should seek alternative accommodation.

- **Ground 6:** This ground is for situations where the landlord, or in some cases your landlord's landlord, needs to carry out substantial building or demolition works which either cannot be done while you are in the property, or where you have failed to co-operate (e.g. in granting access) to allow the works to be done. This ground can only be used by the original landlord who let the property to you. So your landlord cannot sell the property onto a property developer on the basis that he will be able to get you out under this ground. Although this is a mandatory ground, if you suspect that the building works are not actually going to be done, you can require the landlord to prove this.

- **Ground 7:** This ground is only used where the original tenant has died, and the landlord wishes to evict the person who has inherited the tenancy. It is a mandatory ground but it cannot be used during the fixed term of the tenancy. For more information see the section on succession rights in Chapter 19.

- **Ground 8:** This is the most common ground used. It cannot be used unless the tenant is in arrears of rent of at least two months (eight weeks) at the time the notice is served. Note that if your landlord is a registered social landlord, he must follow the pre-action protocol for possession claims based on rent arrears. For further information on this, see page 198.

Discretionary grounds

- **Ground 9:** This ground relates to suitable alternative accommodation. It is most likely to be used for assured tenants who have security of tenure, as assured shorthold tenants can be evicted more easily using Section 21. If you have an assured tenancy, and your landlord suggests alternative accommodation which is to be let to you on an assured shorthold basis, this will not be suitable. For the alternative property to be suitable, it must be another assured tenancy or something with equivalent security of tenure. The accommodation must also be suitable for the needs of yourself and your family. For example, you must be able to commute to work and your children be able to get to their schools and it must be a suitable size to accommodate yourself and your family without overcrowding.

  If you are unhappy about the accommodation on offer, you should seek legal advice. Bear in mind that although the property may not be to your liking, it may still be considered suitable by the court, and your landlord may win his case. If so, you will probably be better off accepting it now and avoiding legal action (which you may lose, in which case you may be ordered to pay your landlord's legal costs). Alternatively, it might be better to enter into discussions with your landlord now and try to persuade him to select another property which you would prefer.

- **Grounds 10 and 11:** These are the discretionary rent arrears grounds, i.e. that you are in arrears of rent but not necessarily the two months (eight weeks) needed for Ground 8 (Ground 10), and that you have been persistently late in paying rent (Ground 11). They are discussed further in the court proceedings section below.

- **Ground 12:** This is for breaches of the tenancy agreement other than rent arrears. Note that for the judge to make an order for possession, the breach must be something serious. The judge will not be evicting you because you fail to clean the windows regularly. Examples of situations where a possession order is more likely is where you are keeping a pet without permission, where you are running a business at the property without permission, or where you have taken on unauthorised lodgers or subtenants.

- **Ground 13:** The condition of the property has deteriorated and this has either been caused by the tenant or his visitors, or he has failed to prevent it.

- **Ground 14:** Where the tenant is causing a nuisance to other occupiers or neighbours, or is using the property for illegal purposes.

- **Ground 15:** The condition of the furniture has deteriorated.

Grounds 12, 13, 14 and 15 are standard 'bad tenant' grounds. If there is any truth in what the landlord is alleging, you should try to rectify things as soon as possible.

- **Ground 14A:** This ground is only available to registered social landlords. It is for situations where a partner has left a property due to the violence or threats of violence of the partner staying in the property, and is unlikely to return.

- **Ground 16:** This ground is where a property was let to an employee who has now left the employer's employment.

- **Ground 17:** This is where the tenant has obtained the tenancy by giving false information to the landlord.

Dealing with Section 8 notices

If a notice is served on you which is on the basis of rent arrears, particularly if the rent arrears are more than two months (eight weeks' worth), you should take urgent action to reduce the arrears, at least to under the two months' (eight weeks') level. If your landlord is a registered social landlord, see the sections on the pre-action protocol.

If you want to be re-housed by the local authority, you should contact the Homelessness Officer immediately. Remember, however, that if the notice is based on any of the 'bad tenant' grounds (e.g. Grounds 8, 10, 11, 12, 13, 14, 14A, 15 and 17) where you are at fault, you may be considered to be 'intentionally homeless' as any eviction which takes place will be based on your bad behaviour. If this happens, you will lose any entitlement you might otherwise have had to be re-housed. However, until the local authority have processed your claim you must not move out.

Housing Benefit delays

If the rent arrears are caused by delays in the payment of Housing Benefit, be aware that this is not a defence to possession proceedings (unless your landlord is the local authority – see the parts of the chapter on the pre-action protocol). You should contact your Housing Benefit Office urgently and tell it that you are under threat of being evicted if it does not progress your claim speedily. As Housing Benefit Offices are usually part of the local authority, you can also consider using the complaints procedure outlined in Part 4, although due to the urgency you might want to contact your councillor (see Part 4 for more information) now rather than later. Make sure that you tell your landlord what you are doing so that he is aware of the situation. Most landlords are fairly sympathetic to Housing Benefit delays, although they cannot be expected to wait forever for their rent.

Evictions by private landlords are generally either under the serious rent arrears ground or under the Section 21 procedure, as these are simpler and more certain. The majority of claims for possession under the other 'bad tenant' type grounds are generally brought by registered social landlords, so the following paragraphs will mostly apply to these cases.

Non-rent arrears cases

If the grounds in your notice are non-rent arrears grounds, particularly if they are 'bad tenant' type grounds, read the notice very carefully (it may be quite long). Is the information given correct? If it is not, you should write and tell your landlord (or the officer or solicitors who served the notice on you). However, at the same time try to gather evidence to prove that the matters claimed are untrue. It is also very important that you seek legal advice, as you will have a defence if any possession proceedings are started, and the sooner you have legal advice on this the better.

However, if the information given about you in the notice is substantially true, then you should think about what you can do about it. Is your behaviour really unacceptable? Do you need support to help you with a drugs habit or alcohol addiction? Are your children out of control? Difficult though you may find it, it is best to try to tackle these problems. There are many organisations which can help. Your Rent Officer may be able to advise you. If you do not want to speak to him (or your landlord) about it, there are lots of other people or organisations you can go to for help – your social worker (if you have one), your doctor, the Citizens' Advice Bureau, your local priest (or equivalent), or if it all becomes too much for you, you can always ring or visit the Samaritans (0845 790 9090 from the UK, 24 hours a day, seven days per week). But do make sure that you do something.

If your landlord is a social landlord, it will normally be happy to let you stay if you are able to resolve your problems. However, it is better to start now, as if you let things drift and do nothing, a claim for possession is very likely, and this will put you under additional pressure. Also, if you have been trying to sort things out and a claim for possession is brought by your landlord, the judge at any possession hearing will be far more sympathetic and will probably give you more time to deal with things before making an eviction order.

Generally, where one of these notices has been served on you, it is wise to take some legal advice, even if you think that you understand the situation and do not object to the landlord's action. Whatever you do, do not ignore it or you may lose your home.

Notices seeking possession – for secure tenants

These are the notices which must be served on secure tenants (i.e. local authority tenants) before a claim for possession is started. They come under Schedule 2 of The Housing Act 1985 but are similar in concept to the Section 8 notices described above. For example, they:

- must be in the prescribed form;
- must set out in full the wording of the 'ground' relied upon;
- must give a date after which possession proceedings will start, which for most grounds must be at least four weeks after service of the notice and be a rent due date or the end of a period of the tenancy; and
- will have a life of 12 months.

There are no mandatory grounds for secure tenancies. The discretionary grounds are as follows:

- **Ground 1:** This ground covers situations where rent has not been paid and/or where you are in breach of your tenancy agreement in some other way. If the claim is based on rent arrears, you should already have been contacted by your landlord under the pre-action protocol.

- **Ground 2:** This is where either you or people staying with or visiting you have caused a nuisance or annoyance to neighbours or in the locality generally, or where you have been convicted of using the property for something immoral or illegal or have committed an arrestable offence (e.g. if property has been used as a brothel or for the growing of cannabis). Note that in serious cases where this ground is being used, the local authority does not have to serve a notice first and it can go straight to issuing proceedings.

- **Ground 2A:** This is where a partner (e.g. spouse, unmarried partner, etc.) has left a property due to the violence or threats of violence of the remaining occupant, and is unlikely to return.

- **Ground 3:** Where the condition of the property has deteriorated.

- **Ground 4:** Where the condition of the furniture in the property has deteriorated as a result of your ill-treatment of the property or furniture, or your neglect of the property (e.g. failing to deal with minor problems so that they become serious), or your failure to prevent others from damaging the property or furniture (e.g. your children or visitors).

- **Ground 5:** Where the tenancy was only granted to you because of false information that you gave the landlord.

- **Ground 6:** Where you have tried to 'buy' a secure tenancy by paying the original tenant a sum of money to assign it to you.

- **Ground 7:** This is where your property is in a building which is mostly used for non-residential purposes, where you, or the person the property was originally let to, were employed by the landlord, and you have been behaving in an inappropriate manner and it would not be right for you to continue to live there.

- **Ground 8:** This is where you were a secure tenant of another property, and the property you are living in was provided to you to live in while building works were being carried out at your previous property, and the building works at your previous property have now been completed and it is available for you to live in again.

Dealing with notices seeking possession

There are no mandatory grounds for possession so it is never a foregone conclusion that a possession notice will actually result in your being evicted, but you should still treat these notices very seriously. Service of a possession notice on you is, after all, the first step towards your losing your home. As these notices are very similar to the Section 8 notices discussed at page 205, please read the sections on Section 8 notices, in particular the part on non-rent arrears cases (if this applies to you).

Introductory and demoted tenancy notices

Introductory tenancies can only be granted by social landlords who have an introductory tenancy scheme. A demoted tenancy is where a social landlord has applied to the court and obtained a demotion order, normally because of antisocial behaviour on the part of the tenant. See further on demotion at page 218. Unlike most tenancies with social landlords, tenants with introductory or demoted tenancies can be evicted by the landlord as of right and there is no defence the tenant can raise.

If you have an introductory or a demoted tenancy and your landlord wants to terminate this, he is required to serve a notice on you first. This 'notice of proceedings' (which is not the same as the notice seeking possession, and which is sometimes called a Section 128 notice), must contain certain prescribed information including:

- a statement that the court will be asked to order possession;
- the reasons why possession is sought;
- the date after which possession proceedings may be started: this date must be at least four weeks after the service of the notice on you, and it must be a rent due date or the last day of the period of the tenancy;
- your right to request a review;
- information about where you can obtain legal advice.

If you want to stay in the property, you need to request a review of the decision to seek possession. This request must be made within 14 days of receiving the notice, so you should deal with it very quickly. The review is carried out by the housing authority and must comply with the prescribed procedure.

The housing authority can overturn the decision made to seek possession at this review hearing. However, if the decision to seek possession is upheld, you do not need to leave immediately, as your tenancy can only be brought to an end by your landlord obtaining a court order for possession. To do this, it must issue court proceedings. However, note that there is no requirement to serve any further notice seeking possession – the preliminary notice discussed here is sufficient.

Notices to quit

This is the form that used to be served for all tenancies. However, it has now been replaced for assured and assured shorthold tenancies by the Section 8 and 21 notices, and for secure tenancies by the notices seeking possession. It is therefore only used now for tenancies protected under the Rent Act 1977 (although it will only be effective in limited cases – see page 215) and for common law tenancies (for details about when a tenancy is a common law tenancy see the section on the different types of tenancy in Part 1).

If a notice to quit is served for any other tenancy type (e.g. if you have an assured shorthold tenancy), it will be void and you can safely ignore it (although it might be wise to write and tell your landlord that he has not served the correct notice).

If an old-style notice to quit is appropriate for your tenancy, note the following points:

- It cannot be used to end your tenancy before the fixed term has ended.

- If your tenancy has a break clause, your landlord should end the tenancy by complying with the terms of the break clause first, and then serve the notice to quit.

- The notice must end not less than four weeks after the date it is served on. If the tenancy is monthly and runs from month-to-month from the third of the month to the second, the notice must end on the second of the month. However, most notices include wording which will prevent the form from being invalid if the wrong date is given by your landlord by mistake.

- There are some notes which all notices to quit must include, otherwise they will be invalid. You can see this information in the box below.

Prescribed information for notices to quit

- If the tenant or licensee does not leave the dwelling, the landlord or licensor must get an order for possession from the court before the tenant or licensee can lawfully be evicted. The landlord or licensor cannot apply for such an order before the notice to quit or notice to determine has run out.

- A tenant or licensee who does not know if he has any right to remain in possession after a notice to quit or a notice to determine runs out, can obtain advice from a solicitor. Help with all or part of the cost of legal advice and assistance may be available under the Legal Aid Scheme. He can also obtain information from a Citizens' Advice Bureau, a Housing Aid Centre or a Rent Officer.

Dealing with notices to quit

If your tenancy is a common law tenancy where the fixed term has ended (or will have ended by the time the notice expires), then this notice will be sufficient to end your tenancy (and your right to live in the property) and you will not have any defence to a court claim for possession. You should therefore either seek alternative accommodation or contact the Homelessness Officer at your local authority if you want to be re-housed.

If your tenancy is a protected tenancy under the Rent Act 1977, the effect of this notice is to end the 'contractual' tenancy. However, the contractual tenancy will be replaced immediately by a 'statutory tenancy', i.e. a tenancy imposed by statute (in this case the Rent Act). This can only be ended if the Rent Act allows this. As Rent Act tenants have long-term security of tenure, there are only a few circumstances under which this should worry you:

- If you are in arrears of rent. Although there is no mandatory rent arrears ground as there is for an assured tenancy, this does not mean that you cannot be evicted for rent arrears. You should therefore try to get your rent paid, or any Housing Benefit problems sorted.

- If your landlord wants to re-house you and has offered alternative accommodation. The comments made for Ground 9 in the Section 8 notice section above will apply here also. There is a lot of case law on the landlord's right to evict the tenant on the basis that he has provided suitable alternative accommodation and you should therefore be wary of rejecting offers made by your landlord. Judges are far less reluctant to make possession orders against tenants under this ground as they know that they will not be made homeless.

- If your landlord previously lived in the property as his main home, and a notice under Ground 1 was served on you before your tenancy agreement started (Case 11 in Schedule 15). Here, your landlord will be entitled to an order for possession as of right as this is one of the few mandatory possession grounds under the Rent Act. However, as no Rent Act tenancies have been created since January 1989, most landlords who are entitled to recover possession under this ground will have already done so.

- A similar mandatory ground is also available for landlords who bought the property intending it to be a retirement home (Case 12). If Cases 11 or 12 apply, you will not have any defence to a claim for possession and you should either arrange for alternative accommodation or contact the Homelessness Officer at your local authority if you want to be re-housed.

There are a few other mandatory grounds under the Rent Act but they are quite rare. If they are going to apply to your case, your landlord will almost certainly tell you at the time that the notice is served on you, and you can take legal advice.

If you think that your landlord is just serving a notice to quit on you to scare you into leaving, where he does not have a legal right to make you go, then it is arguable that this is harassment and you can consider complaining about him to the Housing Officer at your local authority. He will write to your landlord on your behalf explaining that he does not have any right to possession.

Other notices

The notices discussed earlier in this chapter are the main types of statutory notices used to bring a tenancy to an end and upon which proceedings for possession can be based. If you get any other form of notice, the likelihood is that it will not be valid. For example, a letter from your landlord just asking you to leave will not normally have any legal effect.

If you receive any form of notice or request to leave your home, the best thing to do is to obtain legal advice from a solicitor or other legal adviser who understands housing law. You may also want to speak to the Housing Officer at your local authority as requests asking you to leave where no proper possession notice has been served can be classed as harassment, which he can deal with for you.

The pre-action protocol – requirements after the possession notices have been served

This pre-action protocol only applies to social landlords who are seeking to evict tenants based on rent arrears.

After the possession notice has been served:

- Your landlord must try to get in touch with you again to discuss matters, i.e. the amount of the arrears, the cause of the arrears, repayment of the arrears and the Housing Benefit position.

- If an agreement is reached with you (e.g. for you to pay off any arrears by instalments together with the current rent), your landlord must agree to hold off issuing proceedings so long as you keep to this.

- If you fail to make payments under the agreement, your landlord must warn you that you are at risk of court proceedings being issued and give you clear time limits within which you must sort things out.

- If you are unable to resolve matters, then your landlord must see if any 'alternative dispute resolution' procedure (known generally as 'ADR') would be a suitable alternative to court action. This might be appropriate, for example, if you are withholding rent because you consider that your landlord is not complying with his repairing covenants. ADR and mediation (which is similar) can be very effective in suitable cases. Cases are run by a wholly independent mediator or arbitrator who, instead of imposing his own decision on you, will seek to find a solution which will be satisfactory to both parties. Arbitration and mediation are well worth considering. Do not write them off thinking that the arbitrator/mediator will automatically be on the side of the landlord – he will not!

Demotion of tenancies – social landlords only

This is a special procedure now often used by social landlords, which was introduced by the Antisocial Behaviour Act 2003, for use against tenants who behave in an antisocial way. It is not available to private landlords. It involves taking away your security of tenure for a period of 12 to 18 months so that if you 're-offend' (i.e. behave again in an antisocial way) during this time, your landlord will be able to evict you easily. Most of your other rights will remain during this period apart from, in some circumstances, your right to buy. However, if your landlord does not take any further action, at the end of the period your tenancy will normally automatically revert to what it was before.

Demotion can be claimed either on its own or as part of a claim for possession. The procedure is as follows:

- The landlord must serve notice on the tenant. There is a prescribed form for secure tenants but not for assured tenants. However, in both cases the notice must describe the behaviour complained of and should specify the ground (see possession notices sections at page 200). Notices served on assured tenants must give (in most cases) at least two weeks' notice, and those served on secure tenants must give at least 28 days' notice. The notice has a life of 12 months.

- The landlord must then issue a claim for demotion in the relevant County Court for the property, after the notice period has expired. There are special forms for this type of claim. The case will be set down for hearing normally four to 18 weeks after the issue of the claim.

- At the hearing the judge will hear and decide the case. For a complex case, it may be adjourned to longer hearing.

A claim for demotion needs to be taken very seriously. Although your home is not immediately at risk, if the order is made, then it means that during the demotion period your landlord will be able to evict you as of right and without having to give a reason (although he will still have to obtain a court order). You should therefore try to prevent the order being made if you can. If at all possible, you should obtain legal advice. If you are on a low income or benefit, you will normally be eligible for Legal Aid, assuming that you can find a firm which does housing Legal Aid work. The sort of defences you can raise are as follows:

- That the conduct complained of is not severe enough to warrant a demotion order.

- That you were not the person or persons causing the problem (e.g. it was your family or friends), particularly if you tried to prevent the antisocial behaviour.

- That your behaviour has now improved.

- That the consequences of demotion would be disproportionate to the behaviour complained of.

- That there is an alternative to demotion which would be more suitable (e.g. an injunction or antisocial behaviour order, or the adjournment of the proceedings).

- That the claim to demote your tenancy is in breach of the discrimination legislation. If you are disabled, this defence will be particularly relevant. To justify the decision to seek a demotion order, where the behaviour complained of is due to your disability, your landlord will have to prove that the demotion claim is necessary to avoid endangering the health or safety of any person and that it is reasonable for the court to make the demotion order. For more information on disability, see the special section in Part 1. You may also be able to obtain help from the Disability Rights Commission, which has a helpful website at www.drc-gb.org.

If the demotion order is made, then you can continue to live in your property for the time being, but you are at risk of being evicted if the antisocial behaviour continues.

Possession proceedings – the right to be evicted through the courts

This is a very important right which all tenants have under the Protection from Eviction Act 1977. However, as you are now much closer to the moment when you could be evicted from your home, it is even more important that you deal with things properly.

If your landlord issues proceedings for possession against you, you should receive the following from the court – generally by post:

- A copy of the claim form(s) completed by your landlord;

- A notice giving the date and time of the court hearing (in all cases apart from claims made under the accelerated procedure (see page 221));

- A blank defence form for you to use; and

- In some cases, additional information from the court. For example, if there is an advice service run at your court, you will probably receive a leaflet about it.

If your landlord is a local authority or registered social landlord, there are still parts of the pre-action protocol for it to comply with, which are discussed on page 227.

When the papers are served on you, before doing anything, you should read them carefully and see if there are any defences available. There may be some technical defences you can raise:

- Take a look at the 'statement of truth' on the claim form, which will be towards the end of the form. Who has signed it? If it is anyone other than your landlord (or an officer of your landlord company) or your landlord's solicitors, then the claim form is invalid. Claims are regularly rejected by the courts because they have been signed by the landlord's letting agent. The only time someone else can sign for the landlord (other than his solicitor) is where that person has a properly drafted Power of Attorney, and you will be entitled to see a copy of this.

- Check to see what the expiry date of the possession notice is, and then look at the claim form to see the date the proceedings were issued. Had the notice period given in the notice expired? If the landlord has started the claim too soon, he may not be able to succeed. This is particularly so in claims under Section 21 and also for some rent arrears claims.

- If the fixed term of your tenancy has not expired yet, and your landlord is seeking to evict you under one of the 'grounds' in either the Housing Act 1985 or 1988, then take a look at your tenancy agreement. There must be provision somewhere for your landlord to end the tenancy in this way. This is normally done in a special clause often called a 'forfeiture clause' (even though forfeiture is no longer used for most tenancies). The vast majority of tenancy agreements will include this clause, and it will be included in all printed tenancy agreements sold by law stationers. However, if your landlord has drafted his own tenancy agreement, it is worth checking. If the clause is not there, your landlord will not be entitled to evict you until the fixed term of your tenancy has ended. (You can see an example of a forfeiture clause in the section on tenancy agreements in Chapter 8 page 114.)

- Your landlord will normally have needed to serve a possession notice on you first. The court form will give details of when this was served and its expiry date, and in many cases a copy of the notice will be annexed to the claim form. Take a look at it. Have you ever seen it before? If the notice was not served on you, then your landlord's claim may fail. However, be careful in raising this defence. Most landlords will be able to prove service of the notice. You will not be able to defeat the claim simply because you have not read it, or because your dog ate it when it was put through the letter box, or because a 'kind friend' hid it from you thinking it might upset you (to give a few examples).

We will now take a look at some specific types of claim and see what other defences might be available to you.

Accelerated possession proceedings

You can tell if this is the procedure being used because you will not be given a hearing date and the claim form will have 'accelerated procedure' written at the top. This is the procedure which is normally used to evict tenants who have failed to leave after they have been served a Section 21 notice. It cannot be used in any other circumstances.

In most cases you will have no defence to the possession claim. However, consider the following points:

- Is your tenancy an assured shorthold tenancy? If your landlord is a private sector landlord and your tenancy started after February 1997, then it probably will be. Take a look at the section on tenancy types in Chapter 2 at page 36. For example, if your annual rent is over £25,000, you will have a common law tenancy. The accelerated procedure can only be used for assured shorthold tenancies.

- Has the fixed term of your tenancy expired? If not, has it been ended under a break clause (see page 107)? If the answer to both of these is 'no', then your landlord cannot use this procedure to evict you at this time.

- Was the notice properly drafted? Take a look at page 202 for guidance on Section 21 notices. Many landlords have lost their claim because they put the wrong expiry date on the notice. Also, if the notice was served at or before the time you signed your tenancy agreement, it may not be valid (as you cannot serve notice to end a tenancy which has not yet begun).

- Is your property a House in Multiple Occupation (HMO) and if so, does your landlord need to have a licence? If he does, but he is unlicensed, then he cannot succeed in a claim for possession under this ground.

- Did your landlord take a damage deposit? If so (for all deposits taken after 6 April 2007, or where an existing tenancy was renewed after that date), is this protected under an authorised tenancy deposit scheme? If not, again he cannot succeed under Section 21. (See further on damage deposit protection schemes in Chapter 7.)

- Check again to see whether the notice had expired at the time the court proceedings were issued. If not, this will be fatal for your landlord's claim.

- Check again the signature on the statement of truth. It is most commonly this type of claim where letting agents will sign for their landlords, not realising that this will invalidate the claim.

Claims for possession for introductory or demoted tenancies

These tenancy types are only available where the landlord is a social landlord.

If possession proceedings are issued against you, there is, unfortunately, no defence you can raise. The proper time for objections to have been made was (for demoted tenancies) at the court hearing when your tenancy was demoted and (for both demoted and introductory tenancies) at the time the notice of proceedings was served on you. It is now, I am afraid, too late.

However, it will take several months for the proceedings to wind their way to a conclusion, so this should allow you some time to find alternative accommodation.

Rent arrears claims

These can be brought for all the different tenancy types. Consider the following points:

- If your landlord is a social landlord, has he followed the pre-action protocol?

- Work out your tenancy type. Has your landlord served the correct form of notice on you? Note that if you have a common law tenancy, it needs to be an old-style notice to quit, unless your landlord is 'forfeiting' your lease, in which case no notice need be served – this can only be done for Rent Act and common law tenancies, and your landlord will need to tick the forfeiture box on the second page of the summons form.

- Do you have any dispute with your landlord? Are there outstanding repairs due on your property? If so, this could form the basis of a defence to his claim, even though you may be in arrears of rent.

- Are you disabled and if so, are the rent arrears due to your disability? If so, you may have a defence under the discrimination legislation. Contact the Disability Rights Commission for help and advice (www. drc-gb.org).

- If your landlord is a local authority and your arrears are due to Housing Benefit delays, then it should not be bringing these proceedings.

- If your landlord is not the local authority and your arrears are due to Housing Benefit not being paid, then you need to sort this out as soon as possible. Consider contacting your local councillor (see Part 4 for more information about this). Remember that for claims brought by non-local authority landlords, Housing Benefit delays are not a defence.

- If you can clear the arrears, you will be able to defeat your landlord's claim (although you may still be ordered to pay some legal costs). If you can get the arrears to under two months'/eight weeks' worth, you may be able to escape an order for possession, or even if one is made, it will almost certainly be suspended on terms, which means that you will be able to stay at the property.

Note that for rent arrears claims, your landlord must also provide with the particulars of claim, a schedule of rent arrears, which must be in a similar format to the table at page 134. In particular, the schedule must give a running total of the arrears. If this is not included with the paperwork, your landlord will be in breach of the court rules.

Note on terminology

Forfeiture: This is a very old common law procedure, and was commonly used to end tenancies before the statutory codes came into force. The landlord could 'forfeit' the lease/tenancy if the tenant breached any of the tenancy agreement terms. Forfeiture is now prohibited under the Housing Act 1988, and landlords can only forfeit common law tenancies (where the statutory codes do not apply) and tenancies under the Rent Act 1977. Normally forfeiture is only used for non-payment of rent.

If your landlord wishes to forfeit your tenancy for non-payment of rent (assuming this is possible), he does not need to serve a notice on you first and can proceed to issue a court claim for possession immediately. However, there are complicated rules under which you can obtain 'relief from forfeiture' if you subsequently pay the rent arrears. For more information on this you should seek legal advice.

Note that for common law and Rent Act tenancies, landlords can also bring forfeiture for other types of breach, but they need to serve a special notice first under Section 146 of the Law of Property 1925. This is very rare and if it happens to you, you should seek legal advice.

'Bad tenant' grounds

These cases are where the landlord is claiming possession because of something you have or have not done, such as behaving antisocially, damaging the property and/or its furniture, or obtaining the tenancy under false pretences. For a list of all the grounds that may be used, see the notices section at pages 206 to 213.

The good news is that these grounds are always discretionary (i.e. the judge will only make the order if he considers it reasonable to do so), so you will be able to have your day in court and persuade the judge that he should let you stay in the property. Judges are generally sympathetic towards tenants (they do not like being responsible for making someone homeless), so in the vast majority of cases you will get a fair hearing and will normally be given at least one chance to sort things out. The bad news is that for serious cases (in particular for claims under Ground 14 for assured tenancies or Ground 2 for secure tenancies), your landlord does not need to serve a possession notice on you first, or he can serve the notice at the same time as the proceedings are issued. So you may get very little warning.

First of all, when you are served with the court forms, you must read them carefully. Are they correct in what they claim? If the allegations are not correct, is there any way you can prove this? Gather together any documentary evidence you may have, compile a list of people you think may be prepared to speak up for you, and go and get legal advice as soon as possible. These claims are complex and you will not be able to defend your case properly without skilled legal help. If you do not know where to go, a good place to start is to ring Shelterline on 0808 800 4444. At the very least, the adviser should be able to recommend someone local you can go to for advice.

If the allegations are substantially true, then this does not necessarily mean that you are going to be evicted. There is still time to sort things out. If you have not done so already, give careful thought as to how you can improve things. Seek help and advice; not just legal advice, but also help for your problem. There are organisations that can help you, if you are willing to be helped. For example, if you have an alcohol problem, consider joining Alcoholics Anonymous.

Remember that the judge will not want to evict you; he will want to give you a chance. Make sure that you take that chance and do not abuse it. You cannot expect to be given 'second chances' forever. If you are being evicted because of antisocial behaviour, the judge must also consider the rights of your neighbours, who may be complaining about your behaviour. If you do not mend your ways, it is unfair to them for the judge to do anything other than order your eviction, after you have been given a reasonable opportunity to sort things out.

If you are disabled and your behaviour is as a result of your disability, you should have a defence under the discrimination legislation, particularly if your landlord is a social landlord. Note that in this context, conditions induced as a result of addiction to nicotine, alcohol or drugs are specifically excluded. Otherwise, for your landlord to succeed, he will have to prove that the possession order is necessary to avoid endangering the health or safety of any person (e.g. neighbours) and that it is reasonable for the court to make the order. For more information on disability, see the background information section in Part 1. You may also be able to obtain help from the Disability Rights Commission, which has a helpful website www.drc-gb.org.

'Estate management' grounds

These are cases where the reason the landlord is seeking possession is not (necessarily) because you are a terrible tenant but because he needs the property back (and the notice-only procedure under Section 21 is not available). The two main grounds here are Ground 6 for assured tenancies, where the landlord is going to do building or demolition works, and where the landlord is providing suitable alternative accommodation.

Ground 6 has been discussed briefly at the notice stage. If you suspect that your landlord is not actually going to do the works specified, then you should get legal advice on whether you can defend the claim. If the problem is simply finding somewhere else to live, you should now speak to the Homelessness Officer at your local authority. You may be entitled to be re-housed.

Suitable alternative accommodation has also been discussed at the notice stage. There is a long string of case law on this topic and if you are unhappy about the accommodation on offer, the best thing is to speak to a solicitor who specialises in housing work to see if any of these will apply to you. As usual, Shelterline on 0808 800 4444 is a good place to start.

Common law tenancies

If your tenancy is a common law one, then there will not normally be any defence to a claim for possession after the fixed term in your tenancy has ended.

However, if you once had a protected, secure or assured tenancy and your landlord is claiming that you have lost statutory protection, perhaps because you have not been living in the property, there may be a defence (e.g. if you are able to show that the property was always considered by you to be your home). Again, there is quite a lot of case law on this topic, and the best thing to do is to obtain professional legal advice from a solicitor. Again, Shelterline on 0808 800 4444 may be able to help you find a suitable solicitor, if you do not have one already.

The pre-action protocol – requirements after the court proceedings have been issued

As discussed at page 198, the pre-action protocol only applies to claims for possession made by social landlords based on rent arrears. Your landlord will need to confirm to the court the following:

- That at least ten days before the date of the hearing, the landlord has given you up-to-date rent statements and any information he may have about the state of your Housing Benefit application.

- That he has informed you of the date and time of the hearing and encouraged you to attend.

- That if you have kept to the terms of any repayment arrangement made, he will agree to the case being postponed so long as you continue to keep to the agreement.

Note also that if you do not keep to the agreement, your landlord must warn you before going back to court and give you a time limit within which to sort things out.

If the court finds that your landlord has failed to comply with the terms of the pre-action protocol, it can (in all cases) order that he pays your legal costs (if any), and for cases other than those where there is a mandatory ground for possession, order that the case be adjourned, struck out or dismissed.

What do you do next?

In most cases the best thing to do is to obtain legal advice as soon as possible. There is also the defence form, which in many cases you will want to complete and send to the court (this is often referred to as 'filing' your defence). The reasons you might want to do this are:

- Because you want to defend the claim;

- If you do not want to defend the claim, because you want to ask the judge to delay the date for possession; and

- If you do not want to defend the claim, because you want to ask for more time to pay any money judgment or costs order that will be made against you.

In many cases, if there is no available defence and tenants think that they may be able to move out shortly, they will not bother to file a defence. Note that you should be careful about filing your defence too early for accelerated possession claims as this might result in the case being viewed by the judge earlier than he would otherwise have done, which if you do not have a defence, will result in an earlier date for possession. You should aim to get your defence to the court just after two weeks from when it was received by you.

If you want to defend the claim, you should seek legal advice as soon as possible, unless you are very sure of your grounds and want to deal with it yourself. Even then, it is a good idea to at least speak to someone about it.

It is also a good idea to get legal advice before you file your defence, even if you are fairly sure that you are doing things correctly. This is, after all, your home.

If you want to ask the court for extra time in the property, be aware that the standard possession order that is made will be for you to give up possession in 14 days or (in some cases) 28 days after the hearing date. For accelerated possession claims, the judge will almost always make a 14-day order. If you think that you will need more time than this, you have to ask the court. The defence form is a good place to do this.

If your landlord is claiming possession under a mandatory ground, then the judge is only allowed to defer the date for possession by up to six weeks from the date the original order is made, and then only for cases where the defendant will suffer 'exceptional hardship'. For any other type of claim, the judge has a discretion to stay or suspend the order as he thinks fit; for example, on the basis that you repay the arrears by instalments in addition to the monthly rent until it is paid off (after which the order will come to an end). This is known as a 'suspended' possession order.

In most cases, your requests for more time, or for an instalment order for the payment of rent or costs, will be dealt with at the main hearing. If your landlord is claiming possession under the accelerated procedure where there is generally no main hearing, the judge will normally make the order for possession but list the case for hearing just on the question of the possession date and/or an instalment order. (Note that for accelerated proceedings an instalment order will just be for payment of legal costs, as landlords cannot claim for rent in this type of claim.)

Possession hearings

For general information about court hearings, please read the section on background information on court proceedings in Chapter 3. The following are particular points which may be useful for you to know for possession hearings.

- If you have not already obtained legal advice (and really, if you want to stay in the property, you should have obtained legal help by now), your local court may offer a free advice service. This is well worth using as the advisers will normally be very experienced in housing work and will generally be able to represent you at the hearing. Ask the usher when you go to court if you can see one of the advisers.

- If your landlord's claim for possession is based on rent arrears, then he will not normally be able to refuse late payment by cheque, and must credit this to the arrears even though it will not have cleared by the date of the hearing. This was confirmed by a legal case called *Day v Coltrane* and you should mention this to the judge if it looks as if he is not going to allow the cheque. If your landlord has refused to accept the cheque, take it along to the hearing. What will generally happen is that the judge will adjourn the hearing to allow time for the cheque to clear (unless the rent is still more than two months' worth, even taking into account the amount of the cheque, in which case an order for possession will generally still be made now, with the adjournment relating simply to the money judgment for the arrears). However, if you have a history of presenting cheques which subsequently bounce, the judge may be entitled to take a different view.

- You will not (for rent claims based on the mandatory Ground 8 from the Housing Act 1988) be entitled to ask the judge to adjourn the hearing on the basis that you are due to receive some money shortly, or on the basis of anything else which is likely to occur after the hearing date. The judge is only concerned as to whether payment can be made at or before the hearing. So, if some money is due to be paid into your account in time for a cheque made out now to clear, consider taking a cheque along to the hearing.

- As mentioned earlier, the fact that your rent arrears are due to Housing Benefit delays is not a reason for the judge to refuse your landlord an order for possession (unless your landlord is the local authority who runs the Housing Benefit Office). However, if you are evicted from your home due to Housing Benefit delays, then this is very serious maladministration and you are entitled to complain in the strongest possible way. Contact your councillor, MP and even perhaps the local press. It is unacceptable.

- If you have a serious defence (such as a counterclaim for disrepair, or if you are defending a case based on discretionary grounds), the judge will normally treat the first hearing as a 'directions' hearing. This means that he will give 'directions' about the future conduct of the case. For example, he will list what sorts of documents need to be provided and when this needs to be done by, and he may set the case down for a full trial. However, if your case is going to be defended, you should by now have sought independent legal advice and ideally you should be represented at this hearing. A general book such as this cannot give detailed advice on defended possession claims.

- Sometimes the judge will make an order for possession but will 'suspend' this so long as you do or refrain from doing something. For example, this is often used in rent arrears cases where there is no mandatory ground. An order for possession will be made but suspended so long as you pay £x per month off the arrears in addition to the rent. This means that so long as you keep the payments up, your landlord cannot actually evict you. Sometimes possession orders made in cases based on the tenants' bad behaviour will be suspended so long as the tenant refrains from doing the offending behaviour. Again, if the tenant complies with the order, he cannot be evicted. These types of orders are called 'suspended possession orders'.

- Whatever type of case you have and whatever the outcome, it is important that you take detailed notes of what happens at the hearing. In particular, you must make notes about the judge's decision and his exact words (if you can write that fast) when he is giving his judgment. If you are not happy with the decision reached, you will find it very difficult to get proper advice if you are unable to tell your adviser the reasons given by the judge for his decision. If you do not understand what the judge has said or want him to speak slower or more clearly so you can write things down, do not be afraid to ask him. If he refuses, make a note of this too. If you find it difficult to write quickly, consider taking someone along with you to take notes for you. Generally you are entitled to have a friend or adviser to sit with you in court to give you advice and help take notes. This person is often referred to as a 'Mackenzie friend', but note that he cannot speak for you in court.

The order for possession

This is a form which is sent out to you by the court summarising what was decided at the hearing. It will have 'Order for Possession' written at the top and at the top right a box with the details of the case, the court, claim number, parties, etc.

The main body of the order starts by giving the date the order was made and the name of the judge who made it. It will also say who attended the hearing (e.g. 'Counsel for the claimant, and the defendant in person').

Underneath this will be the words 'and the court orders that' followed by the order itself. This will contain the following:

- The order for possession. This will say something like 'the defendant gives the claimant possession of Flat 1, 2 The Grove, Atown, Wessex, XX1 2DD on or before 1 January 2008'.

- Any money judgment. For example, in rent arrears cases there will be a judgment for any rent outstanding at the date of the court hearing.

- There will also often be an order for the tenant to pay rent at a daily rate so long as he is living in the property. This is known as either an 'occupation rent' or the old-fashioned legal term 'mesne profits' (pronounced 'meen').

- An order for costs. This will normally be what is known as 'fixed costs', which is a fixed rate set by the court. It will almost certainly be far less than the sum actually paid by your landlord to his solicitors. If your landlord acted in person, then you will normally just be ordered to pay the court fee and perhaps his travel expenses to court.

- If the order is to be suspended, there will also be a paragraph saying what needs to be done by the tenant. Normally, this will be that you must pay a certain amount each month from the arrears in addition to the normal rent.

- If there was anything else agreed at the hearing, this will also be set out in the order.

There will then be some notes at the bottom warning you what will happen if you do not comply with the order.

When you receive the order you should read it carefully and make sure that it is correct. It is not unknown for the typists in the court office to misread the judge's handwriting and get the order wrong. If you find a mistake, write to the court telling them what is wrong and ask them to correct it. Otherwise, keep it in a safe place.

After the hearing

It will generally take some time for the court to send you the formal order for possession (bearing in mind that to save money courts often send everything by second-class post). So, for a while, you will be dependent on the notes you made at the hearing. However:

- If a possession order has been made and you want to be re-housed by your local authority, you should contact the Homelessness Officer as soon as possible and tell him what has happened.

- If you are unhappy about the judge's decision and you think that he was wrong, take legal advice as soon as possible. It may be possible for you to appeal the decision, but note that you are supposed to do this within 14 days. Extensions of time are allowed sometimes, but it is best to get on with it promptly.

- If an order for possession has been made, but suspended upon your making payments, then make sure that you pay these. If you do not, your landlord will be able to go straight to the bailiffs to enforce the order.

If a possession order has been made against you and you are not eligible to be re-housed, then you should try to find somewhere else to live as soon as possible. The order will specify a date by which you need to have vacated the property. The significance of this date is that your landlord cannot instruct the court bailiffs to evict you until after this date has passed (unless he is specifically given leave to do this). As it generally takes a couple of weeks for the bailiffs to arrange a date to physically evict you, you are probably safe for a bit longer. However, if you cannot get re-housed promptly, you might want to make an application to the court for more time.

Applying for more time

There are several ways you can do this. Sometimes people will apply for time in the defence form. If your case had a hearing then this will have already been dealt with, although if the time given was not long enough you can always apply again. If your landlord was using the accelerated procedure, then the judge who looks as the paperwork will generally make the possession order and then fix a hearing for your application for more time to be considered by a judge (not necessarily the same one that made the possession order).

However, you can also make a separate application after the hearing date or after the accelerated possession order has been made. To do this, you can either make an application shortly before the date on the order for possession, or apply to the courts once you know the date for the bailiffs' appointment, asking for it to be delayed (most people will do this). This is known as an 'application for a stay of execution'. ('Execution' in this context means enforcing the court order, not chopping your head off!)

You can also make this application if your landlord has applied to the bailiffs as a result of your breaching a suspended possession order. Provided that you can show the judge that you will be able to make the payments in future, or comply with the original order, he will probably reinstate the suspended order.

If you cannot get legal help, it is best to go up to the court office and ask it for the form to make the application. The court staff can then help you fill it in, if you are not familiar with this sort of thing. It is also possible to download the form from the Court Service's website at www.hmcourts-service.gov.uk – it is Form N244.

There is normally a fee payable for making the application, which at the time of writing this book is £65. However, if you are on benefit or on a low income, you may be entitled to an exemption from paying the fee. Either you can speak to the court staff about this, or you will find the form (EX160) and a helpful leaflet (EX160a) on the court service website. If you issue the application personally at court and you are on benefit, make sure that you take proof of your benefit entitlement with you.

If you make an application for a stay, it is essential that you attend the court hearing. If you do not, it will be dismissed and you may be ordered to pay your landlord's costs, if he has attended the hearing.

Be aware that if your order was made under a mandatory ground (see page 206), the judge will not be allowed to give you more than six weeks in the property, from the date the order was made. Therefore, if the order was made on 1 June and the bailiffs' appointment is on 11 July, the judge will be able to set it aside and you will normally get a few more weeks as it will take that long for the bailiffs to re-schedule the appointment. However, if the bailiffs' appointment is for 14 July, he will not be able to help you. If your order was made under a discretionary ground (see page 208), then the judge has a discretion to stay and suspend the order as he considers reasonable.

However, in both cases, if it is in the judge's power to order a stay, you will need to give a valid reason why he should do this; for example, that the local authority will not be able to re-house you before the repossession date, or that the breach of a suspended order possession was due solely to Housing Benefit delays. Just saying that it is your home and you do not want to leave will not be enough.

Note on terminology

Tolerated trespassers: In some circumstances where tenants have breached suspended possession orders, particularly with social tenancies, the effect has been to end their tenancy, even though the judge may have re-instated the suspended possession order allowing them to stay in the property. Where this has happened the tenant is said to become a 'tolerated trespasser'. This is far less likely to happen nowadays, as the courts have now devised new forms of order to prevent this happening.

However, it may be a good idea for you to obtain legal advice if this has happened to you, in particular before you pay off all the outstanding arrears (as it may not be possible for the court to correct things after this has been done). If you become a tolerated trespasser this can have serious consequences as where relevant you will lose your right to have the property kept in repair under Section 11, your right to buy, and the right for your family to inherit under the succession rules (discussed in Chapter 19).

Bailiffs' appointments

You will normally be told by the bailiffs when this will be. Often they will come round to see you and will tell you about it in person. You will also receive a formal notification from the court. If you are still waiting to be re-housed by the local authority, contact it as soon as possible. It must re-house you now (if you are eligible).

Ideally, you should make arrangements to move out before the bailiffs' appointment. If not, the bailiffs can use reasonable force to break into the property and remove you. The locks will then be changed and the property made secure by the landlord. If some of your possessions are still inside, you will need to make arrangements with your landlord to collect them.

Remedies

In this chapter advice on dealing with eviction proceedings has been incorporated into the text at the relevant stages.

If you have been properly evicted through the courts by your landlord, then there is nothing further you can do once this process has been completed. You will have had time to object, file defences and so on, as part of the procedure. Most landlords consider tenants get far too much opportunity to delay matters!

However, if by chance you have not been given a proper opportunity to object or put your case (e.g. if you were in hospital and were unaware of the proceedings), then you must seek legal advice immediately. Every day that you delay reduces your chances of getting anything done. If indeed, anything can be done.

Further information

You will find all the court forms and a number of helpful leaflets on the court service website at www.hmcourts-service.gov.uk.

For further information and guidance, you should seek legal advice – see Part 4 on complaints and obtaining legal advice.

CHAPTER 14

The right to your own possessions

Many of the things in your rented property will belong to your landlord, such as the fittings, perhaps the furniture, sometimes things like kitchen utensils and bed linen. Your landlord has rights in respect of these, and can make a claim against you if they are damaged. However, many things in the property will be yours, such as your clothes and personal effects. Perhaps you have your own furniture and other household items. These things are yours and your landlord does not have any rights over them.

Your landlord should not:

- remove your goods if you fail to pay rent.

Or, for any reason:

- destroy or damage any of your property; or
- require you to arrange for it to be covered by insurance.

It is a fundamental rule in English law that you cannot dispose of or deal with something that does not belong to you. The only person who can legally remove your goods from your property is a court authorised bailiff in respect of a court order or fine. If your landlord comes and removes your possessions, however much rent you owe him, this is illegal.

Q I have been living in a cottage for ten years and my old landlord sold it. The new landlord is OK but he has given my stuff away without asking me first. Is this legal?

A Under no circumstances should your landlord give away your possessions! He is not entitled to do this and it is theft, or at the very least harassment. You can speak to The Tenancy Relations Officer/Housing Adviser at your local authority and ask him to write to your landlord, or you may prefer to contact the police.

However, there are times when a landlord's legal inability to deal with a tenant's property can cause him real problems . If you vacate the property but leave it full of your possessions, then it will be difficult for him to re-let it if he cannot clear it. If he cannot dispose of the items, it is not fair to expect him to pay for storage indefinitely if you fail to collect them.

This situation is covered by an Act, rather obscurely called the Torts (Interference with Goods) Act 1977. Under this Act, where a person finds himself in the position of being in possession of someone else's goods (this is known in law as being an 'involuntary bailee'), then he will be able to deal with the goods if he follows the correct procedure. This is as follows:

- The landlord (or bailee) must write to the tenant (or bailor) giving details of the items held, and of when and how they can be collected.

- He must also give a time limit within which this must be done. The time limit must give the tenant a reasonable opportunity to arrange for collection.

- He must also state that if the goods are not collected within the time specified, they will be sold or otherwise disposed of.

- The letter should be sent by recorded delivery (but if you receive it when it has been delivered some other way, it will normally be valid).

- If the landlord does not know the tenant's current whereabouts (e.g. if the tenant has left and has not given a forwarding address), he does not have to send the letter so long as he has made reasonable efforts to trace the tenant.

If you do not respond to the letter by collecting the goods, or if you have not left a forwarding address and your landlord cannot trace you after having made reasonable efforts (and instructing a tracing agent will normally be considered sufficient), then he is entitled to sell the goods or, if they have no value, dispose of them in some other way. As the goods were your property, any proceeds of the sale, technically, should be kept for you. However, if you have left owing the landlord money, realistically you will not be able to recover the money from him as he would be entitled to counterclaim for unpaid rent if you sue him.

If the goods, or the proceeds of sale, are left with the landlord for six years or more, then effectively they will become his, as under an Act called the Statute of Limitations, you will have lost the right to sue him for them.

Remedies

If your landlord has removed all or some of your possessions, then you can treat this as theft and call the police, or you can treat it as harassment and contact the local authority and ask it to deal with it under its powers under the harassment laws (see Chapter 13 for more information). Bear in mind that if you bring a civil claim against your landlord for recovery of your goods, he will be entitled to counterclaim for the value of any rent you owe him.

If your landlord is insisting that you take out insurance for your goods, perhaps with a company which will pay him commission, you can refuse this. Any contract term in your tenancy agreement providing for this will be void under the Unfair Terms in Consumer Contracts Regulations 1999 (see Chapter 8 on the right to be treated fairly). If your landlord is insistent, then this can be classed as harassment and you can complain to the Housing Officer at your local authority.

If your landlord has sold or disposed of your property after following the provisions of the Torts (Interference with Goods) Act, then you cannot do anything about the actual sale. However, you may have a claim against him if he has undersold the items, or if he is refusing to hand the proceeds of the sale over to you. Unless, of course, he is claiming properly incurred expenses, such as storage fees and the costs of sale, or you owe him money (e.g. for unpaid rent).

> **Further information**
>
> If you wish to take a claim against your landlord further, you should seek legal advice.

CHAPTER 15

The right to buy

Properties let by private landlords

Historically, tenants have never had the right to buy the property they rent. At the end of the tenancy, the property always went back to the landlord. This situation has now changed for long leases (i.e. those for over 21 years), but it remains the same for short lets, even though the tenant may actually live in the property for a long time. This means that if a tenancy is for a fixed term of weeks, months or even two or three years, the tenant will never be in a position where he can demand that his landlord transfers ownership of his interest in the property.

Sometimes where a tenant has long-term security of tenure (e.g. if he has a protected tenancy under the Rent Act 1977), he may be able to persuade his landlord to sell the freehold of the property to him. For example, a landlord may consider this the better option if he cannot (because of the fair rent regime) charge a market rent but is required, under his repairing obligations, to carry out expensive repair works to the property. However, the landlord does not have to sell it. He may prefer to pay the repair bill, increase the rent as much as he can under the fair rent regime, and continue to hold the property as an investment, on the basis that it will be very valuable once the final protected tenant has either died or vacated. The fact that you have lived in your rented flat for 30 years and cannot be evicted, does not mean that you are entitled to force your landlord to sell it to you.

Properties let by social landlords

Up until 1980 the situation was the same as for private landlords – local authority and registered social landlords had a discretion to sell property to their tenants, but tenants did not have the right to demand this. However, this all changed with the Housing Act 1980 when Mrs Thatcher's new Conservative government brought in home ownership for the masses, with the right for council tenants to buy their own homes. This right still remains, although subsequent legislation has amended this and reduced the discounts available.

This is a complex area of law. Your right to buy will depend on many things; for example, whether your landlord is (or was) a local authority or a housing association or other registered social landlord, how long you have been living at the property, and whether your tenancy is a secure tenancy or not. There is not enough space in this book to give much detail; however, all landlords of secure tenancies are under an obligation to publish details of tenants' right to buy, and this information must be made available to tenants on request. If this is something you would like to do, you should speak first to your Rent or Housing Officer and ask for further information.

Here are a few general points:

- You must be a secure tenant.

- You, your spouse or co-tenant must occupy the property as your only or principal home.

- There is a qualifying residence period, which is two years if your tenancy started before 18 January 2005 or five years if it started after that date. However, the qualifying period does not have to be all at the same time or all in the same property.

- Only some tenants of registered social landlords will have the right to buy; mainly those who were formerly local authority tenants. Some will have the 'right to acquire' if their property was provided using a social housing or other grant. Others will not.

- Introductory tenants cannot buy during their introductory period but this will count as part of their qualifying period of residence.

- Demoted tenants do not have the right to buy while their tenancy is demoted, and periods as a demoted tenant do not count as part of the qualifying residence period. Tenants of registered social landlords who preserved their right to buy when their property transferred from a local authority to a housing association may lose the right to buy altogether if their tenancy is demoted.

- You can share the right to buy with your spouse or other non-tenant members of your family so long as they have lived in the property as their only or main home for the 12 months preceding the application to buy.

- You can lose the right to buy in certain situations (e.g. if your landlord has obtained an order for possession (although not always), or if the property is due to be demolished).

- If you sell the property within three years (for purchases before 18 January 2005) or five years (for purchases after 18 January 2005), you will, in most cases, have to pay back all or part of the discount you obtained when you bought it.

The right to buy is an important right and many people have taken advantage of it. However, it is not suitable for everyone. Remember that once you own the property, you will be responsible for it (e.g. for keeping it in repair). If you need to move, you may also find that the property is difficult to sell, depending on where it is and what condition it is in. On the whole, property prices rise over time, but this is not an invariable rule. Many people will remember the property crash of the late 1980s and early 1990s and the hardship it caused.

If you are entitled to buy your property under the right to buy legislation and can afford to do so, then in many, perhaps in most, cases, it will be in your best interests to take advantage of this. However, do think carefully about it and take independent legal and financial advice first, particularly if you find it difficult to manage your finances or look after yourself. You may be better off, long term, staying as a tenant.

Remedies

This remedies section applies to social tenancies only.

If your landlord refuses to sell your property to you, he must give reasons. If you disagree with the reasons given, you should first of all go back to your landlord. However, if you are still unhappy, you do ultimately have the right to challenge the decision in the County Court. You should seek legal advice before attempting this.

Further information

The best source of information about the right to buy is your landlord, who is obliged by law to provide information to tenants. If this is unsatisfactory in any way, then you should either follow the complaints procedure discussed in Part 4 or take legal advice.

CHAPTER 16

The right to sublet

The title of this chapter is perhaps rather over-optimistic as in the vast majority of cases, certainly with private tenancies, you will not have any right to sublet.

> **Note on terminology**
>
> In a situation where there are a number of sublettings, the first landlord is generally called the 'head landlord', the middle tenant is sometimes referred to as the 'middle' (or 'mesne') tenant, and the middle tenant's tenant, is called the 'subtenant'.

Private sector tenants

Most tenancy agreements will prohibit subletting. The reason for this is that the landlord is usually very careful about who he allows to live in his property. However, there is little point in his carefully referencing his tenant, if that tenant is then going to be able to sublet all or part of the property to someone else who may be unsuitable!

If the tenancy agreement provides that subletting is only allowed with the landlord's consent, then the landlord cannot refuse this 'unreasonably'. If there is no written tenancy agreement, then it will be an implied term that subletting is prohibited. If there is a written tenancy agreement but subletting is not mentioned, then the tenant will be entitled to sublet during the fixed term, but not afterwards when the tenancy becomes periodic.

Generally, if you want to take in a lodger (this is where someone rents a room in your house and shares living accommodation with you), you should let your landlord know what you are doing and obtain his permission. So long as the proposed lodger is respectable, and taking him in will not cause the property to be overcrowded or breach any licensing conditions if the property is a House in Multiple Occupation (HMO), the landlord will usually agree; particularly if it means that you will be able to pay the rent more promptly! Bear in mind, though, that if you take in three or more lodgers, you may become subject to the HMO regulations yourself.

Note that if you are a protected tenant (see page 37 for more information) and you sublet the whole of your property, you will almost certainly lose your protected status and security of tenure, and the tenancy will revert to being a common law tenancy. This is because, to have protection under the Rent Act 1977, you need to occupy the property as your residence. If you lose protection, your landlord will be entitled to end your tenancy by serving a notice to quit, and then bring proceedings for possession to evict the occupiers (i.e. the subtenants).

Public sector tenants

All secure tenants have an absolute right to take in lodgers, but see the comments above regarding overcrowding and HMOs.

So far as subletting part of the property is concerned (i.e. renting out a part of your property which is self-contained and where you do not share living accommodation), this can occur with the permission of your landlord, who cannot withhold it unreasonably. If you ask for permission, your landlord must give reasons. For example, these may include overcrowding concerns and future works to the property.

As with protected tenancies, you should not, under any circumstances, sublet the whole of your property. If you do this, it will lose its secure status and your landlord will be able to end your tenancy and obtain an order for possession as of right.

Remedies

If your landlord refuses to grant you permission to sublet your tenancy or take in a lodger, one option is to do this anyway on the basis that his refusal is unreasonable and therefore invalid, and leave it up to him to object. However, you need to be very sure indeed of your position before doing this, because if you are wrong, your landlord will be entitled to bring court proceedings to evict you. In which case not only will you lose your home, but also you will probably be ordered to pay your landlord's legal costs. Your best course of action is to take legal advice before doing anything.

If you are a social tenant, then try the complaints procedure discussed in Chapter 21.

CHAPTER 17

Other rights available to secure tenants/tenants of social landlords

Social tenancies are different from private sector tenancies and there are some rights which are available to secure tenants which are not available to tenants in the private sector. This chapter looks at the most important of these rights.

The right to exchange

If you are a secure tenant (see page 35 for more information), you may exchange homes with other secure tenants or with housing association tenants. These are often called 'mutual exchanges'. Each tenant who is exchanging must get the permission of his landlord, but the landlord can only refuse permission on certain specified grounds; for example, if an order for possession has been made, if the accommodation is not reasonably suitable for the person who is going to take it over, or if the accommodation is supposed to be for people with special needs and the exchange would mean that such a person would not be living there. Exchanges are made by way of a formal document, called a 'deed of assignment'.

> **Further information**
>
> There are websites where you can find details of people wishing to exchange, for example on the Homeswapper website at www.homeswapper.co.uk.

The right to be consulted

Local authorities are supposed to consult their tenants and take their views into account on matters of housing management. This is also the case with registered social landlords (RSLs), and the Housing Corporation has issued a number of policy documents regarding this. Consultation is often carried out through tenants' organisations and if you have a tenants' organisation, this is worth joining, particularly if there is something about your property you are unhappy about. Your landlord is more likely to take action on your complaint if it is put forward by a tenants' organisation on behalf of all tenants.

You can find more information on the Housing Corporation website at www.housingcorp.gov.uk. The Tenant Participation Advisory Service, which has a website at www.tpas.org.uk, can help groups of tenants in England by providing training, conferences, research and information. A similar service in Wales is provided by TPAS Cymru (www.tpascymru.org.uk).

The right to manage

Secure tenants have the right to set up a management organisation in order to manage their properties. RSLs must also encourage tenant involvement. For more information, see the Tenant Participation Advisory Service or TPAS Cymru websites given above.

CHAPTER 18

The right to leave the property

No one can physically force you to continue living at a property if you do not want to. You can move out at any time. However, this does not mean that you will not have to pay rent.

When you sign a tenancy agreement or agree to take on a tenancy, this is a legally binding contract under which you agree to pay rent every month (or week) for the period of the tenancy. This either can be for a fixed period of time, or can roll on from month-to-month or from week-to-week. Most secure tenancies will be periodic. Most tenancies in the private sector start out as fixed-term tenancies, but often these then roll on, on a periodic basis. Your rights will depend on whether your tenancy is a fixed term or periodic tenancy.

Periodic tenancies

If you have a periodic tenancy, then you can end this at any time by giving written notice to your landlord of not less than four weeks, ending at the end of a 'period of the tenancy'. So if your tenancy runs from the first of the month to the last day of the month, then your notice must expire on the first last day of the month after four weeks from the service of your notice on your landlord. So if the notice was served on 15 June, the notice must expire on 31 July. If your landlord tries to make you give a longer notice period in the tenancy agreement, then this clause will be void.

owever, if you leave the property without giving the proper notice period, then your landlord will be able to claim rent in lieu of notice. This will normally mean claiming money from your damage deposit. Note that your landlord cannot claim this if he re-lets the property immediately, as he cannot claim rent twice for the same property.

Sometimes your landlord may be prepared to accept a shorter notice period, in which case you will not have to pay rent in lieu of notice. However, this must be in agreement with your landlord.

Fixed-term tenancies

Sometimes you will need or want to move out before the fixed term of your tenancy has ended. For example, you may be moved elsewhere by your job, or you may decide to leave your college course and go back to your parents. However, you may be in some difficulty if your landlord will not agree to let you go early.

The first thing to do is to take a look at your tenancy agreement. Some tenancies have 'break clauses' which allow you to end your tenancy early. These are comparatively rare and most do not allow you to end the tenancy during the first six months. If your tenancy agreement has one, then to end the tenancy you must follow the procedure set out. For example if it requires you to give two months' written notice to your landlord, that is what you must do.

If your tenancy does not have a break clause, then you are legally obliged to pay rent until the end of the fixed term. Strictly speaking your landlord can sue you for this. However, if he does, your landlord will be expected to 'mitigate his losses'. This means that if he is able to find a suitable tenant to replace you, he should do this.

Therefore, your best chance to end your obligations under the tenancy is to try to find a replacement tenant yourself. Provided that he is suitable and passes your landlord's referencing procedure, then your landlord will have no excuse not to end your tenancy and re-let to the new tenant found by you. He is entitled to expect you to pay for any costs incurred (e.g. the costs of referencing and getting the tenant to sign a new tenancy agreement). However, this should not be too expensive (Lawpack publish inexpensive tenancy agreement forms – see www.lawpack.co.uk) and it will certainly be cheaper than paying rent to the end of the term.

However, if neither you nor your landlord are able to find a replacement tenant, then unless your landlord agrees to let you go (and he does not have to) you will be responsible for the rent for the remainder of the term.

If, on the other hand, you want to leave at the end of the fixed term, this is your right. You do not have to give your landlord any notice and any terms in your tenancy agreement providing for this will be void. In particular, your landlord cannot charge you rent in lieu of notice if you go on or before the last day of the tenancy without telling him first. However, your landlord is entitled to ask you whether or not you are leaving, and you should let him know if you intend to leave at that time or whether you want to stay on. If you do stay on, even by one day, then the tenancy will become periodic, and your landlord is entitled to the notice period discussed on page 251.

Additional points

These are the basic rules. However, note the following:

- You may be entitled to leave before the end of the fixed term if your property is in serious disrepair. For further information about this, see Chapter 10 on your contractual rights regarding disrepair.

- The rules discussed in this chapter are based on the fact that you are the only tenant. If you are only one of several joint tenants, then the rules will only apply if all of you want to leave at the same time. If your co-tenants want to stay on, then the situation will be different. You will normally still remain liable for the rent unless you are able to find a new tenant to replace you and have him sign a new tenancy agreement with your landlord and the remaining tenants. For more information on this, see the background information section on shared houses and joint and several liability in Part 1.

Remedies

There is nothing you can do to force your landlord to end your tenancy early if he does not want to, other than perhaps finding another suitable replacement tenant yourself. If you cannot do this, then he is quite within his rights to sue you for the whole of the rent. However, he cannot do this in advance, i.e. he can only sue you for rent which has fallen due, and not for future rent.

If your landlord is claiming rent in lieu of notice to which he is not entitled, then you can simply refuse to pay it. Problems about deductions from the damage deposit should not occur for damage deposits taken after 6 April 2007, as they will be subject to the statutory damage deposit protection scheme. Unfortunately, if deductions are made from deposits taken prior to that date, which are not the subject of a damage deposit protection scheme, then your only option is to sue your landlord for its return in the County Court.

CHAPTER 19

The right for your family to live in the property after your death (succession)

This chapter is about what will happen to a tenancy after the tenant dies. However, it may be helpful to start with a bit of general explanation and terminology.

When a person dies the property (i.e. his personal property and land) that he owns at the time of his death is known as his 'estate'. In some cases the deceased person will have made a Will and will have specified how he would like this distributed (in which case he is often described as the 'testator'). However, if this has not happened, then his estate will pass in accordance with the rules of intestacy. There is not enough space in this book to describe these rules, but generally the property will pass to the deceased's spouse and family.

For the property to be distributed in accordance with the Will or the intestacy rules, someone has to be appointed to do this. This person is called the 'personal representative' (although note that there is often more than one) and his legal authority to deal with the estate is known as the 'grant of representation'. There are two types of personal representative, depending on whether or not there is a Will. If there is a Will, executors are appointed under probate. If there is no Will or it is invalid or the executors named are unwilling to act, then an administrator is appointed under 'letters of administration'. These are both issued a special court office called the Probate Registry.

Vesting is the legal term used to describe the passing of the deceased person's property to another person upon his death. If there is a Will, then the deceased's property vests in the executor(s). If there is no Will, then the property vests in a government official called the Public Trustee until legal authority is granted to the personal representatives. Someone who inherits under a Will or intestacy is called a 'beneficiary'.

The rest of this chapter is written on the basis that the tenant has died, and that you are either a member of the tenant's family or are one of his personal representatives (or both). I will refer to the deceased tenant as 'the tenant'.

What happens after the death of the tenant will depend on what sort of tenancy is involved. For information on the different tenancy types, see Chapter 2.

Joint tenants

If the tenancy is in joint names, and at least one of the other tenants are still living at the time of the tenant's death, then his share will normally pass automatically to the other joint tenant or tenants. This is known as the 'right of survivorship'. There is no need to do anything to make this happen – it is automatic.

The rest of this chapter is written on the basis that the tenant was the sole tenant.

> **Note on rent**
>
> The tenant's estate will be liable for rent until such time as the tenancy is ended or vested in a new tenant. If no one wants to live at the property, it is best to end the tenancy as soon as possible. The personal representatives will be in exactly the same position as the tenant would have been had he been alive, so the notice rules set out in Chapter 18 on the right to leave the property will apply.

The common law

This applies to all tenancies where there are no special rules. The tenancy will count as part of the tenant's estate and will pass to his personal representatives or (if none are appointed and there is no Will) to the Public Trustee, to be dealt with in accordance with the provisions of the Will or the intestacy rules.

Assured and assured shorthold tenancies

If there is a fixed term, then the remainder of the fixed term will pass in accordance with the deceased tenant's Will or intestacy, and if the beneficiary moves in before the end of the fixed term, he will become the new tenant. However, this will not be the case if he moves in afterwards.

If the fixed term has ended, then normally a periodic tenancy will arise under the provisions of Section 5 of the Housing Act 1988 (this is called a 'statutory periodic tenancy'). This will pass, under the succession rules. The succession rules set out in the 1988 Act provide for the tenancy to pass to the tenant's spouse, civil partner or co-habitee (which can include same-sex relationships). However, this will not happen if the deceased tenant himself inherited the tenancy under these rules.

If no one inherits under the succession rules, then the tenancy will pass in accordance with the tenant's Will or intestacy. However, in that case the landlord is entitled to recover possession under Ground 7 in Schedule 2 of the 1988 Act, which is a mandatory possession ground (see Chapter 13 for more information on mandatory grounds and the eviction procedure), provided that possession proceedings are started within 12 months.

Tenancies under the Rent Act 1977

The succession rules set out in the 1977 Act were amended by the Housing Act 1988. They are a bit complicated, but basically they work as follows:

- If the tenant was married, his spouse will succeed to the tenancy provided that the spouse was living with the tenant at the time of the death.

- 'Spouse' includes a civil partner, a person living with the deceased as man and wife and same-sex partners.

- Spouses will inherit a statutory tenancy under the Rent Act 1977.

- If there is no surviving spouse, then any member of the deceased's family residing in the dwelling at the time of death will succeed.

- Family members will succeed to an assured tenancy under the Housing Act 1988.

- There can only be a second succession if, on the death of a successor who was a spouse, there is a member of the family of both the original tenant and the successor, residing in the dwelling at the time of the successor's death and for two years beforehand. Such a person will succeed to an assured tenancy under the Housing Act 1988.

- These provisions (if they apply) override anything that the tenant may have put in his Will about the tenancy.

Secure tenancies

The rules here are rather complex, and will sometimes depend on when the tenant died. Only a brief summary is given here. Note that there was no right of succession before 3 October 1980.

Generally, only the following can succeed on the death of the tenant:

- The deceased tenant's spouse or civil partner; or

- Where there is no spouse/civil partner, another member of the family.

This is unless the deceased tenant was himself a successor. Note that cohabitees are not counted as spouses but as members of the family. In both cases the potential successor must have been living in the property as their only or principal home and family members must have been living with the tenant for the past 12 months.

Government guidance has been issued which recommends that, on the death of a tenant, local authority landlords should normally grant a new tenancy to adult sharers and carers, either in the same property or in suitable alternative accommodation.

If no one is entitled to succeed, the tenancy will pass according to the tenant's Will or intestacy, but in most cases it will just be surrendered to the landlord.

Note that if the tenant had a suspended possession order made against him, this may have legally ended the tenancy (i.e. the tenant may actually have been a 'tolerated trespasser'), in which case, there will be no succession rights.

Introductory and demoted tenancies

Here the tenant's spouse or family will generally succeed but they will succeed to an introductory or demoted tenancy.

Remedies

If you have a difference of opinion with the landlord over whether you are entitled to succeed to a tenancy or not, one solution is to remain in the property and force the landlord to evict you through the courts. You can then defend on the basis that you are a successor tenant, and the judge will decide. However, bearing in mind that if you lose you may make yourself liable for your landlord's legal costs, it is best to obtain legal advice before doing this.

Further information

For social tenancies, the landlord is the best source of advice. If there is no Will, then you may also be able to seek advice from the Public Trustee, who has a website at www.officialsolicitor.gov.uk. Other than this, probably the best place to obtain advice is a solicitor who deals with trusts and probate work.

Part 3

Tenancy outline

CHAPTER 20

Brief outline of a tenancy from start to finish

Finding a property

It is important when looking for a property to make sure that you choose a good letting agent or landlord. The property may be cheap or convenient, but will you be able to get essential repairs done? Here are a few tips:

- If you are looking to rent from a local authority or registered social landlord, note that they have very long waiting lists. You may need to rent privately until they can offer you a property.

- You can normally express a preference when applying to a social landlord about the type of accommodation you would like, but due to the scarcity of accommodation available, do not expect to be offered exactly what you want.

- When looking at properties with letting agents, try to use those which are members of one of the following four organisations: ARLA (the Association of Residential Letting Agents), RICS (the Royal Institute of Chartered Surveyors), NALS (the National Approved Letting Scheme) and NAEA (the National Association of Estate Agents). Agencies which are not a member of any of these may be fine, but if they are not, you will not have a professional organisation to complain to if you are not happy (for more information, see the background information section on letting agents in Part 1).

- When dealing with a landlord direct, unless you have a personal recommendation, it is best to use one which is a member of one of the many landlord accreditation schemes. You can find out about these from the Housing Officer at your local authority.

- If you are a student, first try the accommodation listed in your Students' Union or your university's accommodation office, as these are generally landlords who have been specially approved and who have had to meet stringent standards.

- Other good places to find accommodation for rent are postcards in shop windows, local newspapers and the internet. If you are working for a large company, it may also be able to help, particularly if you are moving from another area of the country to start a new job.

The rest of this chapter is written on the basis that you are a tenant in the private sector, unless specifically mentioned otherwise.

Choosing your co-tenants

If you are planning to share a property with someone else, note that you should be careful to choose someone you can trust if you are going to sign the same tenancy agreement. Remember that you are potentially making yourself liable for his share of the rent if he does not pay. For more on this, see the background information section on shared houses and joint tenants in Chapter 2 at page 46.

Applying for a property and referencing

Generally, before agreeing to take you on as a tenant, your landlord will want some personal details from you and he will want to take references. Often you will be asked to pay a deposit at this stage. You will probably need to complete a form giving all the necessary information and you will have to provide identification. Provided that you do not have a bad credit record or a criminal record, and are able to show that you can afford to pay the rent, you should be all right. Do not tell lies in an attempt to obtain a property – remember that this is a ground for possession. If you are worried about paying the deposit, see Chapter 7 on your right to have the deposit returned to you.

If the landlord is worried about your ability to pay the rent, he may ask you to provide a guarantor. This is where someone signs to confirm that if you fail to pay your rent or any other sums due (e.g. for damage to the property), he will pay on your behalf. This is a very serious commitment, so only close friends and relatives will normally be prepared to do this. It is very common, for example, for student lets, for the students' parents to provide guarantees.

Q My boyfriend has been declined for various things after credit checks, despite having a credit card and two current accounts. He has never been in arrears or had an unauthorised overdraft. We suspect the reason for this is that the property where he is renting a room is blacklisted. The owner does not live in the house, but there have been bailiffs that have come to seize property from there. Is there anything that can be done to avoid this situation? It is especially worrying as each credit reference check reduces points on his credit reference.

A Your boyfriend should get in touch with the various credit reference agencies and ask to see his file, which he is entitled to do (although there will probably be a modest fee payable). If the information on this file is incorrect, he can require them to change it. Credit reference agencies are organisations which store information about us all and which can provide references for a fee. You can find them on the internet or you can ask your local CAB to let you have their details.

Taking on a property

There is normally a lot of paperwork involved at this stage. This is quite normal; indeed, you should be suspicious if there is little or no paperwork.

In particular, it is not a good idea to take on a tenancy where you are not given a tenancy agreement. The main documents involved at this stage are as follows:

- **The tenancy agreement:** You should read this before signing it to make sure that you agree with it. If you are unhappy, take legal advice. However, note that many clauses which seem very harsh may actually be invalid under the Unfair Terms in Consumer Contracts Regulations 1999. For more information, see the section on tenancy agreements in Chapter 8. Make sure that you are provided with a copy of the tenancy agreement. Your copy should have the landlord's original signature and his copy should have yours, although often both copies are signed by both.

- **The inventory:** This is a list of all the contents of the property. Inventories are not provided by all landlords but ideally they should be. They are often very detailed and give information about the condition of the items and the property. Indeed, they are sometimes called a 'schedule of condition'. Generally, you will be taken round the property by the landlord, his agent or a special inventory clerk, often on the day, or the day before, you move in. He will discuss the inventory with you, and afterwards ask you to sign it to confirm that it is correct. Needless to say, you should be very careful about doing this as it can be used later, for example, in disputes about the damage deposit. Make sure that you are provided with a copy of the inventory in the form that you agreed (i.e. with any notes you may have added regarding the condition of the property and its contents).

- **A rent book:** This is only required if your tenancy provides for you to pay rent on a weekly basis.

- **Notices:** Your landlord may serve some notices on you (e.g. a notice regarding the right of his mortgage company to recover possession in certain circumstances). Note that if a Section 21 notice is served on you before the tenancy agreement is signed, it will not be effective as you cannot serve notice to end a tenancy which has not yet started.

- **The gas certificate:** The landlord is required to serve this on you under the gas regulations, if there are gas appliances. If this is not provided, it is a criminal offence. For further information, see the section on other specific hazards in Chapter 10.

- **A standing order form:** Most tenants pay rent on a monthly basis and most landlords will want this paid by standing order. This is the best way to pay rent if you can, as rent will be paid automatically and you will not run up any arrears and risk eviction.

- **A letter of authority to the Housing Benefit Office:** If your rent is going to be paid by Housing Benefit, your landlord will often ask you to sign this letter, as without a letter of authority the Housing Benefit Office will not give him any information about your application or entitlement. Unless you hold strong views on this, it is generally best to sign. The benefit will go towards paying your rent after all. Also, it will mean that your landlord will bother you less about it, if there are delays in payment. The letter may also authorise the Housing Benefit Office to pay the rent directly to him. This is often a good idea, as it will mean that you will not be tempted to use the money for something else. However, note that if you are going to receive a Local Housing Allowance rather than Housing Benefit, this cannot be paid directly to your landlord, except in special circumstances.

- **Manuals:** You should be provided with copies or written instructions regarding all appliances and installations. Many landlords will provide an 'introductory pack' with not only manuals but also useful telephone numbers and details of local facilities.

- **Information about your landlord's tenancy deposit scheme:** All deposits taken in respect of private lettings under assured shorthold tenancies after 6 April 2007 must be protected under one of the authorised tenancy deposit schemes, and your landlord must give you information about the scheme protecting your deposit, within 14 days of your tenancy starting. However, many landlords will provide this information at this stage. For more information about the tenancy deposit scheme see Chapter 7.

You should also be provided with keys to the property. Ideally, there should be a set of keys for each tenant.

> **Q** I am a private renting tenant who has been renting for almost six months. A week before I signed the tenancy agreement I was told that I had to take out household contents insurance for my possessions. I was informed that if I failed to do this, I would be

unable to move in. With the time span being so short, I was already organised to move into the property and so I had little choice but to take out the household contents insurance from my landlord's agent. The initial six months of my insurance have almost ended now and the agent is pestering me to take out further insurance. I have nothing of value and do not understand why the agency can insist that I insure my personal possessions. Is it able to do this?

A Your landlord is not entitled to insist that you take out insurance for your own property. I suspect that he is urging you to use this particular company because he is receiving commission. If he continues to insist, I would suggest that you speak to the Tenancy Relations or Housing Officer at your local authority. It is arguable that your landlord's persistence could be construed as harassment, which is a criminal offence, and local authorities have the power to assist tenants with this. You could also speak to your local Trading Standards Office.

After you have moved in

Have a look around the property and make sure that it is in good order. If you find anything wrong, make sure that you let your landlord or his agent know as soon as possible. If you do not, particularly if the item is marked as satisfactory on the inventory, you will be blamed for any damage and you may be charged for repairs or the cost of replacement when you leave.

If you think this is likely to happen, it may be worth taking a few photographs (preferably with a camera which dates the photos) or even a video to prove the condition of the property at the time you moved in. Keep a record also of any scratches, holes in carpets, damaged paintwork, etc., which the landlord may seek to charge you for at the end of the tenancy.

If you are a student, you should be exempt from paying Council Tax, so make sure that you provide the local authority with any documentation it may require regarding this. Your Students' Union will help you if you do not know what to do.

If your landlord has not already provided a gas certificate (if there are gas appliances at the property), then you should ask for this, and if it is not provided, speak to your local Health and Safety Executive. If you have not already received the information about the statutory damage deposit scheme (if this applies to you), this should be received within 14 days of the date you paid the deposit.

Apart from this, while you are at the property your landlord should leave you alone, other than to carry out the regular inspections, and respond to any requests you may make regarding essential repair work.

Q According to my tenancy agreement from a property agency, I cannot open a business but I have a website, an e-commerce business, and it is so small that I will not have to pay tax or Council Tax. What should I do? If the landlord personally allows me to do the business, is it legal?

A No landlord who is properly advised will ever consent to a tenant running a business from his rented property. The reason is that if the business use becomes significant, the law governing the tenancy may change and the tenancy may be governed by the laws relating to business tenancies, which a landlord of residential lettings will not want. If your e-commerce site is small and does not bring in much income, I would suggest you describe it as a hobby rather than a business. If it turns into something larger, you should rent proper office space and run it from there. Note that people who own their own homes do not normally have this problem.

At the end of the fixed term (if any)

If your tenancy has a fixed term, towards the end of this period, your landlord will probably want to know whether you wish to stay on or whether you will be leaving. Although you do not have to give your landlord formal notice to quit if you are leaving at or before the end of the fixed term, it is courteous to let him know what you are going to do. As discussed in Chapter 18, you will need to serve a notice to quit if you wish to end a periodic tenancy, otherwise you will be liable for a further month's rent.

If you want to stay on, your landlord may want to issue you with a new tenancy agreement or a 'renewal' for a further fixed-term period – normally six months or a year. This is common practice with letting agents. You may be happy with this as it will give you security for a further period. However, it is not essential and legally there is no reason why you should not stay on in the property indefinitely on a periodic basis.

However, bear in mind that most private sector lettings nowadays will be assured shorthold tenancies where you do not have security of tenure. If you refuse to sign a new tenancy or renewal document, it would be quite within your landlord's rights to decide to end your tenancy.

Some landlords or (usually) letting agents will want to charge a 'renewal fee' at this stage. If this is fairly modest, then it should be paid, as it will be deemed to be in respect of the cost of drawing up the renewal document. However, if the fee demanded is fairly high, then this may not be justified. If you want to object, you could consider speaking to your local Trading Standards Office. However, bear in mind that if your tenancy is an assured shorthold tenancy, you will not have any security of tenure, and your landlord may decide to evict you anyway if he considers that you are being a nuisance.

If you decide to leave, there will normally be a 'handover' meeting where the property is checked against the inventory and any deductions from your damage deposit will be agreed. If this does not happen, and you suspect that your landlord will be seeking to make unjustified deductions from your deposit, you may want to consider taking photographs of the property or even a video to prove that it is in good condition. Some tenants keep back the last month's rent payment if they think that their deposit will not be returned to them. However, if your deposit is subject to one of the statutory tenancy deposit schemes, you should not need to worry about this.

You also need to make sure, if the utilities have been put in your name, that the utility companies are informed of your departure and that meter readings are taken at the time that you leave.

You should also arrange for your post to be redirected to your new address, and you should give your landlord a forwarding address.

Part 4

Further information

CHAPTER 21

Further information

Making complaints

If you have a problem with your landlord or a letting agent, you should always see whether any formal avenues of complaint are open to you before taking legal action. If so, you should try following these first. Courts are very pushed for time, and unnecessary claims are frowned on. If you go to court and the court finds that you could have had your problem easily solved by a complaints procedure, it is possible that you may be ordered to pay your opponent's legal costs. Taking a claim to court should always be the last resort.

If your problem is a complex one, it may be worth taking legal advice first on how best to deal with the complaints procedure, plus the adviser may be able to help you draft the letter or complaints form. Also for some, particularly for serious, problems it may be appropriate to consider legal action at an earlier stage, perhaps bypassing the complaints procedure altogether. If so, your adviser will tell you.

If you deal with the complaint yourself, always check if there is an official complaints form you can use. These can usually be found on the relevant organisation's website. If possible, complete this on-screen and print it off, as handwriting is often difficult to read.

If there is no complaints form, then you should send a letter, again preferably typewritten. Set out your complaint fully, but concisely. It is a good idea to tell the story in chronological order. Short paragraphs and bullet points will be easier to follow than long paragraphs. It may also be a good idea to include copies of any relevant documents (never send originals).

Sign and date the letter or form and make sure that you have taken a copy of everything, for your own records, before it goes out. If you do not trust the organisation, take the letter or form around personally and ask for a receipt, and/or take an independent witness with you to prove that the form or letter was delivered.

Make detailed notes of all telephone conversations and meetings, and make sure that these are signed and dated. Keep these, along with all correspondence and other relevant paperwork, in a clearly marked folder, so you do not lose it. If your complaint fails and you have to go to court, this documentation will be important.

Social tenants

Local authority housing

The Housing Office

You should always first take your complaint to your local authority's housing department and speak to one of the Housing Officers. If no action is taken, then send in a formal letter of complaint, making sure that you keep a copy. If the matter is still not dealt with, contact your Housing Officer's manager, with a copy of the original complaint made and setting out the problems you have experienced since. You should get a formal written response to this letter (if not to your original letter) and if the local authority is unable to deal with your problem, the written response should set out why.

If you are unhappy with the service provided by the housing department, the next step is to speak to your local councillor.

> **Note**
>
> Your local authority should have a leaflet on making complaints which will normally be available in your housing department. Make sure that you get hold of one. There will also be information on making complaints on your local authority's website.

Your local councillor

Local authorities are run by elected representatives known as 'councillors', and there will be at least one (more likely two) councillor(s) for the area you live in. If you have a problem regarding local authority housing, a councillor is a good person to speak to. He knows the system and he will be able to guide you. Plus he may be able to speak to the right person on your behalf and/or (if appropriate) raise the matter at the local authority's housing committee.

Do not feel intimidated if your councillor is not from a party you support or if you did not vote for him. He will not (or should not) allow this to influence him in the help that he gives you.

You will be able to find out who your local councillors are and their contact details via your local authority's website or through the 'write to them' website at www.writetothem.com. If you are not on the internet, you can also find out by ringing your local authority's switchboard.

If both your local housing department and your local councillor are unhelpful, the next step is normally a complaint to the ombudsman. Although if your problem is a serious one, you should also consider getting legal advice and taking legal action, if you have not done this already.

The ombudsman

An ombudsman is someone who has been appointed to investigate complaints about a particular organisation. He will be able to help with:

- delay or neglect in responding to enquiries or providing a service;
- failure to follow the agreed policies, rules or procedures of the organisation;
- rudeness, discrimination or unhelpfulness of officials;
- incorrect and/or misleading information and advice given by officials;
- failure of officials to provide advice and information.

If you have been unable to get your problem dealt with satisfactorily by your local authority and your councillor has been unable to help either, going to the ombudsman is the next step. However, you should not go to the ombudsman before you have exhausted the other avenues of complaint open to you through the local authority's structure. Note, also, that the ombudsman will be looking more at the way you have been treated by the local authority, than at your problem itself.

If you are in England, you should use the Local Government Ombudsman (see www.lgo.org.uk). If you are in Wales, you should use the Public Service Ombudsman for Wales (www.ombudsman-wales.org.uk).

Your MP

You can also consult your Member of Parliament (MP) in the same way that you can your local councillor. All MPs hold local 'surgeries' which are often advertised in the local paper. If he considers that your problem has merit, your MP may be able to assist by writing a letter on your behalf or (if he has time) speaking to those in charge on your behalf. However, bear in mind that there is a limit to what your MP can do for you and do not expect too much, particularly if he holds government office as he will have less time for constituency matters. Generally, for housing matters, it is best to speak first to your local councillor.

You can find contact details for your MP from the UK parliament's website at www.parliament.uk or you can write to him at www.writetothem.com.

The Local Government Monitoring Officer

Finally, it is also possible to make a complaint to the Local Government Monitoring Officer. This is an officer of the local authority. If he thinks it is likely that a council officer or committee is about to or has contravened the law, or caused maladministration (e.g. as a result of a letter received from you), he must prepare a report to present to the council, which must be considered within 21 days of it being sent. Although there is no obligation for the council or the committee to consider compensation and there is no right of appeal if the council takes no action as a result, this may be a further way of putting pressure on a local authority (e.g. to meet its repairing obligations). Your local councillor will probably be able to provide you with contact details for the Local Government Monitoring Officer, or ring the general local authority telephone number and ask for details.

Registered social landlords

The procedure for registered social landlords (RSLs) is very similar to that for local authority landlords.

The Housing Office

Again, you should always speak first to the Housing or Rent Officer responsible for your property, followed up with a letter if no action is taken on your problem. Again, if this proves unsatisfactory, take your complaint to the next level of management.

Councillors and MPs

If this does not produce a response, you can also consult your local councillor and/or MP for problems with RSLs in the same way that you can for council housing. There are often strong links between the council and the local housing associations, which will often have been created specifically to take over housing which was formerly owned by the local authority. Again, it is generally better to consult your local councillor rather than your MP for housing problems, at least at first. Again, if your problem is a serious one, consider taking legal advice and starting legal action at this stage.

The ombudsman

Finally, if your complaints have not been dealt with satisfactorily, you can complain about this to the ombudsman. The relevant ombudsman for RSLs in England is the Housing Ombudsman Service. He has a website at www.ihos.org.uk and you will find a complaints form you can use on the site. For Welsh registered social landlords, you should use the Public Service Ombudsman for Wales (www.ombudsman-wales.org.uk), whose services cover RSLs as well as council housing.

Educational establishments

This section applies if you are a student and you rent accommodation from the college or university you are studying with.

The accommodation office

As with social landlords, your first step should always be to speak to the accommodation office, which looks after your accommodation.

The Students' Union

For any complaints which are not dealt with satisfactorily by the accommodation office, you should speak to someone at your Students' Union, who should be able to help.

> **Note**
>
> There is a lot of helpful information on the website of the National Union of Students at www.nusonline.co.uk.

Finally, if you rent from a private landlord but the letting was advertised via the college/university accommodation office, it may be helpful to make a complaint to the accommodation office. The office may be able to speak to the landlord on your behalf. Even if it is not able to help in your particular case, it may decide not to allow the landlord to advertise via it again, particularly if it receives a lot of complaints

Tenants of private landlords

Contrary to what some people think, there is no central organisation responsible for all private landlords and with whom they need to register. There are many different kinds of private landlord, but a large number are just private individuals who own a few houses which are rented out to tenants. If you have a problem with your landlord, you should, as with all organisations, make your complaint first of all to your landlord direct. If he fails to respond, or to respond adequately, consider one of the following before turning to more formal legal remedies.

Your local authority

Local authorities have an important regulatory function and can be a useful source of help. They can be particularly helpful if your problem relates to disrepair, as discussed in Chapter 10. Plus they also enforce the Protection from Eviction Act 1977; for example, if your landlord is threatening to evict you without obtaining a court order first or if he is harassing you.

If your property is a House in Multiple Occupation (HMO), even if it is not an HMO which needs licensing, again your local authority will often be able to help, as there are various regulations which apply to HMO properties which local authorities have the power to enforce. If your landlord is breaching the terms of his licence or if you think he ought to be licensed but is not, again you should contact your local authority.

Local authorities vary in size and in the services they offer. If you ask for their Housing Advice Service, the Housing Officer there should be able to refer you on to the correct department if your problem is not something the Housing Advice Service can deal with. Matters of disrepair and HMOs are often looked after by the Private Rented Section or the Environmental Health Department.

You can find links to local authority websites and their contact details via www.localauthoritydirectory.co.uk.

Trading Standards

Trading Standards enforces some of the various regulations, such as the furniture regulations, which landlords are subject to (apart from the gas regulations – see page 280). It also has powers under Part 8 of the Enterprise Act 2002 where businesses are not complying with the consumer legislation.

If you believe that your landlord is flouting the various legislation and regulations which exist to protect tenants, Trading Standards may be a good source of help. If you wish, the Trading Standards Officers may be able to contact your landlord on your behalf, and in serious cases they may be prepared to bring a prosecution.

So far as Trading Standards' powers under the Enterprise Act are concerned, these can only be used against businesses, so they will not be much help against the amateur landlord with just one property. However, for larger landlords, it is well worth complaining, as the more complaints it receives, the more likely Trading Standards are to take action against the company concerned. Its powers are extensive and, as a last resort, it can close the business down altogether, although it is more likely to seek an undertaking from the company to cease the offending conduct.

You can find details of your local Trading Standards Office via the telephone directory or via its website at www.tradingstandards.gov.uk.

The Health and Safety Executive

This organisation is responsible for policing the gas regulations, and are the people you should contact if your landlord is not complying with these; for example, if you have not received your annual gas certificate or if you suspect that your gas appliances are faulty, and your landlord is not responding to your requests.

You can find your local office either via the telephone directory or via its website at www.hse.gov.uk.

Local accreditation schemes

If your landlord is a member of one of the many local accreditation schemes, he will have had to sign up to its code of conduct. If you consider that your landlord has breached this code, it is worth contacting the scheme's administrators. They will speak to the landlord concerned. This should result in the landlord dealing with the problem, as if he does not, he will risk expulsion from the scheme.

You will probably know if your landlord is a member of one of these schemes; indeed, you may have found your property through the scheme's advertising programme. For example, many landlords who advertise in student accommodation offices are members of local accreditation schemes. Most schemes are either run by the local authority alone or run in partnership between various organisations, such as local authorities, local universities and colleges, and local landlords' associations.

Most accreditation schemes are registered with the UK Accreditation Network, and you can find out more about it via its website at www.anuk.org.uk.

Local landlords' associations

Many landlords are members of local landlords' associations. Like accreditation schemes, these also require their members to comply with their code of conduct. Again, an association will normally take complaints about one of its member's breach of the code very seriously, and the landlord will risk expulsion from the association if he fails to rectify or deal with the problem.

You may not know whether your landlord is a member of an association, but you can always contact your local organisation to find out. There are many landlords' associations and space does not permit me to set them all out in this guide. Many regional associations are members of the National Federation of Landlords, which has a website at www.nfrl.org.uk. Alternatively, your landlord may be a member of the National Landlords Association (formerly the Small Landlords Association), which has branches all over the country. Its website is at www.landlords.org.uk. Your local library or Citizens' Advice Bureau may also have details of landlords' associations in your area.

Letting agents

If you have chosen an agent who is a member of one of the four main professional organisations, these all have a complaints procedure you will be able to use. Also, it may be worth complaining to your local Trading Standards Office (this applies to all agents).

Trading Standards now has new powers under Part 8 of the Enterprise Act 2002 where businesses are not complying with consumer legislation. Ultimately, it can close a business down, but more normally it will seek an undertaking from the business to stop the offending conduct. The staff at Tradings Standards Offices are generally very helpful and will probably be able to give you some advice, even if your problem is not something they can help you with. Also, the more people who complain about 'cowboy' letting agents, the more likely it is that something will be done about them.

> ### Further information
>
> The National Approved Letting Scheme – www.nalscheme.co.uk.
>
> The Association of Residential Letting Agents – www.arla.co.uk.
>
> The Royal Institute of Chartered Surveyors – www.rics.org.
>
> The National Association of Estate Agents – www.naea.co.uk.
>
> For information on the Enterprise Act 2002, see the Office of Fair Trading's website at www.oft.gov.uk.
>
> To find your local Trading Standards Office – www.tradingstandards. gov.uk.

Obtaining legal advice

This book can only act as a general guide – for more complex problems it will generally be essential that you obtain professional legal advice. This section gives information on sources of free and paid for legal advice.

Free advice

Shelter

Shelter is a housing charity which was set up in 1966. Its mission is to help people find and keep a home, and it campaigns for decent housing for all. It has the following free services:

- Shelterline – a free telephone helpline on 0808 800 4444. Lines are open seven days a week from 8am to midnight. It can give immediate advice and guidance, and then suggest specialist or local support services to help you in the longer term.

- Housing aid centres. There are over 50 of these, in various parts of the country, where you can obtain face-to-face advice and assistance. Housing aid centres in your area are one of the best places locally to obtain advice as the office is generally staffed with at least one solicitor, who will be a specialist in housing law. You can find a list of the centres and contact details on the Shelter website.

- The Shelter website has online information on your housing-related rights, and information about Shelter and its services. You will find the website at england.shelter.org.uk. There is also an equivalent website for Scotland.

Law Centres

Law Centres are 'not-for-profit' organisations set up to provide free legal advice to people in their area. Because their funds are limited they concentrate on areas of law where there is the greatest need and least supply. This will normally include housing law, and in most Law Centres you will be able to see an experienced housing law solicitor. All advice and help is given free of charge.

Law Centres in your area, will be an excellent local source of advice that you can rely on. However, it is expensive to run a Law Centre and funding is hard to come by. Because of this many areas do not have a Law Centre.

To find a Law Centre near you, see the search engine on the website of the Law Centres Federation at www.lawcentres.org.uk. You will also find a list in the Links and Contacts section of my website at www. landlordlaw.co.uk.

The Citizens' Advice Bureau (CAB)

This is a very large charity which provides free advice and assistance throughout the country. They have over 3,000 offices and advice centres, so unless you live in a very remote area there should be a CAB office or advice service somewhere near you.

CAB offices are mostly staffed by volunteers, with a few paid staff. Some larger offices may also employ a solicitor. Unlike Shelter, who are specialists in housing, the CAB cover many areas of law, and are generally particularly good at debt advice and Housing Benefit.

However, as housing law is quite a specialist area, the quality of the advice you will receive will depend on the amount of housing law training received by the adviser who sees you. Most advisers are fairly good;

however, I have known a few cases where clients were wrongly advised. When making an appointment to see a CAB adviser you should therefore make it clear that you require advice on housing law, so that the office can make sure that you see the adviser with the most housing law experience.

Even if your local CAB office does not cover housing law, it will be able to give you some initial advice and should be able to refer you on to specialist help.

You can find details of your local CAB from your local telephone directory, library or other information service, or via the CAB national website at www.citizensadvice.org.uk. All CAB offices will offer face-to-face interviews; some will also give telephone and email advice.

The CAB also has a national advice website, which has extensive information and legal advice on most areas of law, including housing law. This can be found at www.adviceguide.org.uk.

The Disability Rights Commission

This is a special organisation set up to assist the disabled and help them enforce their rights. If you are disabled and are encountering discrimination, you should contact the commission for help. It has a telephone helpline on 0845 762 2633, but if you have internet access, you are probably best looking at its very helpful website at www.drc-gb.org.

Other discrimination commissions

You may be able to obtain advice regarding racial discrimination from the Commission for Racial Equality on its website at www.cre.gov.uk, and sexual discrimination from the Equal Opportunities Commission, which has a website at www.eoc.org.uk. Note that there is also a Commission for Equality and Human Rights being set up, which is scheduled to come into being in October 2007. It has a website at www.cehr.org.uk.

Court advice services

Many courts, particularly the larger courts, will offer a housing advice service for defendants in repossession cases. Some of these are run by the local CAB, some by local firms of solicitors, some by other legal charities, and many are run by several organisations in partnership.

If such a scheme is available at your court, you will be able to see a housing adviser before you go into court, and usually the adviser will also be able to represent you at the hearing. However, do not rely on this being available. Many courts are unable to provide this service. Plus, if you have a housing problem, particularly if this has resulted in eviction proceedings being brought by your landlord, you should obtain legal advice as soon as possible. Often by the time the court hearing takes place, it is too late to do anything other than ask the court to grant you a little more time to find somewhere else to live.

To find out if your court offers an advice service, ring its general switchboard and ask. You can find contact details for all County Courts via the Court Service's website at www.hmcourts-service.gov.uk. Generally, courts with a court advice service will include a leaflet about this when sending you the court summons forms.

Solicitors

Free interviews

Many firms of solicitors will offer an initial free advice interview for half an hour to an hour. Here you will be able to seek initial advice from a solicitor, plus they may be able to help you draft a letter or court document.

However, that firm will normally be offering the initial advice as a marketing exercise in the hope that it will attract paying clients. If you return to the firm for further help, this will normally be on the basis that you will be paying for its services, so make sure you fully understand how much this will be. For further information on this, see the 'paid for' advice section at page 290.

Most firms who offer an initial free interview will advertise this in the local press and/or in *Yellow Pages*. It also worth asking if this is offered when you ring up a firm to book an appointment (it can only say no!).

An initial free interview at a solicitors' firm will be particularly useful if you just want a piece of 'one-off' advice or need someone experienced to check a letter or document for you.

Legal Aid

If you are on benefit or a low income, you may also be able to obtain free advice from a firm which offers Legal Aid. If you are able to find a Legal Aid firm which offers a housing service, this will be a very good source of help and advice, so long as you meet the Legal Aid eligibility criteria. All Legal Aid firms have to meet stringent standards set by the Legal Services Commission and (if they offer a housing law service) they will receive regular training in housing law and practice.

However, as the fees offered to solicitors by the Legal Services Commission are fairly low (compared to private fee paying work), and the level of administration involved is high, more and more solicitors' firms are dropping out of Legal Aid work. This has resulted in 'Legal Aid deserts' being created – large areas of the country where there are no solicitors' firms who do Legal Aid work, or only firms which have already used up their quota of 'new matter starts'. Therefore, even if you qualify financially for Legal Aid, you may find it hard to find a Legal Aid solicitor in your area who can help you.

You can find details of solicitors who are part of the Community Legal Service (i.e. those who offer Legal Aid) at www.clsdirect.org.uk. This site also has an online calculator which will work out whether you are financially eligible for Legal Aid.

When going to see your solicitor you will need to take the following:

- Proof of identity (photo-based is best, i.e. passport, etc.).

- A recent (within the last month) letter or statement of entitlement to benefits or Pension Credit. You can get one from the Jobcentre if you have not got a recent one (an account statement from the Post Office will not do).

- If you are employed, take your most recent wage slips or statements, preferably for the past three months.

- Bring current statements of tax credit entitlement (Working/Child/family) and Child Benefit entitlement.

- Any proof of costs of childcare due to work.

- If you are not receiving Income Support/Jobseeker's Allowance/Pension Guarantee Credit and have a partner, you will need to provide evidence of his income and benefits as well.

Telephone helpline

This is now provided by the Community Legal Service for those who qualify for free legal advice. The telephone number is 0845 345 4 345 and you can obtain free advice about benefits, tax credits, housing, employment, education or debt problems.

Local authority advice centres

All local authorities are legally obliged to give advice and assistance to all homeless people who apply to them, plus many of the housing-related criminal offences are enforced by local authorities. So, for every local authority you should be able to find someone who will at least be able to give you some advice and assistance.

The size of the housing advice service will really depend on the area covered by the local authority. Some rural authorities have very few housing-related problems in their area (and indeed very few rented properties) and may only have one officer who will deal with this. Others, particularly those in the large urban conurbations, will have dedicated housing advice centres with excellent facilities.

In particular, local authority advice services should be your first port of call for the following types of problem:

- Where your landlord has committed a housing-related offence, such as harassment.

- Where you are threatened with eviction and you wish to be re-housed.

- Where your property is in poor repair, although you may be passed to the local authority's Environmental Health Department.

- Where your landlord ought to be licensed or you believe that he has breached his licence conditions.

For your local authority's contact details and websites, see www.local authoritydirectory.co.uk.

Housing association and RSL advice services

Many of the larger registered social landlords will arrange for advice services to be made available for their residents. For example, the CAB may maintain an office there, or there may be regular advice surgeries run by the CAB or a local solicitors' firm.

If an advice service is run by your landlord, you will probably find notices giving details of the times and dates in the Housing Office. Otherwise, ask your Housing Officer if this is something provided.

Advice services for students

Students are generally well served for legal advice, particularly in the larger colleges and universities. Advice for housing problems can generally be accessed via the accommodation office or the Students' Union. Sometimes also a local solicitors' firm will be available to provide additional advice, or will run surgeries for students. For information on what is available, speak to your Students' Union.

Note that there is also a considerable amount of information on the website of the National Union of Students at www.nusonline.co.uk.

Your insurance company

Strictly speaking this is not 'free' as you will have paid for the insurance, but many insurance products include a legal help service (e.g. a telephone advice service), which can cover housing matters. Check your insurance policy, your broker, or your insurance provider's website for more information.

Your trade union

Again, this is not really 'free' as you will be paying your union dues, but many unions, particularly the larger ones, will offer a legal advice service, which may include housing advice. For more information, contact your union representative.

Internet

Although there are many sites on the internet which provide free information, sites where you can obtain free 'one-to-one' advice are less common. Other than my own Q&A service, I have not been able to find any genuine free one-to-one specialist housing advice service on the internet. If you know of any please email me and let me know so it can be included in the next edition of this book.

Landlord-Law

This is my own service where I answer ten questions received from the public (via my special form) every two weeks free of charge, and publish them in the Q&A section of the site. Questions tend to be a balance between those asked by tenants and those asked by landlords, although it depends on what questions have been received in any one week. Anyone can submit a question but there is no guarantee that your question will be one of the ten answered.

> **Note**
>
> The best place to find out about legal services available on the internet is the excellent website maintained by Delia Venables at www.venables.co.uk. Particularly recommended is the 'New on the Legal Internet' section.

Giving back

If you have been helped by one of the not-for-profit organisations discussed in this book, do consider giving them some financial or other help once you are in a position to do so. All charities and not-for-profit organisations are run on a very tight budget and donations are always very welcome. For example, why not consider leaving a donation to them in your Will?

You may also be able to help in other ways. For example, the CAB is always looking for volunteers to be advisers or to help in other ways such as reception work. This sort of work is particularly suitable for retired people as they will have a lot of experience which can be used for the benefit of others. It is also suitable for young people and students, non-working parents, indeed anyone wanting some work experience and to do a bit of good in the community.

Paid for advice

If you are not financially eligible for Legal Aid, and there is no Shelter office or Law Centre near you, you may have no alternative but to pay for a legal professional. This means solicitors (and legal executives who mostly work in solicitors' offices), as the other qualified legal professionals – barristers – can generally only be consulted through a solicitors' firm.

You should be very wary about paying for legal advice offered by any organisation or person who is not a qualified solicitor or legal executive, or a member of a solicitors' firm. Many people have negative views of solicitors, particularly as they are perceived to be expensive, and seek to avoid using them on principle. However, the main reason solicitors are so expensive is that it is very expensive to run a solicitors' practice and comply with all the legal requirements which are there to protect clients.

One of the expenses involved is professional indemnity insurance. No solicitors' firm is allowed to stay in practice unless they have insurance to cover all claims up to a financial limit of £2 million (and many firms have cover for more than this). This means that if the solicitor you see makes a mistake, you can claim compensation. If you pay someone for legal advice and he is not covered by insurance, then if you suffer any loss as a result of his advice, you will have no comeback. Even if you suffer no financial loss as a result of the solicitor's advice, there is also a solicitors' complaints service you can use. You can find out more about this on page 295 below.

Choosing a solicitor

If you are consulting a solicitor regarding a housing law problem, it is important that you see someone who specialises in this area of work. The solicitor you saw about your divorce, or who drafted your Will, will not normally be suitable.

Housing law is specialised and it is easy for someone, even a qualified solicitor, who does not understand this area of law, to get things wrong.

However, some high-street firms of solicitors may be reluctant to turn away work and may just refer you to someone in their litigation department. If this person has no experience in housing law, he will have to look things up as he goes along. This is not really a good idea as:

- the solicitor will have no past experience to draw on; and

- you may get charged (if you are paying on a time costing basis) for the time taken by the solicitor to look things up.

You, therefore, need to ensure that the person you are seeing has experience in housing law. How do you do this? Here are some suggestions:

- Find a firm which offers a housing Legal Aid service. This is the best solution. The firm will be used to dealing with tenants and all its housing advisers will have received proper training. It will normally be delighted to have a fee paying client, as it will not have to go through the administrative hoops involved in Legal Aid work.

- Look for advertisements for firms who offer a service to landlords. Although their main client base may be private or social landlords, they will usually be quite happy to take on a fee paying tenant client, so long as they do not act for your particular landlord (in which case they would not be able to act for you as they will have a 'conflict of interest').

A good place to find details of solicitors who provide a service for landlords is on the internet, for example, the following:

- The 'Find a Solicitor' section in my website at www.landlordlaw.co.uk (go to the 'Links & Contacts' section).

- The free information site LandlordZone at www.landlordzone.co.uk (see the 'Solicitors & Legal' section in the Directory).

You can also do a search on the Law Society's directory at www.lawsociety. org.uk. Follow the link for 'Find a Solicitor' and select 'Landlord and Tenant – Residential'. However, bear in mind that just because a firm is listed in the directory as dealing with this area of work, it does not mean that it necessarily has a specialist housing law solicitor.

Solicitors' charges

Solicitors can be expensive but it is easy to forget this and run up a large bill. The solicitors' professional rules specify that a firm should tell you in advance what the work it is doing for you is likely to cost, and keep you informed if its costs are going to exceed this initial estimate. Information about the firm and the method of charging to be used in your case is generally set out in a letter sent to you when the solicitor first starts acting for you, known as a 'client care letter'. This letter should also confirm the work that the firm will be doing for you, tell you who will be acting in your case, and give information about the firm's complaints procedure.

Here are some of the main methods of charging used by solicitors:

- **Charging by the hour:** This is the most common method of charging and probably the least popular with clients. However, sometimes it is difficult to see how solicitors can be paid fairly any other way. For example, with litigation it is impossible to know at the beginning whether a case will settle after a few weeks or run on for years into an expensive trial.

  The people working on your case are called 'fee earners'. All fee earners are allocated an hourly rate by their firm (which varies according to their status and experience) and they will charge on this basis. Sometimes they will reserve the right to charge an uplift on this (e.g. 50 per cent); for example, if the work they have done is unusually complex or urgent.

  The charging rates used by solicitors may seem high to you, but remember that it has to cover all the firm's expenses, such as staff salaries, premises expenses, IT and library expenses, training, insurance, etc. It is not just in respect of that solicitor's own salary!

  The majority of solicitors will record the time they spend on your case on time sheets, and this data is then fed into a computer. For the purpose of time recording, time is divided into units usually of six minutes each, so this is the minimum time that will be entered whenever they do any work on your case. Standard telephone calls and letters are generally entered as one unit each. So if your solicitor's hourly rate is £150, each time you ring him to ask him how your case is coming on this will cost you a minimum of £15. Time recording is the standard method of charging which will be used if no other fee structure is specified.

- **Fixed fees:** This method is often used when the solicitor knows from the start the amount of work involved in a case. It is obviously preferable from the client's point of view as he knows where he stands and he can budget properly. It is most commonly used in conveyancing and debt collecting work, and for straightforward drafting jobs such as tenancy agreements. However, solicitors are sometimes willing to agree a fixed-fee for other work and it is often worth asking a solicitor if he would be prepared to act for you on a fixed fee basis.

- **Conditional fees:** Until 1995 solicitors were not permitted to charge on a 'no-win, no-fee' basis for court claims. However, they are now allowed to use a special type of agreement called a 'conditional fee agreement'. Under these agreements a solicitor will still charge on a time costing basis. However, he will only get paid if the case is won, when, because he has taken the risk of losing his fees, he will be paid a success fee which will normally be an 'uplift' on his fees of an agreed percentage. The percentage will depend upon the risk taken by the solicitor in bringing the case but must not be more than 100 per cent.

Note that only cases where you have a significant financial claim (such as a personal injury or disrepair claim) will be suitable for a conditional fee agreement. The reason being that the case must be one where, if you win, your opponent will be ordered to pay your legal costs; for example, a solicitor will not normally be prepared to act on a conditional fee basis to defend a claim for possession.

Because an unsuccessful litigant is usually responsible for his opponent's costs, conditional fee agreements must be backed by an insurance policy which will cover these fees in the event of the case being lost, together with any disbursements, i.e. expenses incurred. Many conditional fee agreements relate to personal injury claims so it is important that there is provision for disbursements to be paid, as medical reports can be very expensive. Likewise for disrepair claims, there will be the cost of surveyors and other reports on the property. In all types of claim, there will be court and similar fees.

Before acting on a conditional fee basis your solicitor will require you to sign a form of agreement. These are extremely long and complex, and you should make sure that you understand it properly before signing it.

- **Legal Aid/the Community Legal Service:** This has been discussed on page 286. Note, however, that if you receive a benefit as a result of the work done (e.g. an award of damages), you will normally have to use at least part of this to refund the Community Legal Service for the money it paid for your legal costs, insofar as these have not been paid by the other side under a costs order. This is known as the 'statutory charge'. Your solicitor should explain this to you if it is likely to affect your case.

How to minimise or control your solicitor's costs

Here are some tips on how to minimise the costs that you pay:

- Do your own research before consulting a solicitor. This book will help you. If you understand your problem and have some familiarity with the area of law involved, you will understand the solicitor better and he will have to spend less time explaining basic legal concepts to you.

- Make sure that your papers are in order before handing them over. Put correspondence and other documentation into chronological order – this will be a great help to your solicitor and will enable him to get a grip on your case earlier. He will also be grateful to you for having saved him from a boring job. If he has to sort out the papers himself, he will of course charge you for his time for doing this, which (if the bundle of papers is a large one) could work out quite expensive for you.

- Make sure that you are quite clear about your solicitor's charges before you agree to let him handle your case. Do not be afraid of speaking out about this at your first meeting with him. In fact, if your solicitor does not give you clear information about how he proposes to charge, you should seriously consider going to another firm.

- If the type of work involved is not suitable for a fixed fee, and the solicitor is going to charge on a time costing basis, you can always stipulate a maximum amount which the solicitor cannot exceed without your permission. Make sure that this is put in writing.

- You can also ask your solicitor to invoice you at regular intervals, such as monthly. This is a good idea as it will spread out the cost, and you will not be presented with a large bill at the end of the case which you may find hard to pay.

- All solicitors are now obliged to send a 'client care' letter to new clients giving information about their proposed charges, along with other information about the firm and your case. Make sure that you read this letter, particularly the section regarding the solicitor's fees, and make sure that this agrees with what was discussed with you. If your solicitor has agreed not to exceed £500 without your permission, check that this is mentioned in the letter. If not, write back setting out what was agreed and stating that your instructions are conditional upon this.

- Although a timely reminder now and again is a good idea, do not pester your solicitor (e.g. by ringing him up several times a day). Remember that if he is charging on a time costing basis, you will be charged for every call that you make.

- You should always assist your solicitor in every way you can. If he requests information or documents from you, these should be sent as soon as possible. If you delay, you could prejudice your case. In litigation matters there are strict time limits for disclosing documents in a case. If you do not disclose a document in time, you may not be able to use it at trial. Remember that if a solicitor has to keep writing to you requesting information, you will be charged for this work.

- Listen to your solicitor's advice. If he considers that your claim is not a strong one, think very carefully before proceeding. He is probably right. If you do not agree and want to proceed, consider taking a second opinion first.

- When you receive your bill from your solicitor, check that it agrees with the figures set out in the client care letter or any subsequent costs letter. If it is for more than was agreed, write to your solicitor referring to the relevant letter and ask for the bill to be reduced to the agreed sum.

Complaints against solicitors

- Complain to the firm. If you are unhappy about the service provided by your solicitor, the first thing to do is to complain to the solicitors' firm concerned.

All firms should have a written complaints procedure, which they should provide to you on request. There will also normally be a partner whose job is to deal with complaints. You should have been told who this person was in your 'client care letter'. If this was not done or you have lost the letter, ring the firm up and ask the receptionist who its 'complaints partner' is. Then write to this person giving details of your complaint. The firm should respond to and deal with your complaint within the time limits set out in its written complaints procedure.

Note that firms cannot make a charge for investigating a complaint against themselves.

- Contact the Legal Complaints Service. This is an independent body set up to deal with complaints about solicitors. It will expect you to have tried to resolve your complaint first with the firm concerned. However, if this has failed, then it will investigate your complaint for you. There is a telephone helpline on 0845 608 6565, which is open Monday to Friday from 8am to 6pm, and it is probably best to telephone first for initial advice. You can also find out more about the Legal Complaints Service and how it operates from its website at www.legalcomplaints.org.uk.

Further reading

These are all books which I have found helpful, or which offer more detailed guidance on the matters covered in this book.

Small Claims Made Easy by Veronica Newman, published by Lawpack.

Small Claims Kit published by Lawpack.

Residential Lettings by Tessa Shepperson, published by Lawpack (this is my book for landlords).

Residential Lettings Kit published by Lawpack.

Student Housing Rights Guide by Martin Davis and Graham Robson, published by Shelter.

Repairs: Tenants' Rights by Jan Luba and Stephen Knafler, published by LAG.

Defending Possession Proceedings by Nic Madge, Derek McConnell, John Gallagher and Jan Luba, published by LAG.

...and finally

Shelter has an excellent subscription website service, called Shelter Legal, which has a lot of detailed legal information which is particularly helpful for legal advisers. I used it a lot when writing this book. You will find it linked from the 'Housing Policy & Practice' section of Shelter's website at england.shelter.org.uk.

Useful websites and telephone helplines

Useful websites

Online legal resources and legal sites

British and Irish Legal Information Institute	www.bailii.org
Community Legal Service Direct	www.clsdirect.org.uk
Court Service	www.hmcourts-service.gov.uk
Delia Venables	www.venables.co.uk
Department of Constitutional Affairs (for the Civil Procedure Rules)	www.dca.gov.uk/civil/ procrules_fin/index.htm
Landlord-Law	www.landlordlaw.co.uk
Law Commission	www.lawcom.gov.uk
Law Society	www.lawsociety.org.uk
Neil Addison's harassment site	www.harassment-law.co.uk
Office of Public Sector Information (where you can find Acts of Parliament since 1988)	www.opsi.gov.uk/acts.htm

Office of Public Sector Information
(where you can find Statutory
Instruments since 1987)   www.opsi.gov.uk/stat.htm

Residential Property Tribunal   www.rpts.gov.uk

UK Parliament (where you can find
House of Lords' decisions in the
'Judicial Work' section)   www.parliament.uk

Ombudsmen

Independent Housing Ombudsman   www.ihos.org.uk

Local Government Ombudsman   www.lgo.org.uk

Public Service Ombudsman for Wales   www.ombudsman-wales.org.uk

Not-for-profit advice organisations

Homeswapper   www.homeswapper.co.uk

Commission for Equality and Human Rights   www.cehr.org.uk

Commission for Racial Equality   www.cre.gov.uk

Disability Rights Commission   www.drc-gb.org

Equal Opportunities Commission   www.eoc.org.uk

Law Centres Federation   www.lawcentres.org.uk

National advice website   www.adviceguide.org.uk

National Association of Citizens' Advice Bureaux   www.nacab.org.uk

National Union of Students   www.nusonline.co.uk

Shelter   www.shelter.org.uk

Tenant Participation Advisory Service www.tpas.org.uk

TPAS Cymru   www.tpascymru.org.uk

Victim Support   www.victimsupport.com

Government and quasi-government sites

Communities
and Local Government   www.communities.gov.uk

Housing Corporation	www.housingcorp.gov.uk
Offices of Court Funds, Official Solicitor and Public Trustee	www.officialsolicitor.gov.uk
Office of Fair Trading	www.oft.gov.uk
Rent Service	www.therentservice.gov.uk
Trading Standards	www.tradingstandards.gov.uk
Welsh Assembly	new.wales.gov.uk

Landlords' and agents' organisations and sites

Association of Residential Letting Agents (ARLA)	www.arla.co.uk
National Approved Letting Scheme (NALS)	www.nalscheme.co.uk
National Association of Estate Agents (NAEA)	www.naea.co.uk
National Federation of Landlords	www.nfrl.org.uk
National Landlords Association	www.landlords.org.uk
LandlordZone	www.landlordzone.co.uk
Royal Institute of Chartered Surveyors (RICS)	www.rics.org
UK Accreditation Network	www.anuk.org.uk

Other organisations and sites

Association of Law Costs Draftsmen	www.alcd.org.uk
CORGI	www.trustcorgi.com/consumers.htmx
Legal Complaints Service	www.legalcomplaints.org.uk
National Housing Building Council	www.nhbc.co.uk
NICEIC	www.niceic.org.uk
Write To Them (for details of MPs)	www.writetothem.com

Telephone helplines

Accident Line	0870 607 8999
Community Legal Service	0845 345 4 345
Gas Safety Advice Line	0800 300 363
Legal Complaints Service	0845 608 6565
National Grid Transco	0800 111 999
Samaritans	0845 790 9090
Shelterline	0808 800 4444

Index